D0207979

ELECTING FDR

American Presidential Elections

MICHAEL NELSON

JOHN M. MCCARDELL, JR.

ELECTING FDR

THE NEW DEAL CAMPAIGN OF 1932

DONALD A. RITCHIE

UNIVERSITY PRESS OF KANSAS

Published
by the
University
Press of Kansas
(Lawrence,
Kansas 66049),
which was
organized by the
Kansas Board of
Regents and is
operated and
funded by
Emporia State
University,
Fort Hays State
University,
Kansas State
University,
Pittsburg State
University,
the University
of Kansas, and
Wichita State
University

Photographs on pages 66, 83 (Clifford Berryman cartoon), 93, 131, 156, 173, and 179 (from the *New York World Telegram and Sun*) are from the Library of Congress; on pages 31, 34, 59, 117, and 128, from the Hoover Library; on page 128, Clifford Berryman cartoon from the National Archives and Records Administration; and on page 174, from the Senate Historical Office.

Library of Congress Cataloging-in-Publication Data

Ritchie, Donald A., 1945–

    Electing FDR : the New Deal campaign of 1932 / Donald A. Ritchie.

    p.   cm. — (American presidential elections)

    Includes bibliographical references and index.

    ISBN 978-0-7006-1550-6 (cloth : alk. paper)

    1. Presidents—United States—Election—1932. 2. Roosevelt, Franklin D. (Franklin Delano), 1882–1945. 3. Political campaigns—United States—History—20th century. 4. United States—Politics and government—1929–1933. I. Title.

    E805.R58 2007

    973.917092—dc22   2007028024

British Library Cataloguing-in-Publication Data is available.

Printed in the United States of America

10 9 8 7 6 5 4 3 2 1

CONTENTS

An electoral landslide whose outcome seems inevitable in retrospect does not always seem that way in prospect. In 1864 Abraham Lincoln defeated George McClellan by 212 to 21 electoral votes, but less than three months before the election Lincoln had written, "This morning, as for some days past, it seems exceedingly probable that the Administration will not be reelected." On the Sunday before the 1980 election almost every political pundit and pollster judged the contest between Jimmy Carter and Ronald Reagan too close to call. Two days later Reagan bested Carter in the Electoral College by 489 to 49.

One of renowned U.S. Senate and Washington press corps historian Donald A. Ritchie's great achievements in *Electing FDR: The New Deal Campaign of 1932* is to recapture the suspense and uncertainty that, until the votes were counted, marked the 1932 election between Governor Franklin D. Roosevelt of New York, the Democratic nominee, and the reelection-seeking Republican president, Herbert Hoover. To be sure, Ritchie does not dispute the sweeping character of the victory won by Roosevelt and his party: a 472–59 majority for FDR in the Electoral College, along with coattails that brought ninety-seven new Democrats to the House of Representatives and twelve to the Senate. In a concluding chapter that surveys the transformative character of the New Deal and the lasting partisan realignment ushered in by Roosevelt's victory, Ritchie also makes a persuasive case that 1932 was an election of extraordinary and lasting importance.

But, oh, the suspense that preceded these outcomes! Roosevelt's nomination by the Democratic National Convention was hard-fought and, until the fourth and final ballot, far from certain. "Had his party chosen one of the 'stop-Roosevelt' alternative candidates," Ritchie notes, "the Democratic presidential candidate might well have run to the right of Hoover." And, Ritchie adds, that is what probably would have happened if Al Smith, the party's presidential nominee in 1928, had thrown his support to another candidate instead of remaining aloof in the vain hope that Democrats would turn to him again. Bookmakers at the Democratic convention judged Hoover the five-to-one favorite in November, Ritchie reports. Throughout the campaign, Hoover consistently regarded FDR as the Democrats' easiest candidate to beat, and he was not alone in that judgment.

Roosevelt did win, but even that did not end the uncertainty over who would become president. On February 15, 1933, an Italian immigrant named Giuseppe Zangara shot at Roosevelt from close enough range to hit five other people, including a fatal wound to the mayor of Chicago, Anton Cermak. "Had Zangara assassinated Roosevelt," writes Ritchie, "[vice president-elect] John Nance Garner would have taken the oath as president, . . . and a dramatically different administration would have followed" under the laconic, conservative Texan. That FDR was nominated by his party and elected by the country, emerged unscathed from an assassination attempt, and served as president for more than twelve of the most challenging years of American history, Ritchie shows in this splendid book, was many things, but none of them were inevitable.

"History doesn't repeat itself," Mark Twain observed, "at best it sometimes rhymes." Specific elections are rooted in distinct personalities and transient issues that cannot be replicated but can highlight the recurring refrains of the American political process. The election of 1932 involved the Great Depression and Franklin D. Roosevelt's deft challenge to Herbert Hoover's maladroit administration; beyond these particulars, it offers instructive instances of how candidates responded to a national calamity and how voters evaluated their performances. In that election, an economic crisis displaced the cultural issues that had dominated politics during the previous decade. An incumbent party that had rewarded itself too generously with credit for good times suffered the consequences of the economy's breakdown. The election also serves to remind incumbents not to take their party support for granted or to underestimate their opponents.

"The trouble with history is that it can tell you what happened but not what might have happened," Jeffrey Skilling complained at his trial for fraud in the Enron scandal. The history of any election starts with knowledge of who won and lost, which seems to leave little suspense in its retelling. Yet knowing the election results, especially with such a lopsided vote as in 1932, can create a misleading sense of inevitability. Even the participants later recounted it through hindsight. In his memoirs, Herbert Hoover insisted that he held little hope of reelection but felt obliged to fight to the end. But not until late in the campaign did he begin to doubt his chance of reelection, which affected his strategies. History needs to weigh original assumptions and alternative possibilities as well as the actual results.

"Only the President himself can know what his real pressures and his real alternatives are," President John F. Kennedy admonished. "If you don't know that, how can you judge performance?" Kennedy expressed these concerns when he declined to participate in a 1962 poll of historians rating presidential performance. In 1996, I had the opportunity to serve as one of the judges for the *New York Times*'s "ultimate approval rating" of the presidents. Recognizing the subjective nature of the process, I considered twelve key questions in making my rankings: (1) did the president provide dynamic leadership? (2) did he promote a positive domestic agenda? (3) did he establish effective foreign policies? (4) did he exert influence over Congress? (5) did he make strong nominations to the courts? (6) did he build national unity? (7) did he articulate and communicate his programs? (8) did he strengthen his political party? (9) did he preserve the dignity of his office? (10) did he inspire trust? (11) did he rise to the challenges of his times? and (12) did he leave the nation better off than it was before? Under these criteria, I placed Franklin D. Roosevelt third, after Washington and Lincoln—precisely where the other judges placed him. I rated Herbert Hoover slightly higher than did the others, putting him in the "below average" category; on the overall poll, he finished next to last as a "failure." The same criteria proved applicable for evaluating whether the voters made the right decision in 1932 when they selected the challenger over the incumbent.

My research profited from the assistance of the archivists and librarians at the Herbert Hoover, Franklin D. Roosevelt, and Harry S. Truman presidential libraries; the Library of Congress; the National Archives; and the Senate Library. Lynn Smith of the Hoover Library and Jessica Kratz of the Center for Legislative Archives helped identify appropriate illustrations for the campaign. Special thanks go to Tony Badger and Gareth Davies for inviting me to test some of my conclusions before their American history seminars at Clare College, Cambridge, and the Rothmeir American Studies Centre at Oxford. I also owe a great deal to several historian friends: Judi Jennings, for her observations on Quakers and on the Edwardian era; James Sayler, for his work on Arthur Krock and Joseph Alsop; Matthew Wasniewski, for advice on Walter Lippmann; and Rodney Joseph, for closely reading each chapter, raising pertinent questions, and suggesting improvements. Dale Larson, an economist, steered me toward current economic scholarship. The book is dedicated to Fred L. Israel, an inspiring professor of history at the City College of New York who set me off on the path to become a historian, and to Richard A. Baker, whose leadership of the Senate Historical Office has made the rest of the journey so satisfying.

INTRODUCTION

> *When the future historians write of these troublous times and the unselfish*
> *leadership of those who conducted us through them . . . Herbert Hoover*
> *will have his place among the wisest, ablest, most courageous and patriotic*
> *of our Presidents.*
> —Senator Wesley Jones (R-Wash.), radio address, February 15, 1932
>   (*Congressional Record*, 72nd Cong., 1st sess., 1932, vol. 75, pt. 4, 4212)

> *When the impartial historian shall calmly review the history of the Hoover*
> *administration, he must reach the conclusion that the present occupant of*
> *the White House is the most vacillating, timid, inept, and impractical man*
> *who has ever been responsible to lead a democracy in a national crisis.*
> —Senator Millard Tydings (D-Md.), speech in the Senate, June 13,
>   1932 (*Congressional Record*, 72nd Cong., 1st sess., 1932, vol. 75, pt.
>   12, 12776)

Herbert Hoover poses an enigma for historians, just as he did for the voters in 1932. Having demonstrated such ample abilities prior to his presidency, he was transformed into a luckless leader between his triumphant election in 1928 and his defeat four years later. Hoover's presidency grappled with the Great Depression, but Franklin D. Roosevelt's victory marked more than a momentary reaction to the hard times. Confronted with the same economic crisis that drove Hoover from office after one term, Roosevelt offered a profusion of programs for recovery, relief, and reform that led to his election to an unprecedented four terms, and his party retained the majority in Congress throughout his presidency. The 1932 election marked a profound reversal of political fortunes, as decades of Republican ascendancy gave way to a half century of Democratic dominance.

The election represented such an obvious watershed that the challenge has been to disprove it. The political scientist Samuel Lubell speculated that the real turning point had occurred in 1928, when urban ethnic minorities shifted allegiance to the Democrats, enabling Al Smith to carry the nation's ten largest cities (although he lost much of the South and the election itself). Later studies disputed Lubell, finding evidence that the 1928 election results reflected Smith's religion and his stand against Prohibition rather than a transfer of party loyalty. Without Smith's name on the ballot in 1930, Democrats did not retain the same levels of urban ethnic support in local and congressional races. Other scholars have also pointed to the congressional races in 1934 and the presidential election of 1936 as pivotal moments, arguing that by then, the voters had a clearer sense of what Roosevelt intended. In those elections, African American voters shifted significantly from Republican to Democrat, and Roosevelt's New Deal political coalition more fully emerged. Since those elections hinged on voter approval of New Deal programs, however, they required the New Deal to have been in place, leading back to the election of 1932.

Not only did the direction of federal policy shift from conservative to liberal as a result of the election, but the election redefined liberalism in the process. Both Franklin Roosevelt and Herbert Hoover went into the campaign regarding themselves as liberals, although Roosevelt spoke of creating a "new liberalism" whereas Hoover lamented that "true liberalism" ended with his defeat. The classical liberalism of the eighteenth century had combined political freedom from despotic governments and established churches with economic freedom of private enterprise and cultural freedom to express individual rights and liberties. By the nineteenth century, classical liberalism had collided with the Industrial Revolution, with its business consolidation, exploitation of labor, and government corruption. Gilded Age liberals called on government to stay clear of free market forces, shun programs to help the needy, and adopt civil service reforms to undermine dishonest political machines. The industrial era caused populist and progressive reformers to draw different conclusions. They argued that government had an obligation to counteract mounting social and economic ills, and they advocated more direct democracy to purify the political system. By the twentieth century, liberals were defined as those who favored some form of state activism to promote individual rights and social welfare, and conservatives were those who viewed the state as a threat to rights and welfare. American liberals and conservatives both reacted to developments in Europe, from the social welfare state to the rise of Communist and Fascist regimes, debating the merits of greater security through central planning and the parallel threat of greater regimentation.

Roosevelt's New Deal expanded federal authority and altered the relationship between the government and the people. Before the New Deal, the closest federal agency to the average citizen had been the post office. After the New Deal, citizens counted on a wide federal safety net that provided old-age pensions, unemployment insurance, maximum work hours and minimum wages, federally insured bank deposits, regulated stock exchanges, subsidized farm prices, rural electricity, and expanded veterans' benefits. Voter approval solidified these innovations until even conservative presidents recognized that the people would judge them by their effectiveness in responding to disasters and improving the quality of life.

History looks back upon events, but elections often appeared differently before the votes were counted. With hindsight, political analysts have asserted that the Great Depression guaranteed any Democrat could have won in 1932, making Franklin Roosevelt's election a foregone conclusion. Yet for much of that year, Hoover expected to win a second term, and well-informed contemporaries gave him a reasonable chance of succeeding, anticipating that the economy would turn the corner by the time of the election. Earlier in 1932, Roosevelt had come under fire for lacking presidential stature or for being just "another Hoover." He also came perilously close to losing the Democratic nomination. Had his party chosen one of the "stop-Roosevelt" alternative candidates, the Democratic presidential candidate might well have run to the right of Hoover. Had both major parties fielded conservative candidates, progressive Republicans stood ready to launch an independent third party, and Socialists and other radical parties expected large gains from the masses of people feeling dismayed and disillusioned by the mainstream parties. After Roosevelt received the Democratic nomination, his chief rival, Al Smith, boycotted his candidacy for months, raising fears that Smith's sizable bloc of loyalists would withhold their support from the Democratic ticket. The notoriously fractious Democratic Party could well have gone into the election divided, enabling President Hoover to win a second term despite the wretched economy.

Franklin Roosevelt won and developed into one of the nation's strongest chief executives, yet astute political observers in 1932 underestimated his capabilities, writing him off as mentally and physically incapable of handling the demands of both a national campaign and the presidency. Although he entered the Democratic convention as the front-runner, his opponents counted on his delegates deserting him after a few ballots. Among those who worked behind the scenes to ensure his nomination was Herbert Hoover, who viewed Roosevelt as his weakest and most vulnerable rival. Roosevelt's nomination misled Hoover into thinking he could conduct a "Rose Garden" campaign from Washington, dispatching surrogates to speak for him while he remained at the White House handling official business. That miscalculation cost Hoover months of campaigning and left him at a disadvantage when he finally realized how strong an opponent he faced.

The election served as a test of presidential leadership. Although Hoover bore the burden of the Depression, he held the considerable advantages of an incumbency. As president, he could dominate the news, control his party's convention, and deploy cabinet officers to represent him. Republicans also held a traditional lead in voter registration and campaign contributions. Yet Hoover's presidency split the majority party and squandered many of its assets. The rigid ideological stance he adopted caused confusion about his creative responses to the economic crisis and allowed his opponents to depict him as unsympathetic to national needs. Hoover recognized that public confidence was key to economic recovery, but he failed in every effort to restore it, enabling his challenger to promise a new deal because the old solutions were not working. Placed on the defensive, Hoover campaigned on fear rather than hope, contending that things could have been worse and warning that his opponent would lead the country in dangerous directions. The voters overwhelmingly opted to risk a change rather than ride out the storm with a leader in whom they had lost faith.

Beyond a failed economy and a failed presidency, the 1932 campaign reflected a failed friendship as well. Hoover and Roosevelt had once belonged to the same social set and shared similar outlooks on politics and policies, regarding themselves as Wilsonian liberals. In 1920, Franklin Roosevelt had expressed the hope that Herbert Hoover would be elected as president, enthusing that "there could not be a better one." There was even talk that the Democrats should run a Hoover-Roosevelt ticket that year. Hoover instead went with the Republicans, and Roosevelt ran for vice president as a Democrat. During the 1920s, the two men drifted apart: while Hoover gained a seat in the cabinet and greater national prominence, political defeat and polio left Roosevelt sidelined. They were both elected to high office in 1928, with the Republican Hoover winning the presidency and the Democratic Roosevelt becoming governor of New York. From that moment on, they were potential rivals.

After the stock market crashed in 1929 and the economy entered free fall, Hoover and Roosevelt diverged in their responses. The classic self-made man, Hoover grew acutely sensitive to anything that might reduce equality of opportunity and self-reliance. Born into wealth and social privilege, Roosevelt learned to cope with a physical paralysis that made him more sensitive to others stricken by forces beyond their control. Assuming that they knew each other well because of their earlier friendship, neither man appreciated how much they had changed during the intervening years. Roosevelt exaggerated Hoover's abilities and kept expecting him to mount a more effective campaign. Hoover underestimated Roosevelt's abilities and the threat posed to his presidency. Once they perceived their mistakes, a personal bitterness crept into the campaign. Their relationship grew even more antagonistic during the long months between the election and the inauguration, when the Depression entered its bleakest phase. On March 4, 1933, they barely spoke as they rode together to the inaugural ceremonies.

They never stopped fighting that election. Driven from office, Hoover sought to rally public opinion against Roosevelt's New Deal and spent thirty years campaigning for historical vindication. Roosevelt found it advantageous to keep running against Hoover as a symbol of the old order the voters had rejected. It would take decades for the Republican Party to emerge from Hoover's shadow. Roosevelt's presidency resulted in a major political realignment, mobilizing organized labor, new immigrants and their families, and southern whites and northern blacks as the core of the modern Democratic Party. The groups that Roosevelt attracted stayed in the Democratic ranks, although he failed in his effort to convert his party into a predominantly liberal body. Southern conservatives retained powerful congressional chairmanships and resisted some of his liberal initiatives, creating party divisions that long outlasted Roosevelt's presidency.

An understanding of the New Deal must begin with the election of 1932. During the campaign, Roosevelt altered, moderated, and reversed many of his positions to broaden his popular base. Yet his speeches also outlined many of the programs he would advance, and they made clear that he planned to conduct a flexible and experimental presidency, reserving the right to reverse direction if a policy did not work. A reporter once pressed Roosevelt on whether he considered himself a communist, a socialist, or a capitalist. When he rejected each label, the reporter asked, "Well, what is your philosophy then?" "Philosophy?" Roosevelt responded, "I am a Christian and a Democrat—that's all." As the challenger and the candidate of a party that had lost the last three successive presidential elections, he adopted a strategy of appealing to disaffected voters of all ideological stripes. Inconsistencies in his positions reflected his efforts to select from and satisfy the conflicting perspectives of his diverse political supporters. The New Deal continued many of those contradictions, with Roosevelt blending programs from many sources. His lack of fixed views and his pragmatic approach to the issues made him difficult to define as a candidate but ultimately successful as a president.

1

THE POLITICS OF PROSPERITY

The candidate strode across the stage at Madison Square Garden as a wildly enthusiastic, overflowing crowd cheered. He waited solemn-faced through a few minutes of uproar and then held up his hand to silence the vast arena so he could begin a nationally broadcast address, the defining speech of his campaign. It was October 1928, and Herbert Hoover proclaimed the Republican Party responsible for an era of unparalleled prosperity. "Our people have more to eat, better things to wear, and better homes," he said. Wages had increased, the cost of living had decreased, and people's jobs had become more secure. "We have in this short period decreased the fear of poverty, the fear of unemployment, the fear of old age; and these are the fears that are the greatest calamities of human kind." Two Republican administrations had laid the foundations for a new era of progress and prosperity, and as he sought to lead the nation forward, Hoover pledged: "We are nearer today to the ideal of the abolition of poverty and fear from the lives of men and women than ever before in the land." Those noble words would constitute America's greatest unfulfilled campaign promise.[1]

Four years later, Democrats threw those words back at Hoover and his party. Having taken credit for a decade of prosperity, Republicans would be saddled with the blame for the depression that followed. Hoover, portrayed as the Great Engineer who took complex problems through to positive solutions, would be overwhelmed by the magnitude of the economic crisis, and his innovative responses would fail to reverse the economy's downward slide. An overwhelming majority of Americans would revile the Great Humanitarian who had fed the starving people of Europe for his stubborn opposition to federal relief for Americans in distress. Rather than lead the nation to the abolition of poverty and fear, his presidency witnessed their unprecedented spread. In a stunning reversal, Hoover's failures would drive him from the White House and relegate his party to minority status for decades.

Forged in a depression during the 1890s, the Republicans' identification as the party of prosperity ended with the Great Depression of the 1930s. In 1893, when the economy had collapsed, a conservative, hard-money Democrat, Grover Cleveland, had led the nation as president and Democrats held majorities in both houses of Congress. Cleveland thought the federal government had no business intervening in an economic crisis, apart from sending troops to suppress labor unrest and restore civil order. Cleveland's Democratic Party paid the political penalty, and for a generation, people tagged it as the party of the "empty dinner pail." Republicans won majorities in Congress in 1894 and the presidency in 1896. In that colorful contest, the conservative Republican William McKinley triumphed on a platform built solidly on preserving the gold standard and high protective tariffs. The Democrats had rejected Cleveland's conservatism and nominated a fiery young populist, William Jennings Bryan, who advocated reviving the economy through the free coinage of silver. Bryan's inflationary policies were aimed at easing the burden of debt for western farmers at the expense of eastern bankers. Bankers and industrialists lined up behind McKinley, and industrial workers joined their employers in voting for him, seeing little benefit in Bryan's agrarian radicalism. Republicans emerged from the 1896 election with a robust voting base that combined professionals and laborers in the urban industrial Northeast and Midwest, whose swelling populations held a commanding share of the Electoral College.[2]

The depression of the 1890s also convinced American reformers that the government had to step in to regulate big business and industry for the protection of small businesses, workers, and consumers. President McKinley's assassination in 1901 thrust his reform-minded vice president, Theodore Roosevelt, into the White House, and Roosevelt's activism created friction between the Republicans' "standpat" and progressive wings. In 1908, Roosevelt handpicked his successor, William Howard Taft, but he quickly grew dissatisfied with Taft's inadequate commitment to reform. Roosevelt walked out of the Republican Party in 1912 and ran as the Progressive "Bull Moose" candidate for president against the incumbent Taft and the Democrat Woodrow Wilson. The three-way race allowed Wilson to win the presidency with a plurality of the popular vote and returned the Democrats to the majority in Congress. Wilson absorbed much of Roosevelt's reform agenda in his New Freedom legislation, creating the Federal Reserve Board and the Federal Trade Commission, among other accomplishments. Despite the Republicans' reunification in 1916, he attracted enough Progressives to his camp to win a narrow reelection over Charles Evans Hughes.

During Wilson's second term, the entry of the United States into the world war in Europe further reshaped the federal government. His wartime administration created a host of emergency agencies that took direction of the economy by increasing war production, reducing home consumption, controlling inflation, and suppressing dissent. Wartime agencies reflected the progressive ideal of having panels of experts rather than politicians make policy decisions and run the government. The high cost of the war required the introduction of a graduated income tax, but even with the tax revenues, the federal debt soared from $1.2 billion to $25.5 billion. The United States also sold on credit vast amounts of food and military supplies to the Allied nations, for which it expected repayment. Britain and France therefore emerged from World War I deeply in debt to their American ally. The victors imposed heavy reparations on vanquished Germany, expecting to use them to repay their war debts to the United States, and to make these reparations, Germany depended on loans from the United States. Thus, all of the nations were locked into a shaky financial interdependence.[3]

Reduced foreign competition during the war boosted the demand for American farm products, encouraging farmers to borrow heavily to buy more land and plant more crops. Overproduction of crops and renewed foreign competition after the war drove down agricultural prices, making it harder for farmers to meet their mortgages and loan payments. Farm regions slid into a prolonged depression that made the prosperity of the 1920s a cruel joke for farmers. Younger people in particular began abandoning the countryside in search of jobs in the cities. On the industrial side, the termination of government economic controls, along with the return of soldiers to civilian life, led to a postwar recession. Strikes and social unrest rocked the last years of the Wilson administration. Negotiating a peace treaty to end the war and creating the League of Nations to prevent future conflicts distracted the president. The mood of the nation was turning isolationist, and while campaigning for the Treaty of Versailles, Wilson suffered a debilitating stroke. His incapacity deprived the nation of his leadership during the turmoil of postwar reconversion, and the voters would hold Wilson's party accountable at the polls.

As Herbert Hoover later explained, Americans in the 1920s had grown "tired of the war, the economic controls, the debt, and the huge taxes they paid." The bitter aftertaste of government crusades buried the Progressive Era, but before the reform movement expired in the postwar period, it produced two additional constitutional amendments that would rearrange the political landscape. The Eighteenth Amendment, ratified in 1919, prohibited the manufacture and sale of alcoholic beverages. And by granting women the right to vote, the Nineteenth Amendment, ratified in 1920, doubled the potential pool of voters. Both changes occurred as public opinion was taking a sharp turn to the right. Progressives found themselves on the margins of the Republican Party, and the Democratic political coalition that had elected Wilson came apart. Alienated by the war and postwar diplomacy, industrial workers, who were largely first- and second-generation immigrants, gravitated back to the Republicans. Newly enfranchised middle-class women were more likely to exercise the right to vote than women in the working class, and they further expanded the Republican base. In 1920, the Republicans ran a staunchly conservative ticket with Ohio senator Warren G. Harding and Massachusetts governor Calvin Coolidge, and they won in a landslide. Harding, having promised a return to "normalcy," took 60 percent of the vote and made inroads into the Democrats' "Solid South." Reflecting support for his conservative policies and a reaction to infighting among the southern Democrats, Harding won Tennessee and carried on his coattails ten southern seats for Republicans in the House of Representatives.[4]

Democrats in 1920 had nominated the moderate Ohio governor James M. Cox for president and the young, progressive-minded Franklin D. Roosevelt (FDR), assistant secretary of the navy in the Wilson administration, for vice president. They hoped that FDR's distant relationship to Theodore Roosevelt would woo Republican progressives. In deference to President Wilson, Cox and Roosevelt built their campaign on support for the League of Nations, without appreciating that Wilson's foreign policies had driven many Irish, German, and Italian Americans into the Republican ranks. Outspent, outadvertised, and out of step with prevailing public opinion, the Cox-Roosevelt ticket never stood a chance.[5]

During the 1920s, the Democrats' traditional base in the urban North and rural South forced them to straddle a growing divide between city and country. Census figures in 1920 revealed that for the first time, more Americans lived in towns and cities than on farms. That year, Sinclair Lewis's angry novel *Main Street* skewered the insular, small-minded attitudes of rural Americans, while schoolchildren in the countryside were learning from their *McGuffey Readers* that youths lured away by the bright city lights faced moral corruption. An anxious and declining minority, suffering through a prolonged postwar farm depression, rural Americans saw themselves as native-born, God-fearing, self-reliant individuals defending traditional values against the influences of the alien, secular, decadent cities.

For the younger city dwellers, a breezy, live-for-today attitude emerged from the carnage of World War I, expressed in the fads and unconventional behaviors of the Jazz Age (the label was taken from F. Scott Fitzgerald's collection of short stories, *Tales of the Jazz Age*). Their rebellion against Victorian virtues and constraints was matched by innovations in communications, from tabloid newspapers to commercial radio and silent movies. Radio promoted professional sports, movies created stars, and tabloids reduced the news to banner headlines and graphic illustrations. News reporters devoted less attention to politicians and reformers than to athletes, actors, and gangsters. The new media also prompted drastic changes in women's fashion, and as hemlines rose, young women bobbed their hair, smoked cigarettes, and sipped cocktails in speakeasies. Crazes from flagpole sitting to marathon dances came and went. Producers attracted consumers with a dazzling assortment of new items that could be purchased on the installment plan. Cheap loans also encouraged stock speculation, with more investors buying stock on margin (paying only a small part of its cost and borrowing the rest, counting on the rise in the stock's price to cover the difference). Summing up all these trends, Prohibition Commissioner Amos Woodstock commented that "running through the whole miserable mess of sensation and jazz is one idea—that getting money is the test of human success."[6]

Low interest rates, low taxes, and technological innovation sustained economic growth throughout the 1920s. Anxious to protect the international gold standard, the Federal Reserve Board held down interest rates throughout the decade (higher rates would have attracted greater European investments and gold flow into the United States, weakening European banks that were still recovering from the world war). These policies promoted economic growth at home, making mortgages and car loans more affordable, but they also encouraged the buying of stocks with low-interest bank loans. Housing construction that had been delayed during the war took off at a fast clip. Electricity spread to 70 percent of American households (although it reached only 10 percent of American farms). Henry Ford's assembly line churned out inexpensive cars, and industry vastly expanded its capacity for producing consumer goods, with fewer workers needed to do the job. Wage earners' share of the corporate income, having increased over the first twenty years of the century, fell rapidly during the 1920s. The gap between the higher and lower incomes widened, with two-thirds of the population earning the minimum income necessary for a decent standard of living and a fifth of the people living at a bare subsistence level. Inequitable income distribution contributed to overproduction, since the mass of consumers could not afford to buy all the goods being manufactured. Half of all American families had no savings. On the surface, the decade's economic boom seemed limitless, but such troubling statistics indicated the prosperity's precariousness.[7]

A DIVIDED NATION

Social critics blamed Americans' passion for cars for undermining their moral code, and they attributed a decline in churchgoing to the pleasures of motoring on Sunday mornings. But the drop in attendance at traditional churches was more than compensated for by the masses who flocked to hear flamboyant tent evangelists. Rapid cultural changes divided the nation between those attracted by the new freedoms of urban life and modernism in religion and those who wanted to preserve the traditional standards of rural life and get back to "old-time religion." Fundamentalist preachers thundered against jazz, bootleggers, movies, card playing, birth control, modern authors, the pope, and communism, calling on a sinful nation to repent. The onetime professional baseball player Billy Sunday, who attracted large crowds with his athletic style of preaching, captured this spirit in his prayer: "Lord save us from offhanded, flabby-cheeked, brittle-boned, weak-kneed, thin-skinned, pliable, plastic, spineless, effeminate, ossified three-karat Christianity."[8]

Fundamentalists flexed their political muscles by fighting to prohibit the teaching of evolution. In Tennessee, sympathetic legislators enacted a law in 1925 that forbade schools from teaching anything that denied "the divine creation of man as taught in the Bible." To challenge the law, the American Civil Liberties Union recruited John T. Scopes, a science teacher from Dayton, Tennessee, a small town suffering severely from the closure of a blast furnace that had been its largest employer. The Scopes "monkey trial" became a national circus, broadcast over the radio and recorded in newsreels. In defending Scopes, the celebrated attorney Clarence Darrow warned that a ban on teaching evolution in schools could just as easily be extended to mentioning it in books and newspapers. For the prosecution, the former Democratic presidential candidate William Jennings Bryan argued that the people had a democratic right to enact laws to protect their religious beliefs. Scopes was convicted of a misdemeanor and fined $100, which was paid by the *Baltimore Sun*'s caustic columnist and social critic H. L. Mencken, who labeled the South the Bible Belt and lashed out against restrictive orthodoxies. Tennessee's state supreme court overturned Scopes's conviction on a technicality, without invalidating the law, which prevented an appeal to the U.S. Supreme Court. Four decades later, in 1968, the U.S. Supreme Court rejected laws prohibiting the teaching of evolution as unconstitutional.[9]

Tensions between the cities and the countryside spilled into the halls of Congress. The House of Representatives, for the only time in its history, failed to agree upon a reapportionment following the census of 1920. In the past, the House had always increased its membership as state populations grew, but by 1910, so many representatives crowded the House chamber that the members' desks had to be removed and long padded benches installed in their place. Taking this as a sign that the House had grown too large and unwieldy, legislators capped its membership at 435—meaning that after each new census, some state delegations would grow and others would shrink to reflect different patterns of population growth. Fiercely resistant to losing seats, rural representatives argued that the countryside exerted a greater moral influence on the government. They also insisted that the 1920 census had merely registered a temporary shift, caused by the war, and that Americans would surely return to the farms over time (in reality, the farm population would continue to shrink). Congress dragged its feet until 1929, finally agreeing to a reapportionment weighted disproportionately toward rural districts. Not until the Supreme Court's "one man, one vote" decree in 1962 would congressional districts become equal in population.[10]

The urban-rural rivalry also intertwined with American foreign policy. During the 1920s, the United States engaged in a form of selective isolationism, refusing to join the League of Nations or the World Court while participating in negotiations for naval disarmament and an international agreement to outlaw war. American banks and corporations invested heavily in Latin America and Europe, and American troops occupied a number of Caribbean and Central American countries. European war debts to the United States also preoccupied American policymakers. American public opinion firmly insisted on the Allies repaying their war debts, which caused the Allies to continue to insist on reparations from Germany and weakened most European economies. The U.S. Federal Reserve Board's monetary policy protected European banks and governments in part to facilitate the repayment of these war debts, even though that course restricted its policy flexibility at home. With isolationist sentiments rampant, only the bravest or most foolhardy politicians openly challenged public sentiment by espousing Woodrow Wilson's international ideals.

The United States of the 1920s resisted pluralism. Old-stock white Anglo-Saxon Protestants ran the major institutions from corporate boardrooms to university administrations, dominated the nation's economy, wrote its history, and controlled its politics—except in a few larger cities. Housing, employment, and educational biases limited opportunities for racial and ethnic minorities. The old gentry saw disturbing demographic trends in the 1920 census, caused by shifts in immigration patterns. Those who traced their ancestry to Great Britain, Germany, and Scandinavia felt troubled over waves of mostly Catholic and Jewish immigration from Ireland, Italy, Russia, Poland, Bohemia, and the Balkans. Three million Italians emigrated to the United States between 1900 and 1920, tripling the number who had arrived on American shores during the entire nineteenth century, while at the same time, immigration from England declined. "The America of our grandfathers was a land of blond men of Nordic or so-called Anglo-Saxon blood, who lived outdoors, tilled the soil, herded cattle, hunted, fished and sailed the seas from the Arctic to Antarctic," wrote the Washington correspondent for the *Los Angeles Times*. "The America of our grandsons will be a heavily populated country of short, dark-skinned men, living for the most part in the most crowded, complicated and enormous cities the world has ever seen, depending on manufacturing, trade and commerce for their living." Such sentiments convinced Congress to enact discriminatory quotas against "undesirable" immigrants.[11]

Nativist fears led to a revival of the Ku Klux Klan, which appealed to native-born, white Protestants and endorsed political candidates who ran against "Jew, Jug, and Jesuit." The Klan fought successfully to stop the Democrats from nominating New York governor Alfred Emanuel Smith in 1924, keeping him from becoming the first Catholic candidate for president (at least until 1928). Although the Roman Catholic Church constituted the largest single religious denomination in the United States, accounting for three out of every ten churchgoers, members of the combined Protestant denominations far outnumbered Catholics. Most mainstream Protestant churches did not sympathize with the Klan, however, and its violence and vigilantism soon undercut its influence.[12]

Worn with worry over evidence of corruption in his administration, President Harding died suddenly in the summer of 1923, elevating Vice President Calvin Coolidge to the presidency. The laconic Coolidge offered Americans a welcome relief from the lofty oratory of Wilson and the bombast of Harding, and his sharp contrast from his predecessor helped isolate him from the Harding administration's scandals. The conservative Coolidge had rejected the Progressive movement as radical and destructive, and he did not think the government should be blamed "because everybody was not prosperous." A passive administrator, Coolidge made little effort to generate news, and Washington reporters concocted human interest stories about him that shaped his image as a "strong, silent man."[13]

Democrats hoped to make a winning issue out of the Harding scandals, but their ruinous national convention in 1924 demolished their chances. Divided between urban and rural representatives, Catholics and Protestants, and wets and drys (opponents and defenders of Prohibition), the delegates cast 103 ballots over two long, sweltering weeks in New York City. The deadlock eliminated their two most promising candidates, Governor Al Smith and the former treasury secretary William G. McAdoo, and they settled on a capable but colorless Wall Street lawyer, John W. Davis. Some Progressive Republicans broke away to nominate Wisconsin senator Robert M. La Follette on a third-party ticket. Against the Republican Coolidge and the Progressive La Follette, the Democrat Davis polled less than 30 percent of the vote, giving Coolidge more votes than his two rivals combined. A sizable drop in voter turnout indicated a growing indifference to the political process.

The Democrats' New York convention marked the last political appearance of their perennial presidential candidate, William Jennings Bryan. Since his first campaign in 1896, Bryan had traveled the nation as a troubadour in search of an issue as compatible for him as free silver had been, from pacifism to Prohibition. He preached a social gospel of caring for the needy and railed against a survival-of-the-fittest social Darwinism in government policy as avidly as he did against scientific Darwinism in the schools. He remained a staunch defender of rural values, and when he died in 1925, the Oklahoma cowboy commentator Will Rogers reminded his audiences that the plain people felt they were left with no one to fight for them because Bryan had no vice president.[14]

Bryan had considered Prohibition a likely issue on which to ride to political power, and it remained potent throughout the twenties. For decades, rural reformers campaigned against the saloon as a social evil responsible for disease, poverty, the abuse of women and children, broken families, and political corruption. Early in the Wilson administration, the Women's Christian Temperance Union (composed of Protestant women reformers) and the Anti-saloon League (staffed and supported largely by evangelical ministers) gained sufficient support in Congress to propose a constitutional amendment to ban alcoholic beverages. When proponents lost their first vote, they campaigned against those who opposed the amendment. By 1916, the Prohibitionists had secured the needed two-thirds majorities in both houses, drawing their strongest support from rural, Protestant areas in the South and West. Opposition to Prohibition was centered in the more ethnically diverse Northeast and Midwest. During World War I, a bipartisan coalition of dry Democrats and Republicans passed a Prohibition amendment, and the states swiftly ratified it. Having won their moral victory, the drys passed the Volstead Act, over President Wilson's veto, defining the Eighteenth Amendment's restrictions to include beer and wine as well as hard liquor and thereby seriously complicating its enforcement.[15]

The burden of carrying out Prohibition fell upon Republican administrations. Requiring a scale of social management beyond anything that the federal government had ever undertaken, the law ran contrary to the limited-government philosophies of Harding and Coolidge, whose administrations were unsurprisingly lax in prosecuting offenders. Most Americans complied with the law at first. Drinking declined, as measured in fewer arrests for drunkenness and fewer hospitalizations for alcohol-related illnesses. But resentment gradually arose over Prohibition's infringement on personal liberties, and people began flaunting the law. By the mid-1920s, the nation's capital had twice as many speakeasies as it had saloons before Prohibition, and Washington paled by comparison to cities such as New York and Chicago in terms of the number of illegal gin joints. Criminal syndicates that had trafficked in gambling and prostitution jumped at the chance to supply the demand for liquor, purchasing immunity from the local police and politicians. Spreading corruption led to a reform movement aimed at repealing the Eighteenth Amendment, an amalgam of states' rights advocates and those opposed to legislating morality. The wealthy also viewed Prohibition as a threat, calculating that liquor taxes had once accounted for almost 14 percent of all government revenue. When those taxes fell to almost nothing, the moneyed class feared the tax burden would shift onto them.[16]

THE RISE OF HERBERT HOOVER

All the contradictions of the 1920s contributed to the election of Herbert Clark Hoover to the presidency. His rags-to-riches personal story matched the plot of a Horatio Alger novel, that of a disadvantaged lad's rise through pluck and luck. Born in 1874 in the tiny, predominantly Quaker town of West Branch, Iowa—making him the first president born west of the Mississippi River—Hoover was the son of a blacksmith father and a mother who was a Quaker minister. As a child, he spent long hours in silence, sitting on the hard benches of the meetinghouse, where he absorbed the Quaker principles of spiritual equality, peace, simplicity, and hard work. Bert Hoover, as he was then called, was just six years old when his father died, and he and his brother and sister were farmed out to relatives while his mother traveled around preaching. She died when Bert was nine. Raised for the next two years by relatives in Iowa, he was sent by train at age eleven to live with an aunt and uncle in Oregon's Willamette Valley. He spent his adolescence in the Quaker colony of Newberg, before moving with the family to Salem. Shy, quiet, and diligent, he dropped out of day school at fourteen to work in his uncle's real estate office but took night classes at a business school. Oregon senator Charles McNary, who knew the adolescent Hoover, recalled him as reserved and not much fun, sticking to his work and studies rather than swimming or playing ball with the other boys. Years later, when asked about his youthful goals in life, Hoover replied without hesitation that his boyhood ambition was "to be able to earn my own living without the help of anybody, anywhere."[17]

Editorial writers and cartoonists made much of Hoover's orphaned childhood, and that melancholy experience undoubtedly contributed to his character. Psychologists have studied the unusually high number of orphans who became heads of state around the world, including an extraordinary proportion of British prime ministers. Among American presidents, Hoover was the only one to lose both of his parents before he was ten, but others who lost at least one parent in their youth included George Washington, Thomas Jefferson, Andrew Jackson, Abraham Lincoln, Andrew Johnson, Grover Cleveland, Theodore Roosevelt, Calvin Coolidge, and Franklin D. Roosevelt—whose wife, Eleanor Roosevelt, was also orphaned as a child. Psychologists reason that feelings of abandonment and vulnerability can spur both creativity and a desire to succeed and control. Politics and public service offer an attractive path to correct what orphans might consider a bad destiny.[18]

Beyond self-reliance, Horatio Alger's plots typically involved the timely intervention of a benevolent millionaire. In Hoover's case, his millionaire was the railroad baron Leland Stanford, who, in memory of his deceased son, endowed a nondenominational, coeducational, tuition-free university that opened its doors in 1891. Although his Quaker uncle had reservations about him attending a "godless" school, Hoover applied and was admitted to Stanford University's pioneer class. His admission was conditional on overcoming deficiencies in English composition, something he labored over all his life. Stanford graded on a pass-fail basis, but Hoover won academic notice for his energy and originality. He majored in geology and engineering, managed the football and baseball teams, and won election as junior class treasurer (his next elected office would be the presidency of the United States). He earned money for room and board by running a laundry and assisting in the geology laboratory. One lab student, an outgoing, athletic young woman named Lou Henry, caught his eye.[19]

Hoover graduated broke during the depression in 1895, and for a few months, he worked as a mine laborer until a San Francisco engineer hired him to write mining reports. This connection led to a job offer from the British firm of Bewick, Moreing and Company, which sent him to its minefields in Western Australia. He returned to marry Lou Henry after she graduated from college in 1899. Together, they sailed to China, where he managed mines and where they survived the Boxer Rebellion, the Chinese uprising in 1900 against foreign domination. Coolness under fire lifted the American's reputation among his British employers. In 1901, Bewick, Moreing made him a partner, with a share in the profits, and Hoover and his wife moved to London. Instead of settling into a desk job, he journeyed relentlessly to inspect the company's far-flung mining operations and scout new prospects. He was a multimillionaire by the time he retired at age thirty-two, physically and mentally exhausted as a result of "continuous overwork." Hoover then traveled the world as a freelance "doctor of sick mines." Wherever he worked, he studied the local government, economics, and history, accumulating a broad knowledge of world conditions.[20]

From the rough life in the mining camps, the Hoovers joined the elite society of Edwardian England. Their stately new lifestyle included homes in fashionable London neighborhoods (where their two sons were born), a weekend country house in Stratford-on-Avon, numerous servants, and membership in choice British clubs. Hoover's political opponents would later mock him as Sir Herbert, Lord Hoover, and Erbert Oover, spreading rumors that he had applied to become a British subject, but the expatriate Hoover had not been willing to abandon his American citizenship. He could not shake the feeling of being an outsider in a culture that placed the accident of birth over demonstrated merit. However, he did absorb the Edwardian values of privacy, dignity, and formality and the routine of entertaining though large dinner parties. Later, as president, he always dressed formally for dinner, and White House butlers calculated that Hoover entertained more guests at meals than any previous president. Another Edwardian holdover was the high starched collar Hoover retained long after it had gone out of fashion, giving him such a stiff and formal appearance.[21]

Having made his fortune, Hoover contemplated entering public affairs. "I want to get into the big game back home," he told a Stanford classmate, "not the money game either, and not exactly the political game—but the big game and the real game somewhere." He bid unsuccessfully for ownership of the *Sacramento Union,* a newspaper that would have given him a political voice in California. Then, in August 1914, just a week before his fortieth birthday, the outbreak of war in Europe stranded 120,000 Americans on the Continent. The U.S. consul general in London recruited Hoover to head a committee to assist the Americans in returning home. This first government assignment led him to an even higher-profiled effort to provide urgent relief to some 10 million civilians in Belgium and northern France, caught between the German army and the Allied blockade. Feeding the Belgians required Hoover to negotiate between warring nations with a high level of persuasiveness. He excelled at the task, earning international recognition as a humanitarian. Yet he somehow kept his distance from those he assisted. The sight of a breadline elated Lou Henry Hoover, knowing that it meant those "brave people were getting a sufficient supply of wholesome clean food." But her husband avoided visiting the breadlines because seeing people reduced to such dire need brought him to tears. Whenever people talked about his Belgian relief work as a thrilling effort, Hoover called it the most unpleasant thing he had ever had to do.[22]

When the United States entered the war in 1917, President Wilson summoned Hoover to Washington to head the Food Administration. Despite his international publicity, Hoover arrived in the capital a relatively unknown quantity, and he described himself as a "stranger in my own country." Congressional conservatives questioned his citizenship and demanded to know why the president had placed absolute power over food production in the hands of "a gentleman from England." Progressives rose to his defense. Nebraska senator George Norris lavishly praised Hoover's testimony before the Senate Agriculture Committee and declared that no man in the world was better equipped for the job. Liberals and Progressives stood in awe of Hoover's management capabilities and claimed that he was the model of the nonpolitical expert they wanted running the government.[23]

Most governments mandated rationing during the war, but Hoover's skillful use of slogans and mass-marketing techniques encouraged voluntary compliance. "Food will win the war," his agency assured citizens as it called on them to observe "wheatless Mondays" and "meatless Tuesdays" in order to reserve supplies for American troops. Homemakers "Hooverized" by rationing food and consumer goods and signed pledge cards promising "to carry out the directions and advice of the Food Administration in the conduct of my household." Hoover's Food Administration selected the family of Assistant Secretary of the Navy Franklin D. Roosevelt to publicize better management of large households. On her pledge card, Eleanor Roosevelt listed her five children and ten servants over whom she kept a watchful eye, making sure that they utilized all leftovers. (After reading of this in the newspapers, her amused husband congratulated her on inventing a "New Household Economy for Millionaires!")[24]

The food czar displayed a hearty appetite for authority. Drawing on his expertise as a mining consultant, Hoover regarded himself as a problem manager. He believed in hands-on administration and insisted on making all major decisions, demanding complete control over every aspect of his agency's operations. His countless battles with other agencies for jurisdiction led President Wilson to speculate that Hoover would rather see a good program fail if he could not be in charge of it. When the war ended, Hoover returned to Europe as director of the American Relief Administration, organizing shipments of food to millions of starving people in eastern Europe and Soviet Russia. Dismayed by what he saw of communist, socialist, and fascist governments in postwar Europe, the master bureaucrat now turned the word *bureaucracy* into a pejorative in his speeches and warned against regimentation.[25]

A HOOVER-ROOSEVELT TICKET

During the war, the post office delivered a letter to Hoover addressed to "Miracle Man, Washington, D.C." Liberals and progressives looked to him as Woodrow Wilson's presidential successor. Hoover for President clubs sprang up spontaneously around the country, even though members of these groups did not know whether he belonged to either party. Having spent most of his adult life abroad, Hoover had only the vaguest political identity. His hometown of West Branch, Iowa, had been rock-solid Republican, and the only Democrat he could remember from his childhood had been the town drunk. In dormitory debates at Stanford, Hoover argued the Republican position, and in 1896, he cast his first vote for William McKinley. But he bolted the party to support Theodore Roosevelt's Progressive campaign and accepted a post in Woodrow Wilson's wartime government. In 1918, to bolster President Wilson's hand in the peace negotiations, Hoover endorsed the reelection of Democrats in Congress. Republicans who won the majority in both houses of Congress that year never forgot or forgave Hoover's apostasy.[26]

The liberal Supreme Court justice Louis D. Brandeis regarded Hoover as "the biggest figure injected into Washington life by the war" and marveled at his firm grasp of industrial and labor conditions, his public spirit, and his organizing ability. Brandeis found it refreshing that Hoover had none of the airs of a candidate and that the office seemed to be seeking the man. The justice's nephew, Louis Brandeis Wehle, who had worked with Hoover during the war, became convinced that the Democrats should nominate him for president, paired on a ticket with Franklin Roosevelt. Hoover and Roosevelt were members of the same Washington social circle, most likely introduced to each other at a reception that Interior Secretary Franklin K. Lane hosted to welcome his fellow Californian Hoover to official Washington. The war had curtailed formal entertaining in the capital, so a group of junior members of the administration instead met regularly at informal Sunday night gatherings in their homes for bridge, cocktails, light suppers, and discussions of current issues. As one member of the Sunday night set explained, "They had to do something of the sort to keep from working themselves to death." Once the war ended, the young administrators left for overseas missions, and the group drifted apart, although when Lane died, Hoover and Roosevelt cochaired an endowment for his widow. Wehle's idea of a 1920 Hoover-Roosevelt ticket instantly appealed to Roosevelt—but not to Hoover. As Wehle made his pitch, Hoover listened in a characteristic pose, hunched forward over his desk, doodling on the blotter, and casting his eyes downward to hide his expression. Finally, he dismissed the notion of running for president. "I don't believe that I want to get into a situation where I have to deal with a lot of political bosses," he said.[27]

The more people pressed him to run, the more indecisive Hoover grew. He issued a public statement that described himself as an "independent progressive" who would neither seek elective office nor resist a draft. He endorsed both President Wilson's plan for the League of Nations and the Republicans' reservations about the League. He denounced reactionaries in the Republican Party and radicals among the Democrats. Realistically, Hoover could spot the postwar trend toward the Republicans and saw no advantage in becoming the Democrats' sacrifice. He finally reasserted his Republican roots by allowing his name to be entered in the California Republican primary, pitting him against California senator Hiram Johnson, an irreconcilable opponent of the League of Nations. Hoover failed to calculate what little appeal Wilson's League held on the West Coast or what a powerful campaign organization Senator Johnson had built. The senator swamped him in the primary, eliminating him as a serious presidential contender. A bewildered Hoover sought advice from the political commentator Walter Lippmann, whom he had gotten to know in the wartime government. Lippmann explained that Hoover had made a tactical mistake by revealing his party affiliation. As long as Hoover remained undeclared, the Republican old guard had to take him seriously due to their concern that the Democrats might nominate him. Once he withdrew from the Democratic contest, Republicans no longer had anything to fear from him.[28]

Hoover's loyal supporters held out hope that the Republican convention might still turn to him after the front-runners faltered. The convention instead passed over the internationally famous Hoover and chose the parochial Warren G. Harding. Needing to demonstrate his party loyalty, Hoover endorsed the Harding-Coolidge ticket, declaring the Republican platform to be progressive. During the campaign, he spoke out for Wilsonian internationalism but got cool responses from Republican audiences. At a rally in Indianapolis, the crowd listened to Hoover almost in silence and then cheered for the next speaker, a woman who "draped her oratory in the American flag and the wickedness of 'entanglements.'"[29]

After Franklin Roosevelt was nominated for vice president by the Democrats, Hoover sent him a congratulatory note, jesting that he was jeopardizing his new political standing by wishing his Democratic friend success in the campaign. Both men knew that the Democrats stood little chance of winning that election.

Warren Harding wanted the best minds in his cabinet, and that meant finding a place for Herbert Hoover. Instead of being tapped for a top job as secretary of state or treasury, Hoover was offered the lesser post of secretary of commerce, which was a disappointment for him. He held out until he received assurance that he would be given a free hand in reorganizing the department and a say in all economic matters, from business and finance to agriculture and foreign policy. Newspapers began calling him "the Secretary of Everything." For reporters, Secretary Hoover served as a handy "dictionary of dates or a cyclopedia of useful information." He convened scores of conferences with business and labor leaders, keeping his name in the headlines on a daily basis. His hyperactivity made some journalists speculate that the war had spoiled Hoover by amplifying his every action so that he could not settle down into the humdrum routines of an "unromantic department." Justice Brandeis also had second thoughts about Hoover after hearing talk in Washington circles about his insatiable grasping for power and publicity.[30]

Having returned almost as an immigrant to his native land, Hoover established his 100 percent Americanism in *American Individualism,* a small book that he published in 1922. For him, individualism required equality of opportunity, the nation's "most precious social ideal." His personal participation in the "backwash of war and revolution" had confronted him with the troubling rise of totalitarian regimes. He positioned himself as a man in the middle, standing between the old-fashioned, laissez-faire, rugged individualism that had allowed social inequalities to develop and put property rights ahead of human rights, on the one side, and the type of central state planning that led to regimentation and infringement on individual liberties, on the other. He envisioned a system of voluntary economic planning through cooperative arrangements between government, business, and labor. Rather than break up big business under antitrust laws, he argued, the federal government should foster cooperative trade associations to set standards of fair business and labor practices. As secretary of commerce, he put his philosophy into practice by encouraging the formation of trade associations. Secretary Hoover also convened an unemployment conference in 1922 to deal with the loss of jobs during the recession. Although the conference promoted his concept of voluntary cooperation, it also recommended expanded public works to encourage employment and business stability. Before any of its proposals could be carried out, however, the economy recovered on its own.[31]

The event that gave Hoover the most visibility was the disastrous Mississippi River flood during the spring of 1927. Prolonged rain had made the river burst its levees, inundating millions of acres of farmland and displacing thousands of people. President Coolidge named his commerce secretary to head the Special Mississippi Flood Committee to find food, clothing, and medicine for the flood victims. Through voluntary contributions to the Red Cross and free shipping by the railroads, some 600,000 people received relief assistance under Hoover's guidance. Although many federal agencies contributed to this effort, none of the money came from the federal government. The Red Cross even had to reimburse the U.S. Army for equipment it used. Newspapers and newsreels portrayed Hoover as the nation's "family physician"—the person to call in troubled times.[32]

Hoover's flood relief activities demonstrated his strengths and exposed some of his flaws, particularly his penchant for issuing confident statements that ran contrary to the facts. In his speeches, for example, he regularly noted that only six people had died due to the flooding since the Red Cross had begun its efforts, long after reports confirmed additional victims. Nor could Hoover admit the slightest fault in the massive relief effort he led. He exaggerated its accomplishments and ignored some of its biggest problems—namely, its failure to improve the appalling conditions of southern black sharecroppers. In the aftermath of the flood, white landowners were forcibly holding their sharecroppers in camps to prevent an exodus from the Delta. The black press published reports of their conditions, which Hoover ignored.[33]

At the conclusion of his mission, Hoover submitted a costly plan by which the federal government would pay for the reconstruction of the levees in several states. His proposal accepted the legitimacy of federal action, recognizing that the state and local governments along the river lacked the resources to do the job by themselves. President Coolidge blanched at the price tag but reluctantly submitted Hoover's flood control plan to Congress. It covered the riverbanks from Missouri to Louisiana and would cost $296 million over ten years. The Senate raised that figure to $325 million, but the tightfisted Coolidge threatened a veto unless the House capped the expenditures. Congress cut the amount while still allocating more than the president had wanted. Bowing to public opinion, Coolidge signed the Flood Control Act of 1928—the largest appropriation for a domestic program up to that point. Hoover and Congress drew different conclusions from this legislation. Southern Democrats from states bordering on the Mississippi saw the act as establishing a precedent that the federal government would respond to natural disasters with funds, rather than leave the rebuilding to the state governments, unaided. For Hoover, the moral of the story was that a private relief organization had handled all individual needs and that government had limited its response to construction projects. That clash of perspectives would reoccur during his presidency.[34]

Hoover traveled to South Dakota in the summer of 1927 to present his flood report to the vacationing Coolidge. The Secret Service agent who accompanied them on the thirty-mile ride from Coolidge's lodge to a press conference in Rapid City noticed that the two men sat side by side without speaking a word to each other for the entire trip. President Coolidge resented the public acclaim his secretary of commerce was receiving, and he griped that Hoover had been giving him unsolicited advice for years, "all of it bad." While in South Dakota that summer, Coolidge stunned the nation by stating that he did not choose to run in 1928. Republican conservatives hoped that he could be drafted for another term, but Hoover took the president at his word and launched his own bid to replace him. Among the potential Republican candidates, Coolidge probably preferred the Senate's majority leader, Charles Curtis, but the Kansas senator lacked Hoover's stature. Coolidge watched

Hoover's progress toward the nomination with little pleasure, since the two men held such divergent views on the proper role of government. "If you see ten troubles coming down the road," Coolidge advised Hoover, "you can be sure that nine will run into the ditch before they reach you and you have to battle with only one of them." Hoover could not accept this advice because, as he observed, "when the tenth trouble reached him he was wholly unprepared, and it had by that time acquired such momentum that it spelled disaster."[35]

THE ELECTION OF 1928

The oddest aspect of Herbert Hoover's presidential candidacy was that so few Republican leaders favored him, observed Alice Roosevelt Longworth, the wife of Republican Speaker of the House Nicholas Longworth, whereas "most of them were openly or covertly against him." The iconoclastic H. L. Mencken agreed that no one in Washington liked Hoover, other than those who expected to get jobs in his administration. The public, rather than the politicians, mandated Hoover's nomination, admiring him as the embodiment of the American dream. None of those who ran against him could measure up to his record of accomplishments—nor could they match his campaign funds and organization. At the Republican convention, the party's old guard referred contemptuously to Hoover's loyalists as boy scouts, but the candidate had spent nearly eight years in the cabinet studying how professionals played the game, and by then, his organization had lost its amateur status.[36]

Hoover's political identity remained murky, reflecting his discomfort in associating himself exclusively with any faction. Conservatives suspected him of being too progressive. Progressives regarded his activities in the Commerce Department as being too probusiness. Isolationists worried about his internationalist tendencies. And he had not held an elected office since college. To demonstrate his popular appeal, Hoover entered a string of primaries, taking on some popular favorite-son candidates. United only by their contempt for Hoover, the favorite sons—most of them senators—aimed to amass enough delegates to prevent him from gaining a first-ballot majority. In a deadlocked convention, they would select a nominee in the back room. The senatorial group hoped to control the convention's Credentials Committee, but Hoover's forces prevailed and installed one of his supporters, Assistant Attorney General Mabel Walker Willebrandt, as chair of the committee.

The Republican presidential nomination required just a simple majority of delegates, rather than the two-thirds vote that Democratic nominees needed. Majority rule gave undue advantage to the 25 percent of the delegates from the Deep South and border states, where Republicans rarely won elections. The "black-and-tan" delegations from the South consisted largely of African Americans who were deprived of the vote by poll taxes, literacy tests, grandfather clauses, and physical intimidation—despite the assurances of the Fifteenth Amendment. Their only political advantage came through federal jobs from Republican administrations. Shrewd political managers therefore courted the southern black delegates with promises of patronage and payments of their campaign expenses.

To Hoover, this patronage system reeked of corruption, and he refused to allow his agents to make any deals of this type. His campaign manager instead reminded the southern blacks that Hoover had done well in the primaries and would enter the convention as the front-runner: if they hoped to benefit under the next administration, they had better commit to Hoover promptly. Republican reformers in the South—mostly white business owners, lawyers, and other professionals—put forward "lily-white" delegations to challenge the so-called black and tans. Hoover's agents made it clear that they would accept whichever group endorsed their candidate. On the Credentials Committee, Mabel Walker Willebrandt headed a pro-Hoover majority that consistently seated his delegations. For three southern states, they installed lily whites in place of the blacks and tans. The other African American delegates got the message and fell in line. Hoover sailed to a first-ballot victory.[37]

For vice president, Hoover had in mind former Massachusetts governor Channing Cox, a vigorous stump speaker who could help the ticket in the Northeast. But Republican senators complained that no one outside of that region knew Cox. As a gesture to the farm states, they insisted on the nomination of the Senate's majority leader, Charles Curtis. Part Kaw Indian, Curtis was a law-and-order, high-tariff, dry Republican from Kansas. No one ever accused him of being a progressive, but progressive senators trusted him as a "great reconciler" who faithfully kept his word. Regarding Curtis as a political hack, Hoover grumbled that his party could have given him a more distinguished running mate, but he accepted the imposition. Having spent the primaries lambasting Hoover, Senator Curtis now had to eat his words. Amused reporters in the press section nudged each other at the sight of him accepting the

"the indignity of second place on the ticket. His mustache twitched in pain, as he tried to smile. It was only a contorted grin that creased his swarthy face."[38]

The Democrats nominated New York governor Al Smith and Arkansas senator Joseph T. Robinson, a ticket that gingerly patched together their city-country, North-South, wet-dry, Catholic-Protestant divides. As a popular and effective governor of the nation's largest state, Smith had championed urban reform, ethnic pluralism, and the underprivileged. He had grown up on Manhattan's East Side, dropped out of school, and worked in the Fulton Fish Market. He retained his Lower East Side accent as he rose through the political ranks of Tammany Hall, the city's Democratic machine, and into state office. Smith was serving in the state legislature in 1911 when a fire at the Triangle Shirt Waist Factory in Manhattan killed 146 women; some died from the smoke and flames, others by jumping from the eleventh-story windows. Along with a fellow Tammany Democrat, Robert F. Wagner, Smith investigated the disaster and was shocked at the wretched working conditions in the city's factories. Together, Smith and Wagner sponsored a series of pathbreaking laws that established fire codes and set standards for workers' health and safety. Smith went on to serve four two-year terms as governor.[39]

It was fashionable for city dwellers to regard the rural population as backward and themselves as forward thinking, but politicians in the 1920s talked about the "conservative East" and the "radical West." Conservatives generally ran well in the industrial Northeast, whereas progressives remained politically entrenched in the West. Conservatives and populists coexisted warily in the rural South. Al Smith and New York epitomized the ideological confusion of the decade. People in the South and West distrusted New York as the "citadel of conservatism," symbolized by Wall Street and eastern bankers. At the same time, New York was home to more political radicals than all other parts of the country combined. As the state's governor, Al Smith was similarly difficult to pin down ideologically. A political liberal who responded to the needs of a metropolitan, immigrant, industrial population, he sometimes seemed more eager to please the business community that he aspired to join than the working class from which he had emerged—and he privately supplemented his government income with cash and stock options from wealthy friends. On such social issues as woman's rights, Smith tended toward cultural conservatism, yet on Prohibition, he was wringing wet.[40]

"I'm going to beat the pants off Hoover," Smith assured reporters at the start of the campaign. With his engaging public personality and trademark brown derby, the governor generated lively newspaper copy. He exhibited an easy humor and could explain complex issues in everyday language. But for all his winning attributes, Smith faced daunting obstacles. It would have taken a miracle for any Democrat to win against the popular Hoover during the high tide of Republican prosperity, and Smith bore the added liabilities of being a Roman Catholic in a Protestant nation, the son of immigrants in a nativist era, and the product of an urban political machine associated in the rural public's mind with venality. Smith had rarely traveled outside New York and had no experience with the nation's vast rural regions. "You just sit by the window all day and see nothing," the New Yorker commented, shaking his head as his campaign train crossed the West. People who viewed Smith as alien circulated malicious gossip about his wife and warned that the pope would move into the White House after his election. Crosses were burned along the railroad lines on which the candidate traveled, and a minister in Oklahoma City warned his congregation that anyone who voted for Al Smith would be damned to hell.[41]

On economic issues, Smith differed little from Hoover. He agreed that business formed the backbone of the nation and that government should not meddle with the ongoing boom. As a presidential candidate, he rarely mentioned any of the socially advanced legislation he had promoted as governor. For his campaign manager and Democratic Party chairman, Smith selected John J. Raskob, an executive with DuPont and General Motors who not long before had been identified in *Who's Who* as a Republican and a capitalist. The newly minted Democrat Raskob was, like Smith, a Catholic and a wet on Prohibition. The Democratic platform downplayed the party's traditional opposition to protective tariffs, and it sounded vague on farm relief, labor rights, and taxation. Despite this generally conservative tilt, Smith came under fire from Hoover for supporting public ownership of waterpower resources in New York.[42]

Smith's campaign stepped off awkwardly when the candidate telegraphed the convention that regardless of its platform pledge of an "honest effort" to enforce the Eighteenth Amendment, he personally wanted to see Prohibition repealed. Franklin Roosevelt, who had placed Smith's name in nomination, considered this a foolish move, since the candidate's opposition to Prohibition was so well known that he had already locked up every wet vote in the country: Smith's declaration would just make it harder for him to appeal to the drys. Smith had been trying to appease the liberal *New York World,* his strongest editorial supporter. Walter Lippmann, the *World*'s editorial page editor, believed that candidates should speak out forthrightly. "It does seem to me preposterous that a man should claim nomination for President of the United States," Lippmann insisted, "without ever having declared himself on national issues." Leaders of the Anti-saloon League were ecstatic that Smith had injected the Prohibition issue into the campaign for them.[43]

Hoover enjoyed a drink, but politically, he stayed dry (moderation, not necessarily abstention, is a Quaker standard). In his acceptance speech, he proclaimed that the nation had "deliberately undertaken a great social and economic experiment, noble in motive and far reaching in purpose." Headline writers abridged this to a "noble experiment," and the paraphrase stuck, despite Hoover's protest that the press had twisted his words. The term managed to upset both sides, since wets disliked the "noble" part and drys hated the "experiment" part. Hoover defended the Eighteenth Amendment and promised more effective enforcement. Smith insisted that the law had fostered a disrespect for governmental authority. Although Smith alienated the drys in his own party, his stand attracted some wealthy Republicans wets, whose financial contributions helped Democrats to almost match the Republicans in fund-raising that year.[44]

Inside the Smith campaign, Franklin Roosevelt lamented that the candidate concentrated entirely on winning the cities, with their large immigrant and Catholic populations, and ignored the countryside. Smith's advisers mistakenly assumed that the cities dominated the nation the way they did New York State, and they miscalculated the political clout of rural Americans. Hoover proved the more astute political analyst. He anticipated that Smith would do well in the cities of the North and Midwest, and he looked to balance them in the South, which had mostly gone Democratic since Reconstruction. In his acceptance speech, he made a brief plea for religious tolerance and then ignored the issue for the duration of the campaign. His staff refrained from attacking Smith on religious grounds and let Southern Methodists and Baptists do it for them. Campaign buttons proclaimed "Hoover Democrat" and "A Christian in the White House." In Washington, the campaign located its southern division away from the Republican National Committee (RNC) to make it a more hospitable place for anti-Smith Democrats to visit. With southern blacks mostly disenfranchised, Hoover's campaign was

Herbert Hoover talks with reporters during the 1928 campaign. He had made himself highly accessible as secretary of commerce, but as a candidate, Hoover generally kept his distance from the press.

focused on attracting southern white, middle-class professionals and temperance groups.[45]

Southern Democrats accused the candidate of abolishing segregated facilities in the Department of Commerce (which he had), but Hoover's campaign staff categorically denied that any change had occurred under his command "regarding the treatment of colored people." They presumed that despite such slaps, northern blacks would vote the Republican ticket out of traditional loyalty. Hoover's speeches avoided any criticism of the Ku Klux Klan, lynching, or anything else that might offend southern whites. Speaking in Elizabethton, Tennessee—in the traditionally Republican northeast corner of the state, wedged between North Carolina, Virginia, and Kentucky—he linked southern progress to the need for a merit system in the civil service, a coded signal that his administration would cut blacks off from federal patronage. The strategy enabled him to win seven Democratic strongholds: Florida, Kentucky, North Carolina, Tennessee, Texas, Virginia, and West Virginia. Those southern Democrats who voted for him became known as Hoover-crats.[46]

Hoover tried to steer clear of overt references to the religious issue, but they surfaced under the rubric of Prohibition. In September, Mabel Walker Willebrandt delivered a highly charged address to a Methodist ministers' conference in Ohio. She never mentioned Smith's religion but cited his connections to Tammany Hall and to New York's dereliction in enforcing Prohibition. "There are two thousand pastors here," she declared. "You have in your churches more than six hundred thousand members of the Methodist church in Ohio, alone. That is enough to swing the election." Governor Smith interpreted her remarks as an appeal to Protestants against Catholics, and on national radio, he delivered an impassioned address against injecting religion into politics. The controversy put the RNC on the defensive. Despite having encouraged Willebrandt to barnstorm, the national committee issued a disclaimer that she had not been speaking officially for the campaign. Candidate Hoover described Willebrandt's efforts as "freelance," although his aides had reviewed her text in advance. Hoover remained above the fray, while his campaign rode the era's cultural prejudices.[47]

Newspaper correspondents who had covered the Commerce Department were puzzled about the change that came over Hoover during the presidential campaign. Before, he had been easily accessible; now, he was withdrawn, hesitant to speak plainly and risk offending one or the other wings of the Republican Party. In addition, the presidential candidate revealed a "horror of personal publicity." His journalist friend Will Irwin produced a campaign film, *Master of Emergencies*, that had audiences sobbing over its depictions of Hoover's humanitarian efforts. Appalled by its appeal to emotion, Hoover told Irwin that the movie would "get votes only from the morons." In *American Individualism*, he had disparaged "the crowd" as having no mind, only feelings to be manipulated by demagogues on the left and right. As a candidate, he intended to offer informed argument rather than fervent oratory. In fact, he felt terribly uneasy in front of crowds. On the podium, he read rather than spoke, buried his face in the speech text, and went about the task with a minimum of inflection or gestures.[48]

Candidate Hoover delivered seven campaign addresses, each carried over the radio to national audiences. Radio networks had been patched together by 1928 and for the first time could broadcast a candidate's remarks into households across the country. Hoover may not have been anywhere as engaging a speaker as Al Smith on the stump, but radio made his flat midwestern tone sound more "American" than the Democrat's rasping New York accent. For most of the campaign, Hoover kept a low public profile and limited the occasions when he allowed himself to be interviewed or photographed. His public relations agents despaired that he did not appreciate the value of human interest stories. To counteract his stiff and indrawn appearance, his staff spread the word that the candidate could be charming in private. Hoover's aloofness initially helped Smith, who talked freely and garnered a greater share of the news stories. Republicans protested that reporters were deliberately making Al Smith sound more interesting, but this was because Smith permitted the press to quote him directly. As the campaign progressed, the Smith campaign complained that the press was aiding Hoover's candidacy by quoting Smith's off-the-cuff remarks and slang.[49]

In Hoover's place, several Republican progressives stumped vigorously for the Republican ticket, among them Senators William E. Borah of Idaho, Smith Wildman Brookhart of Iowa, and Charles McNary of Oregon. They all trusted that Hoover would approach farm relief more flexibly than the dogmatic Coolidge, and their speeches helped Hoover in the farm states, where the economic slump had made him vulnerable. Senator Borah gave eloquent addresses throughout the western states. Senator Brookhart focused on Hoover's birth state, Iowa. And Senator McNary, the sponsor of the McNary-Haugen farm bills that Coolidge had

Hoover campaigns in Paterson, New Jersey, on September 18, 1928. Uncomfortable appearing in front of large crowds, he gave only seven speeches during his winning presidential campaign.

vetoed, lent his influential name: if McNary supported Hoover, farmers could trust him.

Hoover's lack of zeal for campaigning reinforced his public image of not being a politician, a decided strength at a time when the Harding scandals had left professional politicians in "bad odor." Hoover promised a more active presidency than either Harding or Coolidge had delivered, and his campaign speeches sounded positively idealistic in contrast to Coolidge's well-known reservations about government. Despite Hoover's private concerns about rampant stock market speculation, the Republican campaign linked him personally to the good times. Campaign workers handed out copper coins called Hoover Lucky Pocket Pieces on which was inscribed "Good for four years of prosperity." Republican ads stressed that "a vote for Herbert Hoover is a vote for *experience,* not *experiment*—a vote for the continuance of an administration which has led America to new peaks of achievement—a vote for the party that has wiped soup-kitchens, strikes and bread lines from the land." The most famous—and later infamous—Republican advertisement promised "A chicken in every pot, a car in every garage."[50]

Hoover painted a splendid picture of a new era of perpetual prosperity, a time in which poverty would vanish entirely. "We have not yet reached the goal," he said when he accepted the nomination, "yet, given a chance to go forward with the policies of the last eight years, we shall soon, with the help of God, be in sight of the day when poverty will be banished from this nation." The vision remained the theme of his last major speech on the eve of the election, when he carried the fight to Madison Square Garden in Al Smith's home state. He assailed Smith's policies on public power as being closer to European socialism than to American individualism. His campaign staff had advised him that the power issue was not high in the public's mind, but Hoover was determined to convince the voters of a perfidious threat from the Left. His charges confused social action with socialism, and they convinced the progressive Republican George Norris to endorse Al Smith, but Hoover's warnings resonated with eastern conservatives. Until then, bookmakers had given odds that Smith would carry New York State. After the speech, the odds shifted to Hoover.[51]

On election day, Herbert Hoover carried New York and thirty-nine other states with 57 percent of the vote. The factors that most swayed the voters were the decade's soaring prosperity and Al Smith's religion. Hoover had barely uttered three sentences against religious intolerance,

H. L. Mencken wrote on the eve of the vote, "but the bigots kept on supporting him, and they will support him tomorrow, and he knows it and is counting on it." One of Hoover's wartime aides, Robert Taft, assessed the election results in Ohio for his father, former president William Howard Taft, and concluded that the wets and Catholics had been for Smith and everyone else went for Hoover. Taft noted that it was hard to separate religion from Prohibition and anti-Tammany sentiments, but he stated that "after all this is a Protestant country." No matter how well Al Smith scored among Catholics, wets, and immigrants, these groups together constituted only a minority of the population. Hoover drew strong support from the old-stock, Protestant, and dry voters, as well as from business executives, doctors, lawyers, and teachers. He also attracted the majority of female voters and by far the largest share of African Americans.[52]

Smith's 15 million votes were some 6.6 million more than the Democrats had polled four years earlier. He took about half the urban vote nationwide, with a particularly large margin in New York City. Yet he ran abysmally in much of the South, where many traditional Democrats had either "gone fishing" on election day or voted for Hoover. The Republican candidate carried seven southern states and ran strong in such cities as Dallas, Houston, Birmingham, Atlanta, and Richmond. He profited from intense campaigning by southern Prohibitionists, and riding on his coattails, a record number of Prohibitionists were elected to the next Congress. This victory, however, would prove counterproductive for the drys. The partisan activities of the ostensibly nonpartisan Anti-saloon League outraged southern Democrats, causing them to stray from the fold. As long as the Republicans remained entrenched at the Capitol and the White House, Prohibition would be safe, but if that changed, the Anti-saloon League's political base would shrink as well. Drys could not imagine that just four years after a smashing success, their cause would evaporate. As the party of prosperity, Republicans built an unsurmountable electoral majority throughout the 1920s, leaving open the question of whether they could sustain this support if prosperity faltered. The people held great expectations for their new problem-solving president, without anticipating the catastrophic problems he would soon face.[53]

One of the few to express reservations in the rosy afterglow of Hoover's victory was his onetime friend Franklin Roosevelt, the newly elected governor of New York. Roosevelt spotted a potential defect in Hoover's performance style. He had known and admired Hoover's abilities as the head of a department where he could focus on one problem at a time and bring it to a triumphant conclusion. But he predicted that those talents would handicap a president who needed "a versatility of mind that can take up one subject after another during the day and find itself equally at home in all of them." Roosevelt doubted that Hoover could keep his equilibrium while jumping from one domestic or foreign policy problem to another at half-hour intervals. The presidency, he believed, would require a man with a very different temperament than Herbert Hoover possessed.[54]

2

PREFIX FOR POVERTY

Something about Hoover's name lent itself as a label. Initially, it had a positive ring. During World War I, for example, when people said they Hooverized, they meant that they economized. And in the 1928 presidential election, Republicans talked about an endlessly bullish Hoover market. Yet when the economy collapsed on President Hoover's watch, his name became a prefix for poverty. The homeless built shantytowns they called Hoovervilles. Newspapers became Hoover blankets, patched aprons were Hoover aprons, and pockets turned inside out were Hoover flags. Broken-down vehicles were Hoover cars, and mules pulled Hoover carts. Hunters bagged rabbits and called them Hoover hogs. To be Hooverized now meant to be impoverished.

Such a turn in fortune was inconceivable on election night in November 1928, when a solid majority of Americans registered confidence in Herbert Hoover's abilities. His Democratic opponent, Al Smith, felt so disheartened by the election returns that he told reporters he did not expect to run for office again. The anti-Catholic bias Smith encountered had been deeply discouraging, as had his failure to carry his home state of New York; Smith ran 100,000 votes behind the man he had handpicked to run for governor, Franklin Roosevelt, who eked out a narrow victory. The election changed the political landscape. Assuming that Hoover would have a lock on the White House until 1936, Roosevelt's political guru, Louis McHenry Howe, wanted FDR to wait another four years before running for governor, but Roosevelt had given in when Al Smith implored him to make the race.

The election results caused Howe to revise his timetable. On the morning after the election, he stopped to talk with the *New York World* reporter Charles Michelson on Broadway. "Al Smith isn't going to like this," he told Michelson. "He has lost the state and Franklin has carried it, and the country is not going to forget that when 1932 comes around and the Democrats pick a candidate for president."[1]

THE PARTY ORGANIZATIONS

Between elections, the national party organizations usually slipped into hibernation and left politics to the elected officeholders. A year before the next presidential election, members of each party's national committee would congregate in Washington to pick a date and a place for their convention, name a sergeant at arms, and then adjourn. The committees would reconvene prior to the opening of the conventions to settle credential disputes between rival delegations. The presidential nominees would name new national chairmen, who would set up campaign headquarters (usually in New York or Chicago), form finance committees, hire staffs, line up speakers, print campaign literature, and purchase ads. Once the election was over, the national committees would once again go dormant. Although the victorious party committee could recommend lower-level federal appointees, control of most patronage concentrated political power in the White House. The president acted as his party's national political boss, but the defeated party had no equivalent. Since Republicans occupied the presidency most often between the Civil War and the Great Depression, they built a national political organization around federal patronage. As members of the minority party, Democrats on the national level organized around Congress and state and local political machines.[2]

Republicans broke this pattern in 1918, when they formed a functioning organization well in advance of the next presidential election and appointed a savvy Indiana politician, Will Hayes, as Republican National Committee chairman. Hayes raised and spent prodigiously, promoted party unity, and coordinated strategy prior to the national campaign. The Republican victory in 1920 earned Hayes copious praise and a cabinet appointment. The defeated Democrats aspired to copy Hayes's practices but lacked his party's plentiful finances. Their national chairman, Tennessee representative Cordell Hull, operated out of a two-room office staffed by a secretary and a publicity director—tagged by the Washington press corps as a "poorly paid, unimaginative, and obscure ex-newspaper-man who needed the job." Even so, the Democratic National Committee (DNC) won acclaim for the party's rebound in the 1922 congressional elections, when a recession helped their candidates make strong gains.[3]

After the disastrous convention and election of 1924, the DNC fell into inertia. Expressing concern about this organizational lethargy, the former vice presidential candidate, Franklin Roosevelt, sent a circular letter to all recent convention delegates soliciting their opinions about how to make the party "stronger and more militant." Roosevelt suggested that a full-time national committee could hold frequent party conferences, but with the party's ranks badly divided and its treasury nearly empty, his initiative went nowhere. The journalist H. L. Mencken, himself a registered Democrat, described the party in those days as a loose federation of "discordant minorities" at war with each other, and he judged the distance between the wings of the party as greater than the distance separating them from the Republicans.[4]

Surveying the Democrats' three successive presidential losses, DNC chairman John Jakob Raskob concluded that the few months between the nomination and the election did not provide enough time to organize an effective national campaign. An unassuming-looking man, Raskob had fathered thirteen children and had amassed a personal fortune through his managerial connections with Du Pont and General Motors. He set out in a determined manner to build an ongoing party organization that could plan for the next round of congressional elections and the next presidential contest. As a fund-raiser, Raskob had achieved a political miracle by nearly matching the Republicans in campaign funds, bringing in some $6 million compared with the $1.3 million that Democrats had collected in 1924. Even so, the Democrats ended the 1928 campaign in debt, and the downturn in the economy would seriously complicate their efforts to pay off their obligations. Democratic headquarters depended almost entirely on the largesse of the DNC chairman, who lent the party $30,000 a month to cover salaries and expenses. Some Democrats complained that their chairman had brought the party out of bankruptcy, stood it on its financial feet, and then clamped a mortgage on it.[5]

Chairman Raskob's deep pockets enabled Democrats to rent an entire floor of the National Press Building in Washington and fill its warren of offices with secretaries, stenographers, clerks, and messengers. Visitors compared the party headquarters to a corporate suite, leading some liberals to disavow the Democratic organization as the Republicans' twin. Further reinforcing the corporate image was the man Raskob chose to run the DNC's day-to-day operation, former Kansas representative Jouett Shouse, chairman of the Executive Committee. A suave, dapper man who dressed in spats and carried a cane, Shouse shared the chairman's conservative inclinations and served as the face and voice of the DNC during the Hoover administration.

The DNC also hired Charles Michelson away from the Washington bureau of the *New York World* to be its publicity director. In past elections, leading newspapers had granted leaves of absence to some of their top Washington correspondents to handle publicity for the campaign organizations, depending on each paper's preferred party. When the campaigns ended, the reporters would return to their old jobs and cover the politicians they had just helped to elect. Charley Michelson quit the newspaper business entirely to accept a handsome salary and a free hand in designing Democratic publicity. Reporters described Michelson affectionately as a gray, tousled elf of a man who huddled over his typewriter in a cloud of cigarette smoke, but they would have discounted any press releases issued under his name as so much partisan propaganda. Therefore, he instead devoted himself to writing speeches for Senate and House Democrats, reasoning that if a member of Congress said something quotable, reporters would print it as news. Combining hard data with catchy phrases, irony, and invective, Michelson wrote piles of speeches for an assortment of members eager for material. It became a commonplace around the Capitol that if members of Congress sounded like politicians when they delivered a speech, the words were their own, but if they sounded like statesmen, Charley Michelson must have written them.[6]

While the Democrats built a functional publicity machine, the Republicans neglected their own. During the 1920s, the RNC had plenty of money to run its press operations but spent it mostly on feeding canned news stories and editorials to small, weekly, rural Republican papers. In 1928, the Kansas newspaper publisher Henry J. Allen directed Hoover's publicity efforts, but in April 1929, he accepted an appointment to fill the Senate seat vacated by Vice President Curtis. After Allen's departure, the RNC let its publicity operation expire, dropping all of his assistants from the payroll. Republican national chairman Hubert Work was content to turn publicity matters over to the White House, assuming that President Hoover's press conferences and administrative actions would preclude the need for party propaganda. This strategy left the RNC unprepared for Charley Michelson's explosion of Democratic propaganda.[7]

Other RNC operations also fell into disrepair during the Hoover years. The president had no luck in finding a satisfactory national chairman, and each of his choices only deepened the party's internal divisions. In 1928, he had encouraged a network of independent, volunteer-run Hoover for President groups, to appeal to independent voters. He kept the RNC out of his campaign as much as possible, naming Work, a former cabinet officer, as RNC chairman with the understanding that the candidate rather than the national committee would run the campaign. After the election, the president expressed his displeasure with the RNC's traditional system of patronage rewards, and he expected Work to defer to the White House on patronage decisions. He intended to use patronage for building new Republican organizations in the South and for establishing political leverage with Congress. Having grown used to being able to recommend lower-level appointments through the RNC, congressional Republicans were rankled by the loss of that prerogative. Senate majority leader James "Sunny Jim" Watson conveyed their unhappiness to the president. An old-fashioned, backslapping pol, Watson had led the stop-Hoover forces at the 1928 convention, but he rallied to Hoover's support as president and head of his party. Hoover disliked the majority leader and discounted his advice. For months, he resisted Watson's warnings that Republicans in Congress considered Work inept, until he finally relented and eased Work out of the chairmanship.[8]

Hoover's second choice for the position was intended to signal reconciliation with Republican regulars. Tennessee businessman Claudius Huston promised to return to the traditional ways of handling patronage, but scandal cut short his tenure. Huston headed the Tennessee River Improvement Association, which lobbied against plans for a federal electric power project in the Tennessee Valley. Progressive supporters of public power retaliated by launching a congressional investigation into charges that the Republican chairman was being paid by the "power trust." As the headlines turned ugly, Hoover dithered over Huston's future until it became clear that Democrats would make him an issue in the congressional elections. Hoover then named a third national chairman, an old-school, standpat senator from Ohio, Simeon D. Fess. Senator Fess had once opposed Hoover's appointment as secretary of commerce on the grounds that he was temperamentally unfit to cooperate, but by 1930, he had become the president's devoted advocate. A former professor and given to lecturing his colleagues in the Senate, Fess twitted the progressives as "pseudo-Republicans," not an auspicious approach to party unity.[9]

Intending Senator Fess to act as a figurehead, Hoover placed real authority for directing the party's affairs in the hands of Robert Lucas, executive assistant to the chairman. The forty-year-old Lucas hailed from Louisville, Kentucky, and was a player in Hoover's strategy of reconstructing Republican leadership in the South from black to white. Hoover appointed Lucas as the commissioner of the Bureau of Internal Revenue and invited him to join the influential Medicine Ball Cabinet that exercised each morning on the White House lawn. Lucas gained the president's confidence as the ideal man to revitalize the RNC, but the party chairmanship was an unpaid position and Lucas needed an income to support his family. So, Senator Fess took the chairmanship, and Lucas got a salary and expenses as his executive assistant. Lucas also managed an off-the-books "special fund" for surreptitious use against the president's opponents within the party.[10]

During the congressional elections of 1930, Robert Lucas spearheaded an educational campaign to put the facts about Hoover's administration before the public. The garrulous Senator Fess, finding it impossible not to speak his mind, issued a flood of pronouncements urging Republicans to remain loyal to Prohibition. Fess's bone-dry stand alienated the party's wets, distracting attention from Hoover's programs. The president instructed the chairman not to talk so much.[11]

Ostensibly neutral in all party primaries, the RNC was supposed "to elect, not select" the party's candidates, but news leaked out that Lucas was secretly financing state primary campaigns against progressive Republicans. A congressional inquiry uncovered evidence of the special fund Lucas had used in the Nebraska primary against Senator George Norris, paying for cartoons and literature signed with fictitious names to evade the state's campaign-financing laws. Lucas admitted his actions but justified them by arguing that the independent-minded senator had broken with the party by failing to endorse Hoover for president. Despite these efforts, Norris won the primary and a resounding reelection, whereas many regular Republicans went down to defeat. Revelations of the clandestine campaign activities diminished Lucas's effectiveness, and as party finances plummeted during the Depression, the RNC laid off most of its staff.[12]

HOOVER'S TROUBLED PRESIDENCY

Herbert Hoover took office with a substantial electoral mandate and Republican majorities in both houses of Congress. He enjoyed the admiration of many members of the Washington press corps, whom he had cultivated as secretary of commerce and who anticipated a more open and active presidency. The U.S. economy flourished, and Europe seemed finally to have recovered from the traumatic effects of the world war. At the start of his term, Hoover's chief concern was that his party had oversold him as a "superman," raising public expectations too high for him to satisfy. Indeed, that image quickly deflated after he encountered some of the worst luck of any president, compounded by his own political missteps. Within months, Republicans in Congress split over the new tariff, and on Wall Street, the stock market crashed. If the president had to have such bad breaks, his supporters took comfort in the knowledge that they happened during his first year in office. "Things can keep right on breaking badly, of course," one columnist mused, "but the fact remains that they seldom do."[13]

Many of Hoover's problems stemmed from his own disposition. In a confidential report to his government, the British ambassador to Washington appraised the new president's lack of social charm, conversational ability, and direct human sympathy. Fortunately, the ambassador noted, Lou Hoover possessed "all the qualities which her distinguished husband lacks." The president seemed to combine an absolute confidence in his opinions with a painful sensitivity to any criticism, a mix that was "not likely to make the White House a bed of roses for him, nor perhaps his staff." The ambassador's assessments were not, however, entirely accurate. In small groups, Hoover could be a relaxed and engaging conversationalist. Having traveled extensively, read voraciously, and absorbed vast amounts of information, he could talk intelligently with visitors on seemingly any subject. But in contrast to his capacity to convince a few at a time, he had a limited ability to stir mass audiences, causing the Republican newspaper editor William Allen White to fret, "I don't think he can sublet the job of emotional appeal."[14]

Even in intimate settings, Hoover would talk only as long as he held everyone's attention. As soon as someone else tried to lead the conversation, he would fall back into sullen silence. One of his secretaries commented that even after working closely with the president for a year, he found it hard to carry on a general conversation with him. Hoover complained about how much time he wasted listening to useless advice from others, especially from members of Congress. Sometimes, when a conversation lasted too long for Hoover's liking, he would look up abruptly and utter a violent expletive that would startle his visitor into silence. Having witnessed his brusque and brittle nature, his closest aides did their best to protect "the Chief" from anyone they thought he would not want to hear. The First Lady similarly steered dinner conversations away from subjects he would not want to discuss. Their protectiveness deprived him of the range of opinions and alternatives he should have been getting.[15]

Hoover the engineer pondered problems from all angles, mulling over the many reasons why a decision might fail. Although he scrutinized data, he often seemed to work from hunches or instinct—akin to the divine guidance that Quakers called an inner light. Slow to reach a conclusion, he would act speedily, even impetuously, once he had made up his mind and then become stubbornly defensive of his decision. These qualities, along with an extraordinary ability to tackle and solve problems, made it nearly impossible for Hoover to delegate responsibility. Though he was famous for appointing commissions, he shouldered the largest load of his administration himself, working seven days a week and late into the nights, which pushed him to dangerous levels of exhaustion. Other than for weekend fishing trips, he rarely left the White House. "The public only yields privacy to officials in fishing and in prayer," he once commented, "and they can't pray all the time." Unlike his predecessors, Hoover remained in Washington every summer—an ordeal made bearable only by the installation of the first air conditioning in the White House during his presidency. Visiting Washington in 1931, the British author H. G. Wells sought a courtesy visit with the president and received a begrudging two minutes of his time. Wells recorded the visit as an intrusion upon an "overworked and overwhelmed man, a month behind in all his engagements and hopeless of ever overtaking them."[16]

To accommodate his vision of a strong, take-charge presidency, Hoover ordered a remodeling of the West Wing. First constructed during Theodore Roosevelt's presidency in 1902, the West Wing had previously housed a staff of forty. Architects achieved Hoover's plan for doubling this capacity by converting the basement storage area into offices. On Christmas Eve 1929, a spark from a faulty chimney flue set ablaze files shifted from the basement to the attic; those that were not burned suffered damage from the water used to douse the flames. Renovation of the gutted West Wing had to commence all over again. Dispossessed from the Oval Office, President Hoover operated out of the secretary of the navy's office in the building next door. A visitor described his temporary quarters as a long room stripped for business, with a brightly waxed, uncarpeted floor, nearly empty of furnishings save for a desk and a few chairs in the far corner.[17]

Previous presidents had made do with one secretary; Hoover asked Congress for authorization to appoint three. His appointments secretary, Lawrence Richey, had worked longer and closer with him than the others. A stocky Italian American (whose family name was originally Ricci), he had served as a Secret Service agent and private detective before Hoover hired him in 1917. Richey fit the president's requirement for "a man who could see sharply, hear quickly, walk warily, report accurately and—above all—be faithful to a friendship." He shared and facilitated Hoover's passion for fishing, the one diversion that allowed the president to unwind. He also satisfied Hoover's hunger for inside information, doing investigative work for him at the Commerce Department and the White House. As appointments secretary, he handled the daily calendar, determining who would see the president, and by keeping the shades in his office constantly drawn, he prevented reporters from identifying his visitors. White House staff identified Richey as *the boss*, the man who maintained tight control over all office operations. "We were all scared to death of him," a stenographer confessed.[18]

A second secretary, the owlish Walter Newton, had spent a dozen years in Congress and handled congressional relations. Politically shrewd, Newton found his job complicated by Hoover's disdain for pork-barrel politics and by Larry Richey's intervention in patronage requests. The third member of the triumvirate, George Akerson, a hulky, hard-drinking Scandinavian and a former Washington correspondent for the *Minneapolis Tribune,* became the first officially designated presidential press secretary. Well liked by reporters, Akerson had overseen Hoover's successful press operations at the Commerce Department. He had a harder time making the president more accessible to the newspapers and the radio, battles he regularly lost to the fiercely protective Richey.

President Hoover, according to speechwriter French Strother, "dominated his administration, its purposes, its methods, its mechanisms and its men." Hoover's insistence on writing his own policy speeches limited Strother's role, leaving him only to draft routine presidential pronouncements and compile material that the president could use for dictating his speeches. Others on the staff included a large number of stenographer-typists on loan from other government agencies that paid their salaries. Each stenographer agreed to stay late one night of the week to take dictation while Hoover answered his mail. Even sitting in the same room, they found it hard to hear him because he chewed on an unlit cigar and talked from one side of his mouth, and he avoided making eye contact. "He had the reputation of being a charmer," one of the women recalled, "but he hid it well."[19]

Republican majorities in Congress swelled as legislators rode in on Hoover's coattails, but divisions between party regulars and insurgents complicated his legislative leadership. Senators were especially individualistic and resistant to party discipline. During the presidential campaign, Hoover had offered himself as "everything to everybody and on every side of every proposition," Senator Hiram Johnson charged, but a president had to make decisions and choose sides. For Hoover, this happened early in his term when he attempted to fix the lingering farm depression. Western progressives had allied with southern Democrats to pass the McNary-Haugen farm relief bills that President Coolidge had vetoed. Since Idaho senator William E. Borah had stumped vigorously for him across the farm states in 1928, Hoover felt obligated to honor Borah's request to call Congress into special session to do something about farm relief.[20]

Hoover announced the special session in his inaugural address, amid his celebration of a prosperous American economy. With the nation blessed with abundant resources and opportunity, he harbored "no fears for the future of our country. It is bright with hope." But the special session acknowledged the troubled farm economy. Hoover proposed that Congress create a federal farm board to make loans to farm cooperatives, and at the same time, he called for a "limited revision" of the tariff to raise tariff rates on agricultural imports and thus boost sagging farm prices. He then made the tactical error of trying to distance himself from the tariff debates.

Wanting the federal government to subsidize the sale of surplus farm commodities on the world market, progressives did not think Hoover's farm programs went far enough. The president's refusal to accept their plan for subsidies pitted him against the same progressive senators who so recently had campaigned for him, and they sided with Democrats in opposing higher tariff rates. The regular Republicans on the House Ways and Means Committee, chaired by Representative Willis Hawley, pushed farm products to the side and took the opportunity to raise industrial tariffs to new highs. Hoover's failure to protest encouraged other economic interests to lobby the Senate Finance Committee, chaired by Utah senator Reed Smoot, for further tariff hikes. In retaliation, low-tariff Democrats and Republican progressives slowed the tariff debate over a tedious, fifteen-month process of congressional bargaining that fragmented the majority party. Had Hoover exercised his election mandate and exerted more legislative leadership during these early months of his presidency, he might have prevented the party split from widening.[21]

A thousand economists signed a petition urging Hoover to veto the Smoot-Hawley tariff. Professor Paul Douglas, author of the petition, mused that "poor Hoover wanted to take our advice" but could not bring himself to break with Republican protectionists. The president did not want to put himself in a situation where he depended on Democratic support against his own party's congressional leaders. Ignoring the experts, he signed the tariff, justifying his decision on the grounds that he had persuaded Congress to allow some flexibility for the U.S. Trade Commission in determining rates. He counted on the commission to lower the excessive rates. Not impressed, the progressives pointed out that the Trade Commission had a poor track record on lowering rates. As the economists predicted, the high tariff proved a disaster. Even before its enactment, U.S. trading partners retaliated by raising their tariff rates, freezing international trade. The tariff fight solidified Hoover's ties with Republican regulars and shredded his standing among the progressives. Senator Brookhart apologized for the 200 speeches he made in behalf of Hoover's candidacy. And Senator Borah, once the president's most intimate adviser on Capitol Hill, stopped visiting the White House almost entirely.[22]

During the tariff debate, the Democratic publicist Charley Michelson spotted Hoover's vulnerability: the president was a political novice who did not know how to deal with the seasoned professionals in Congress. A stronger executive would have browbeaten Congress, enlisted his cabinet in the fight, and taken his case to the people. But Hoover had "feared antagonisms for which he had no slide rule of calculations" and had recoiled from the conflict. Such behavior made him appear vacillating, an image the Democrats promptly exploited.[23]

Of all modern presidents, Herbert Hoover seemed the least interested in the pomp and glory of the office. He was the only one—since Wilson renewed the tradition—not to take advantage of the drama inherent in a presidential appearance before a joint session of Congress. Instead, he sent off his State of the Union messages and had clerks of the Senate and House read them in his place. Hoover preferred to deal with small groups of legislators in private rather than address them as a whole in a public setting. His staff advised him that members of Congress could usually be divided into three groups: the supporters and opponents of an idea and those who remained indifferent. They concentrated on building alliances with the indifferent, a tactic that worked for the most part but added to the demands on Hoover's time and attention. He spent many hours conferring with legislators, whom he mostly regarded as parochial and patronage-driven, failing to appreciate that the time they spent in their home states gave them realistic insights into local conditions and public opinion.[24]

As part of his southern strategy, Hoover nominated Judge John J. Parker, a North Carolina Republican, to the Supreme Court in 1930. Trade unions immediately complained that the nominee's rulings were antilabor, and the National Association for the Advancement of Colored People (NAACP) unearthed some of his earlier campaign speeches opposing political rights for blacks in North Carolina. Senate majority leader Watson counted heads and projected that Parker could not win senatorial confirmation, but Hoover would not withdraw the nomination, concerned that retreating would make him appear to lack backbone. As Watson predicted, a coalition of Democrats and progressive Republicans defeated Parker, revealing how far Hoover's congressional prestige had sunk. A frustrated Watson threw up his hands, saying that the president's trouble "was that he showed firmness at the wrong time and in the wrong way!" The nomination fight shook African American support for the president, and newspapers quoted Hoover as saying, "I don't know what this country is coming to if things are to be run by demagogues and Negro politicians." He did win credit from African Americans for inviting to a White House garden party the wife of the sole black member of Congress, Illinois representative Oscar De Priest, over the angry protests of white southerners.[25]

As his congressional relations soured, Hoover could neither forgive his progressive critics nor bring himself to meet them on friendly terms. Politics was "one of the minor branches of harlotry," the Kansas editor William Allen White put it, and Hoover had "a frigid desire to live a virtuous life." At the same time, many of the conservative Republicans had not forgotten the president's original identification with the Wilson administration, and they remained suspicious of his commitment to basic Republican policies. When the economic picture turned bleak and shook public confidence in the incumbents, both regular and insurgent Republicans expressed bitterness that Hoover showed so little interest in their political fate.[26]

HARD TIMES

Congress was still sparring over the tariff when the New York stock market crashed in October 1929. The speculative bubble burst, panicked investors unloaded their stocks, and prices plummeted, ending what F. Scott Fitzgerald called "the most expensive orgy in history." Since two-thirds of all stock had been purchased on margin, the sharp drop in prices left speculators not only broke but also in debt. "All I lost was two hundred and forty thousand dollars," the comedian Groucho Marx quipped after the crash. "I would have lost more but that was all the money I had."[27]

Hoover felt the collapse of stock prices proved him right. As commerce secretary, he had lectured Federal Reserve Board members against their easy-money policy and pressed the board to raise interest rates to discourage the rampant stock speculation. Although the board's governors finally hiked the discount rate in the summer of 1928, bankers continued to make highly profitable margin loans. That prompted the board to push its rates even higher, and the tight money policy caused a decline in business expenditures for new equipment and plants, triggering a recession in the fall of 1929. The October stock market crash further drained the money supply, costing investors and banks billions in assets. Nervous investors shifted their financial assets from stocks and bank accounts to gold, further deflating the economy. Apprehensive consumers cut back on new purchases, stalling the production of consumer goods. Higher interest rates in the United States attracted capital from countries that were weak in terms of the balance of payments, further reducing the market for American exports. Factory assembly lines that had raised the standard of living in the 1920s slowed to a halt.[28]

Hoover's treasury secretary, Andrew W. Mellon, one of the nation's wealthiest men, recommended that the government step aside and let the economy purge the rot from its system, in his words: "Liquidate labor, liquidate stocks, liquidate the farmers, liquidate real estate." As a businessman, Mellon had endured financial panics since 1873, and he doubted that government could do much to moderate them, other than cutting interest rates and taxes. People would simply have to work harder, live within their means, and make do with less. Hoover regarded this laissez-faire approach as callous and instead sought ways for the federal government to reinvigorate the economy. "Mr. Hoover is a most active and tireless President," Mellon commented skeptically, "prolific of new ideas and movements from day to day, which adds to our responsibilities." Hoover held a series of well-publicized meetings at the White House during which he "jawboned" leading industrialists into starting new work and holding the line on wages. He argued that any retrenchment would only depress the economy further and that wage stability would propel consumers' demands for goods. The nation's largest employers pledged cooperation, but as consumer demand fell, they cut working hours and laid off employees. In retrospect, the problem was not wage stability, since falling prices would boost people's purchasing power, but the threat of unemployment, which would discourage consumers from spending beyond the bare necessities.[29]

The prosperity of the 1920s had apparently been less robust than Hoover had described it during his campaign for president. The nation's wealth had soared—but with drastically uneven income distribution. The 30,000 wealthiest U.S. families had made as much as the 11 million families at the bottom. Industry had produced more goods than it could sell. The 1929 plunge in stock prices erased a decade of investments and shut down business expansion and new housing construction, spurring unemployment. To counteract the rising joblessness, Hoover expanded federal building projects and called on state and local governments to spend more for public works. Most responded positively, but state and municipal governments soon exhausted their financial reserves and borrowing capacities. The continuing downturn eventually forced the states to reduce relief programs and raise taxes to cover budget deficits, furthering the deflationary trend.[30]

President Hoover preferred to deal directly with business and labor, rather than seek legislative solutions. His focus on forces outside the government, the columnist Walter Lippmann observed, meant that he spent his energies "in fields where under our political system the President has no powers and no responsibility." Calvin Coolidge's former secretary, Ted Clark, concurred that Hoover's temperament did not fit a government divided between an executive and legislature. "He has never really recognized the House and Senate as desirable factors in our government," Clark advised Coolidge. "Perhaps they are not, but that does not alter the fact that they exist and that they have equal powers." Confident that the crisis could be met through private and voluntary efforts, Hoover held back from proposing legislation to reform the stock markets or provide relief for the unemployed.[31]

Believing that public confidence was the key to economic recovery, Hoover made reassuring statements about the economy's fundamental soundness. He called the slump a depression, thinking that sounded less ominous than a panic. He never said that prosperity was "just around the corner," a phrase routinely attributed to him but actually uttered by Vice President Curtis. Still, Hoover held out the hope of a speedy return to better times. His relentless optimism clashed with the steadily worsening economic indicators. The tightened money supply resulted in unprecedented deflation, as prices fell 10 percent a year. New investments slowed to a trickle. Farmers defaulted on their mortgages, banks failed, and businesses cut hours and laid off many of their workers. Unemployment spiraled from 3.2 percent in 1929 to 8.7 percent in 1930, 15.9 percent in 1931, and 23.6 percent in 1932. Marriage and childbirth rates also dropped, a striking consequence of people's reduced income.[32]

Perplexed over the economy's failure to rebound, Hoover decided that the root cause of the collapse lay in a worldwide depression started outside the United States. He kept a graph on his desk—ready to be thrust upon doubtful callers—that recorded the downturns in the European financial structure and the corresponding pattern of bank failures in the United States. He discounted both the stock market crash and the high protective tariff as contributing factors. But Hoover conceded that the massive war debts that European nations owed the United States were destabilizing the international economy. When Britain and France threatened to default, the president dramatically proposed a one-year moratorium on their war debts—a move that was wildly unpopular among isolationists in Congress. The United States and the leading European governments followed the conventional wisdom that public confidence could best be restored through balancing the budget by cutting spending and raising taxes, which only took more money out of circulation and exacerbated the problem. U.S. officials worried about doing anything that might unleash inflation, but the real problem was deflation, with an acute need for reflation.[33]

Hoover called the presidency a repairman's job, requiring him to fix one emergency after another and leaving him without time to start anything new. Paradoxically, despite his activism, his public remoteness made him appear unresponsive to the people's desperate needs. To counter this perception, Republicans called him "the hardest working man in the country," and they sought to blame his failures on his Democratic and progressive opponents in Congress. Senate majority leader Watson floated a charge that Democrats had been responsible for the stock market crash by stalling the tariff bill, but Democrats fired back that the party claiming credit for the boom ought to bear the burden of the bust. The victors' 1928 rhetoric came back to bite them. Republicans had coined the term *Hoover market* to describe the flush times; Democrats kept the phrase alive once the economy collapsed. Their propagandist, Charley Michelson, supplied congressional Democrats with ready rebuttals to the president's confident predictions—although Democrats reported that their constituents had stopped believing Hoover on their own. "Instead of a master pilot at the wheel, a sad-eyed and sorely disappointed and sadly bewildered man sits, in almost seclusion at the White House, conscious of his failures and not knowing where to turn," a Missouri Democrat declared in the House.[34]

On top of the economic crisis, Hoover had to contend with a natural disaster when a prolonged drought hit the Mississippi Valley in 1930. Scorching heat turned crops brown, depriving farmers of food to sell or eat. The drought offered the president an opportunity to revive his humanitarian image, but instead, his intransigence outraged the afflicted states. Hoover counted on his Agricultural Marketing Act to provide loans to farm cooperatives and on the Red Cross to care for those poorer farmers who lacked the collateral necessary to apply for federal loans. But neither the act nor the organization could cope with the magnitude of the human need.[35]

The worsening crisis made members of Congress eager to vote for federal relief, but at a time when the sum total of the federal government's expenditures amounted to just 2.5 percent of the gross national product, President Hoover worried that congressional pork-barrel projects would throw the budget out of balance. Having lost control of one special session, he resisted calling another and instead appointed the National Drought Relief Commission and charged it with studying the problem. The commission recommended a $60 million relief program. When Congress came back into regular session, the Senate passed the full amount, but Hoover intervened and asked the House to cut the funds to $25 million, with none of the money going for food. Only private relief agencies should distribute food, he believed. Federal money should be limited to "seed and feed," for replanting fields and feeding farm animals. Southern Democrats found it offensive that the administration would feed mules before it would feed people.[36]

When business registered some modest gains in March 1930, Hoover confidently forecast that the unemployment problem would be remedied within the next sixty days. "Gentlemen, you have come sixty days too late," he told a delegation that appealed for expanded public works programs that June: "The Depression is over." Congressional Democrats heaped scorn onto Hoover's false optimism, and a skeptical Governor Franklin Roosevelt advised his friends to measure the presidential prophecy against the facts. Too late, the White House staff realized that the sixty-days claim had been a "destructive mistake," leaving Hoover open to ridicule. If the economy had rebounded, prosperity would have enhanced his stature and he would not have needed to make the prediction. But if he had spoken simply on instinct, trusting that prosperity would return if people believed it would, then his comments were unproductive. The president shook public confidence by creating the impression that the federal government had tried and failed to restore sounder conditions. Political demoralization spread through Republican circles in Washington, particularly in the House of Representatives, where every member faced reelection in November.[37]

Everywhere, signs of distress grew more evident throughout 1930. Homeless shelters overflowed, breadlines formed, street beggars proliferated, and more people rode the rails on freight trains than at any time since the 1890s. Not everyone was hurting, of course. The New York Yankee slugger Babe Ruth turned down a $75,000 contract and demanded another $10,000. Sportswriters questioned whether he should draw a bigger salary than the president of the United States. "What's Hoover got to do with it?" growled the Bambino. "Besides I had a better year than he did anyway."[38]

Hoover's deteriorating relations with the press further hobbled efforts to restore public confidence. He had assumed the presidency with a reservoir of goodwill among Washington reporters, winning high marks from them by dismissing "the White House spokesman," the attribution that reporters previously had to use when quoting presidents at press conferences. He allowed them to quote him directly on some matters, keeping other information on background. Hoover's aloofness, however, soon undercut his good intentions. Standing before the assembled reporters made him feel like a microbe under a microscope. He required them to submit written questions in advance, and he ignored the ones he was unwilling to answer. Reporters despaired when the president put his more striking or forceful expressions on background, knowing the remarks would lose their attractiveness as news if put in indirect form. Hoover's press conferences dissolved into sessions in which he read formal statements, answering only a few questions.[39]

The president kept the bulk of the press corps at a distance while seeing a few whom he counted as friends and invited to his weekend fishing camp—prominent columnists and magazine writers such as Will Irwin, William Hard, and Mark Sullivan. These individuals churned out stories praising his deeds as a "Super-Administrator," but other reporters dismissed them as his "trained seals." Hoover appreciated the informational value of the news but not its emotional side. He resisted providing any human interest stories or allowing any intrusion into his privacy. "What I do in the conduct of my office is the public's business, of course," he told a friendly journalist. "But what I eat for breakfast shouldn't interest anyone." The First Lady guarded her privacy just as intensely and leaned toward unobtrusiveness, receiving little news coverage other than for ceremonial events and her Girl Scout activities.[40]

Even Hoover's weekend retreats became a sore point for the press. To escape the pressures of the White House, the president bought land and constructed a rustic fishing camp on the Rapidan River, deep in Virginia's Shenandoah Valley and a hundred miles from Washington. He wanted reporters to stay far away from the camp, even though he entertained high-level guests and conducted official business there. Required by their papers to keep close to the president in case some news broke, reporters would careen by the carload down the winding Virginia roads after the presidential motorcade and then rent rooms in towns miles away from Camp Rapidan. On one occasion, Hoover rushed back to Washington from the camp on urgent business, and the *New York Times* ran a story noting that his motorcade had made the trip in two hours—speeding at what was then an excessive rate of fifty miles an hour. The story infuriated Hoover, who demanded to know who in the White House was leaking such personal information. (In fact, no one had leaked it; the reporter had simply calculated the time and distance.) After that, Hoover's press secretary decreed that reporters would have to clear all stories in advance with administration officials, an order with which the press corps refused to comply.[41]

The *Baltimore Sun*'s Frank R. Kent agreed that President Hoover lacked the dramatic ability to sell himself and his policies, but Kent also attributed Hoover's poor public relations to the DNC's Charley Michelson for having minimized his assets and magnified all of his liabilities. Michelson had initially aimed his barbs at Republican protectionists as they jacked up the rates of the Smoot-Hawley tariff. Republican legislators complained that Democrats were mouthing Michelson's words on the Senate floor, on the radio, and at political gatherings, creating public doubt about the tariff. The Republicans wanted the RNC to build a parallel publicity office to defend the tariff bill, but as long as Michelson focused his publicity campaign on members of Congress, Hoover was unmoved, and the RNC offered no competition.[42]

The president became agitated only after Michelson began labeling the Smoot-Hawley tariff the Hoover tariff and calling the stock market crash the Hoover panic. In a 1930 article, Kent outlined the Democrats' propaganda efforts, and the RNC printed the piece as a pamphlet entitled *"Smear Hoover": Raskob's Order to His Subsidized Propagandist.* Michelson denied that he had ever resorted to slander or misrepresentation, insisting that he had focused legitimately on Hoover's "official sins of omission and commission." He pointed out that he had received plenty of help from those Republican senators who had never reconciled themselves to Hoover's presidency. The Democratic publicist lifted some of his most potent criticism of the president from past statements by Republican leaders, and he collected the funniest jokes about Hoover from the Republican cloakrooms. (In one instance, a Republican senator breathlessly told his colleagues that kidnappers had abducted President Hoover and left a ransom note demanding a half-million dollars—or else they would bring him back.)[43]

The president was hardly helpless against these attacks. He could count on the national press publishing any of his statements and those of his cabinet secretaries, often in full. Many government agencies employed press agents to grind out news releases, and most of the inhabitants of the White House pressroom reported for Republican-owned newspapers that had endorsed Hoover for president, a factor that muted critical reporting. The RNC belatedly hired its own publicity agent, an Associated Press reporter who generated daily press releases assailing the Democrats and especially their national chairman, John J. Raskob. With so many resources at hand, the administration should have been able to smother Michelson's one-man operation.[44]

Hoover's sensitivity to press criticism led him to create and privately fund a "press intelligence office," which White House secretary Larry Richey directed. Since Hoover insisted on knowing the worst that was being said about him, the office's staff scoured stacks of newspapers and magazines for anything that seemed slanted against the president. Apparently, no item was too small to escape notice, and editors began receiving demands from the White House that they publish corrections or fire offending reporters. Richey compiled lists of those he suspected of disloyalty to the administration, and he used government agencies to investigate them. Acting on his orders, the Bureau of Investigation (forerunner to the Federal Bureau of Investigation [FBI]) uncovered the identities of the anonymous authors of the best-selling exposé *Washington Merry-Go-Round,* Drew Pearson and Robert S. Allen. Richey got them dismissed from their newspapers, but they turned around and launched a hugely successful syndicated column. Richey was also behind a pre-Watergate presidential burglary, in which agents of the Office of Naval Intelligence broke into the office of a Democratic Party operative in search of potentially damaging information about Hoover (nothing significant turned up). Ted Clark, who saw reporters being "abused to their faces by Richey," attributed Hoover's sinking public approval to his poor press relations.[45]

Alienated reporters began to question the honesty of the economic data the administration was providing them. Hoover's statistics on unemployment, the deficit, and general business conditions often proved wrong. Reporters also learned that the president was holding high-level meetings without issuing any formal announcements or commenting on what had been discussed. At one press conference, Hoover informed reporters that he planned to make no announcement after an upcoming conference on unemployment, not even to divulge who had attended. He ordered them not to "waylay" his guests to try to interview them as they left the White House. Journalists remonstrated that it was their job to cover such events and suggested that the president would be better off making the facts known to the public. In the end, they went ahead and reported the conference, despite the administration's silence.[46]

Hoover's credibility suffered another blow when he mishandled the report from his commission to reexamine the laws of the land—most notably its conclusions about Prohibition. Determined to enforce Prohibition laws vigorously, the administration had doubled the number of prosecutions and had sent the notorious bootlegger Al Capone to prison for income tax evasion. Hoover appointed a commission, chaired by former attorney general George Wickersham, with the expectation that it would back his call for stricter enforcement of Prohibition. Instead, a majority of the commissioners concluded that Prohibition was not working. Because the dissenters disagreed about whether the Eighteenth Amendment should be modified or repealed, Hoover declared that the Wickersham Commission's report supported continued enforcement. Once reporters grasped that the president's interpretation had contradicted his own commissioners' findings, they lambasted his misleading assertions.[47]

Reporting on Prohibition emphasized the hypocrisy of its advocates. Police arrested George Cassidy, a rumrunner known as "the Man in the Green Hat," who revealed that he had been selling liquor out of the congressional office buildings. Cassidy counted among his customers more drys than wets, but he pointed out that the drys had held the majority in both houses for the preceding decade. If the entire membership of Congress voted the way they drank, he estimated, there should be enough votes to repeal the Eighteenth Amendment.[48]

Bad press led to the resignation of Hoover's press secretary, George Akerson, in 1930. Although Akerson had once made his boss the capital's best "grapevine" for news, he had lost most of his battles with the administration to open it up and humanize the president's image. Sorry to see him go, reporters were chagrined to learn that the aggressive Theodore "Ted" Joslin, a reporter for the Republican *Boston Transcript*, would replace him. Voicing a common reaction, Hearst News Service reporter George Holmes characterized the appointment as the first time a rat had joined a sinking ship. Joslin set out to improve Hoover's press relations, but he did not count on the depth of the president's animosity toward reporters. "Once I am re-elected I am going to clean that bunch out whatever the consequences may be," Hoover promised him.[49]

WHOSE CAR IS IT?

Halfway into Hoover's term, the congressional elections of 1930 saw the Democrats pick up eight seats in the Senate and forty-nine in the House. These gains, although impressive, represented fewer seats than they had won in the recession year of 1922, and the Republicans, despite suffering significant losses, still retained paper-thin majorities in both houses. Unfortunately for Hoover, the congressional elections did

President Hoover at his desk in the Oval Office in 1932 with his press secretary, Theodore "Ted" Joslin. Joslin's diary documented the president's chilly relations with the Washington press corps.

not end in November 1930 but extended for another year, under the old constitutional timetable still in effect at the time. During this delay, the full impact of the Depression would be felt. As the Republican *New York Herald Tribune,* looking back over the year, put it: "Somewhere in the last three months of 1931 the truth came home to almost everyone that here was no passing squall . . . but a first class tempest."[50]

On election night in 1930, the Republican Speaker of the House, Nicholas Longworth, had sent a good-natured message to the Democratic minority leader, John Nance Garner. Fast friends despite their party differences, Longworth and Garner routinely drove to the Capitol in the Speaker's official car. "Whose car is it?" Longworth telegraphed. "Think it mine," Garner replied. "Will be a pleasure to let you ride." In the immediate aftermath of the election, Longworth held on to the car—and the House—by a two-vote margin, but thirteen months would elapse until the new Congress was constitutionally mandated to convene on the first Monday in December 1931. President Hoover could have called Congress back earlier to deal with the economy, but he wanted nothing more to do with special sessions. During those many months, fourteen members of the House died, including Speaker Longworth. The special elections held to fill the vacancies tracked the impact of the Depression on the public consciousness. As more banks and businesses failed, more elections went to the Democrats, even in traditionally Republican strongholds. On November 3, 1931, a special election in Michigan nudged Democrats into the majority in the House for the first time since 1919. Democrats could not be certain of their majority until November 24, when Democrat Richard Kleberg won a race to replace Texas's sole Republican congressman. (Kleberg's other contribution to his party was to recruit an ambitious young staffer named Lyndon Johnson).[51]

RNC chairman Simeon Fess attributed the losses to a "crazy quilt" of local issues rather than a rejection of the Hoover administration. The RNC insisted that the results actually vindicated the president, since the losses had not been greater. Hoover's White House staff took pains to show how the losing Republican candidates had brought about their own defeats. Yet the congressional results provided an ominous forecast for the next presidential campaign. Republicans realized that the president had somehow failed to give the voters a clear picture of himself and his goals. People could not tell whether he was "cool or friendly, sincere or insincere, confident or vacillating, fearless or temporizing," which did not help his electoral chances.[52]

Republicans held the Senate by a margin of forty-eight to forty-seven, and there was one independent, Henrik Shipstead, the Farmer-Labor senator from Minnesota. Vice President Curtis's tie-breaking vote ensured that his party could hold the majority no matter which way Shipstead sided. However, Hoover counted only forty "real Republicans" among the senators, the rest being progressives who had deserted him. The president astonished Senate Republicans by asking them to step aside and let Democrats organize the chamber and chair its committees. He reasoned that it would be easier to deal with Democratic leaders if they controlled both houses rather than having them "conspiring in the cloakrooms" with the Republican progressives who were against him. Being in the majority would force upon the Democrats a sense of shared responsibility and make it easier for Hoover to veto bills passed by the opposition party, holding them accountable for obstructing his efforts to end the Depression.[53]

Republican senators indignantly refused to hand control of the legislative agenda to the Democrats. Hoover blamed this decision on the fact that Senator Watson liked "the extra importance of being majority leader," as well as the senior Republicans' desire to hold on to their "nicer offices in the Capitol." The president noticed that seniority had enabled a number of his progressive critics to attain important committee chairmanships, and he saw no reason why their desire for status should stand in his way. He seemed not to realize that the chairmanships were "the very pinnacle of the political careers of men in the House and Senate," Ted Clark recorded, "but most of all the thought has never entered his mind that he is asking these sacrifices to make his path to reelection easier and for no other purpose."[54]

Democrats felt exhilarated by their gains but recognized their responsibility for doing something to cure the economy. DNC chairman Raskob joined Senate Democratic leader Joseph Robinson and House Speaker John Nance Garner in signing a statement of cooperation, pledging to work with President Hoover for the welfare of the country. The statement was aimed at reassuring business leaders and avoiding any further business slump, but its concessions offended liberal Democrats who expected their party to offer alternatives to Hoover's programs. Nor was the White House receptive to the offer of cooperation. Hoover's staff advised him that he would need to perform some "deed of courage" to show his willingness to risk his political future for the sake of principle, and they began looking for bills to veto.[55]

Hunger marchers became commonplace. Reports of labor unrest came in from the coalfields, along with protests by farmers in the agrarian heartland. City crime statistics spiked, ranging from petty thefts to homicides and kidnappings—one resulted in the death of the infant son of the famed aviator Charles Lindbergh. "Crime had us in a state of siege," recorded the journalist-historian Claude Bowers. "In sober truth we were on the verge of revolution. With the hammer of the auctioneer knocking down farms to the highest bidder because of nonpayment of taxes, the traditionally conservative, law-abiding farmers were on the warpath." Hard times turned criminals into folk heroes, such as Clyde Barrow and Bonnie Parker in the Southwest and John Dillinger in the Midwest: they claimed to rob the banks that stole from the people. Meanwhile, Hollywood's new talking pictures caught the public mood by glorifying gangsters. In 1931, Edward G. Robinson played the title role in *Little Caesar,* as did Jimmy Cagney in *The Public Enemy,* and both actors scored box office hits.[56]

Although the size of the economic crisis staggered local governments and private charities, President Hoover steadfastly resisted calls for direct federal relief for the unemployed. Nineteenth-century Americans had regarded poverty, indebtedness, bankruptcy, and unemployment as failures of personal character. But social workers of the Progressive Era redefined unemployment as the result of the cycles of the industrial economy rather than individual weakness. By 1931, joblessness had spread among skilled workers as well as the unskilled, the hardworking as well as the slothful, but the president clung to the older way of thinking. He insisted that no one was starving, assuring one reporter that hoboes were better fed than they had ever been; indeed, he added, he had heard about a hobo in New York who got ten free meals in one day. "Surely, Mr. President," the reporter responded, "you are not confusing the unemployed with hoboes, are you?" The cowboy commentator Will Rogers, who headed a special Red Cross mission to feed the unemployed, was dismayed when Hoover rejected his pleas for federal aid. Once people started taking government relief, they would expect it, Hoover explained, and federal funds would only discourage voluntary donations. Leaving the White House, Rogers commented sadly, "I don't think we have anybody in Washington that don't want to feed 'em, but they all want to feed 'em their way."[57]

Throughout 1931, Hoover resisted advice that he call another special session of Congress, thinking he could act more efficiently without congressional interference. Consequently, he was left to shoulder alone both the responsibility and the blame for the deepening Depression. When the new Congress finally convened in December 1931, his annual message reassured the legislators that business downturns had recurred throughout American history and were always transitory. Despite his complaints about an unruly Congress, Hoover got most of the legislation he wanted in the new session, either through persuasion or by threatening vetoes that the opposition could not override. Congressional Democrats had no alternative legislative agenda and instead followed Hoover's lead by creating the Federal Home Loan Bank Act to stimulate home construction and ownership and the Reconstruction Finance Corporation (RFC) to provide loans to banks in jeopardy—modeled after the War Finance Corporation of World War I. The move to provide federal money to banks made sense economically, but it left Hoover vulnerable to charges that he was willing to bail out the banks but not the unemployed. Big bankers, Will Rogers wryly commented, had "the honor of being the first group to go on the 'dole' in America."[58]

The White House planned a strategy that pitted the president against the Democratic majority in the House, despite the Democrats' offer of cooperation and Hoover's private admission that he found it easier to work with Democratic leaders than with some of his own Republicans. The president expressed disdain for Speaker Garner as "a cheap politician," but he also seemed to admire the Democrat's guile and shrewdness. Unlike Garner, Hoover had never learned how to flatter or cajole to strike deals and reach compromise to accomplish his objectives. He saw his relations with Congress in terms of checking its radical ideas and big-spending tendencies. Congressional Democrats viewed the relationship as one that involved provoking the president into expanding relief and recovery programs against his will.[59]

After months of refusing to call a special session, Hoover urged the lawmakers to forgo their Christmas recess in order to pass the RFC bill. Congress ignored this suggestion and recessed until after the start of the new year. The president pointedly ended his own holiday the day after Christmas, pressing for speedy legislative action on his plan. He aimed to create the image of a hardworking president confronting an idle Congress. In the meantime, the favorable response of business interests to the RFC measure had made some progressives suspicious. New York representative Fiorello LaGuardia, who led the progressive Republican bloc in the House, called it a "millionaire's dole" and a "subsidy for broken bankers." Iowa senator Smith Brookhart wanted to know why the taxpayers should pay for the financiers' folly. Despite these protests, however, the RFC bill sailed through to enactment by strong bipartisan margins of 355 to 55 in the House and 63 to 8 in the Senate. Its mission of rescuing troubled banks with federal funds made sense economically and psychologically in terms of restoring depositors' confidence, although it left Hoover vulnerable to charges that he was willing to bail out the wealthy but not the unemployed.[60]

During the spring of 1932, Hoover bombarded Congress with messages stressing the need for federal retrenchment and a balanced budget. He frequently threatened to veto bills and penned seven strongly worded veto messages. In May, he asked permission to address the Senate in person before a vote on a revenue bill to raise taxes, a surprising departure for a president who usually avoided personal appearances before Congress. Even then, Hoover displayed little showmanship. Senate staff observed that the president's entrance into the chamber was "as totally undramatic as that of the most obscure citizens," and he addressed the senators in a monotone, like "a businessman reporting to a board of directors." Nonetheless, the bill passed by a wide margin, and the White House reported a flood of congratulatory telegrams on the president's speech. Senators responded that their constituents also wrote in favor of balancing the budget, while at the same time they protested any increase in taxes or cut in federal spending.[61]

A coalition of Democrats and progressive Republicans generated their own bills to deal with unemployment, with New York's Democratic senator Robert F. Wagner most actively seizing the legislative initiative. Wagner attracted attention for his ability to talk cogently about industrial conditions. In contrast to Hoover, the senator identified the primary causes for the economic distress as internal rather than international, asserting that legislation could fix the problems. Hoover vetoed Wagner's bill to create a system of state labor exchanges, on the technicality that it would disrupt employment programs already under way within the Labor Department (and then he swiftly reorganized the employment service and removed its director). Hoover also opposed calls for unemployment insurance, describing it as a handout that would "endow the slacker."[62]

The president tried to boost business confidence by restraining federal spending and balancing the budget, whereas Senator Wagner instead proposed new public works projects to create jobs. Wagner wanted to broaden the RFC's mission to include relief for the unemployed. He pointed out that when railroad presidents went to Washington seeking public help, they heard no preaching about rugged individualism, but when millions of Americans needed work, the government became devoted to "the preservation of self-reliance." The efforts of the northern liberal Wagner to prime the economic pump through public works attracted the votes of southern conservatives. South Carolina senator James Byrnes voted with Wagner after conditions forced his hometown of Charleston to issue script to meet the city payroll (script were promissory notes that storekeepers accepted in lieu of cash, with the expectation that the city eventually would have the funds to repay them). The crafty Byrnes also advised Democrats to support the president's policies as far as possible, in order to give Hoover the legislative rope with which to hang himself: Byrnes cautioned Democrats that if they tried to develop their own relief agenda, they would only divert attention from the Republicans' failure.[63]

In the House, Speaker John Nance Garner wielded a heavy gavel and a powerful temper that kept his three-vote majority in line. An old-time patronage and pork-barrel politician, Garner had reminded his constituents back in 1916 that northern representatives had plastered their states with unnecessary federal buildings. With the Democrats in charge of the House, he said, "I'll tell you right now, every time one of those Yankees gets a ham, I am going to do my best to get a hog." Yet Garner was also a fiscal conservative who lined up Democratic votes for the president's economic plans to balance the budget. He met with the chairman of the House Appropriations Committee, wrestling from him a pledge not to add a single dollar to Hoover's budget and to trim every appropriation possible. When the federal budget approached a billion-dollar deficit, Hoover proposed tax increases, including a 2.25 percent national sales tax, the burden of which would fall disproportionately on the working class. The Speaker reluctantly endorsed the sales tax, but a coalition of liberal Democrats and progressive Republicans regarded the measure as regressive and managed to kill it in the House, as the chamber rang with "rebellious yells and cheering." Feeling that the revolt had eroded his prestige, Garner took the floor and told the members that it was their paramount duty to maintain the country's financial integrity. He asked all who favored a balanced budget to rise, and almost everyone did. Then he asked those opposed to a balanced budget to rise, and no one stood. Garner's audacious move salvaged some of the tax increases

Texas representative John Nance Garner, known as "Cactus Jack," presided over a narrow, three-vote Democratic majority in the House of Representatives during the last two years of Hoover's administration. Speaker Garner became a contender for the Democratic nomination in 1932.

but not the sales tax. The donnybrook reflected poorly on Congress and bolstered the president's stature. "The Democrats in a week have done Mr. Hoover more good than his Republican friends have been able to do him in a year," a *Chicago Tribune* editorial declared. "They have made his second term seem much more reasonable in his prospects than it was before."[64]

From listening to their constituents, members of Congress understood that the public expected some form of federal relief. Senate Democratic leader Joe Robinson turned to the financier Bernard Baruch to devise a plan for instituting "self-liquidating" public works projects, such as toll roads, sewer systems, and hydroelectric power plants; the states would later repay their RFC loans for these projects out of operating funds. Hoover agreed to the scheme, which the press dubbed the Robinson-Hoover plan. However, Speaker Garner sponsored a more grandiose version of the bill that would fund some 3,500 public works projects through a hike in gasoline taxes. Hoover called it "the most gigantic pork barrel ever proposed to the American Congress" and vetoed the bill. When Congress enacted a scaled-back version, he realized that fearful Republican members would likely override another veto. This time, he signed the Emergency Relief and Construction Act, calling it a "strong step toward recovery." The act represented a pragmatic softening of Hoover's adherence to voluntary efforts, local initiatives, and private relief, but he negated whatever credit he might have earned for trying something new by continuing to defend the old system, reinforcing his image as the chief obstacle to helping the needy.[65]

THE LIKELY CHALLENGER

Hoover kept careful watch over potential rivals, especially the new governor of New York. Although he and Roosevelt had been friends during the Wilson administration and although Roosevelt had refrained from criticizing him during the 1928 campaign, Hoover had taken offense over a circular letter that the Democrat had sent to their wartime colleagues, asserting that Al Smith better represented Wilsonian ideals. Julius Barnes, head of the Chamber of Commerce and a former Hoover aide, passed a copy of the letter to the chief. Hoover was still irritated with Roosevelt when they both attended the Gridiron Club dinner held by the Washington press corps in April 1929. Nor was he amused when the reporters sang:

O, Franklin, Franklin Roosevelt,
Is there something in a name?
When you tire of being governor,
Will you look for bigger game?
Will you wish for something higher;
When at Albany you're through?
When weary of the State House,
Will the White House beckon you?[66]

For old friends, Franklin Roosevelt and Herbert Hoover could hardly have been less alike in background or temperament. In contrast to Hoover's humble beginnings, Roosevelt had been born into wealth and privilege at Hyde Park, New York, in 1882. His father, a genial country gentleman, was a widower who had married again to a woman half his age, the strong-willed Sara Delano. Together, the couple sheltered their son Franklin on their Hudson River estate, surrounding him with nurses, governesses, and tutors, and they took him on extended tours of Europe. Although raised as an only child (his half brother was a generation older), Franklin had a large extended family of aunts, uncles, and cousins, and he enjoyed spending time with the boisterous children of his distant relative Theodore "TR" Roosevelt. TR's offspring considered Franklin soft because he preferred sailing, whereas their strenuous father insisted that they row their boats.[67]

With few local friends of his age, Franklin had little practice in the team sports played at Groton, the elite Episcopal academy where his parents sent him when he turned fourteen. Despite his gregariousness, he found it difficult to fit in with others at the school. His upbringing, his closeness to his parents, and his extensive traveling made him feel older than his age, and the other boys seemed immature to him. Groton emphasized religious study, and Roosevelt's reading aloud from the Bible and great works of literature would help shape his style as a public speaker later in life. Throughout his life, he was sustained by what one cousin called his "simple, rather old-fashioned, but deep and unshakable Christian faith."[68]

Going to Harvard, Roosevelt studied history and government and took classes from one of the nation's most prominent speech teachers, George P. Baker. Intelligent and attractive, Roosevelt devoted more attention to his social life than his classes and satisfied himself with "gentlemen's Cs." In 1900, when his cousin Theodore ran for vice president, Franklin supported him by joining the Harvard Republican Club, and he cast his first vote, for TR, in the 1904 presidential election. Otherwise, Franklin hewed to his father's Democratic loyalties. Contemporaries regarded the young Roosevelt as pleasant, energetic, and ambitious but also lacking in depth and strength of character. They gave him the nickname "Feather Duster" for his light banter, suggesting an image that would dog him for years. Roosevelt's most serious extracurricular effort at Harvard was editing the student newspaper, the *Crimson,* and his severest disappointment came when Porcellian, an elite social club to which his father and TR had belonged, declined to accept him.[69]

Roosevelt's elderly father died while he was a freshman at Harvard, and his mother moved to Boston to be near him. The desire to distance himself from her control of his life may have prompted his engagement during his senior year to his distant cousin Anna Eleanor Roosevelt. The couple possessed strikingly different personalities: Franklin was light and self-assured, whereas Eleanor was serious and insecure. Sara Delano Roosevelt considered her son far too young to marry and did her best to discourage the match, but Franklin and Eleanor wed in 1905. The president of the United States, Theodore Roosevelt, gave the bride away and jovially congratulated the groom on keeping the name in the family.[70]

As a married couple, Franklin and Eleanor never escaped his mother's influence. Sara held the family's purse strings, ran the house at Hyde Park, and built a duplex in Manhattan with connecting doors between her side and theirs. Eleanor resented her domineering mother-in-law but deferred to her. The young couple settled into New York's high society while Franklin attended Columbia Law School. An indifferent student, he passed the New York State bar exam but became bored with practicing law, jumping at the first opportunity to run for office. In 1910, he campaigned as a Democrat for the state senate in heavily Republican Dutchess County. He toured the county in a bright red car, stumped vigorously for good government, and won an upset victory, in large part because Theodore Roosevelt's progressive reform efforts had split the state's Republican Party.[71]

In the state legislature, Roosevelt made good on his promise to fight the political bosses when he led a fight against Tammany Hall's choice of William F. "Blue-Eyed Billy" Sheehan for a U.S. Senate seat (state legislatures elected senators until 1913). Roosevelt and other reformers managed to force Sheehan to withdraw, but Tammany simply nominated another candidate, who was elected. Roosevelt's brash style grated on the

Tammany legislators, among them Al Smith and Robert Wagner. He concentrated on agricultural issues important to his district and paid little attention to the urban, industrial areas that Smith and Wagner represented. He made his most important friendship in Albany with a politically shrewd newspaper reporter, Louis McHenry Howe. A wizened, gnomelike figure in perpetually rumpled suits, Howe spotted the tall, handsome, magnetic Roosevelt, with his famous family name, as a man of destiny. When Roosevelt fell seriously ill with typhoid fever in 1912, Howe quit reporting to run his absentee campaign for reelection. They remained an inseparable team until Howe's death twenty-four years later.[72]

Theodore Roosevelt further split the Republican ranks by running for president as a Progressive in 1912. That year, Franklin Roosevelt endorsed the winning Democratic candidate, Woodrow Wilson, who rewarded him with the post that TR had once held, assistant secretary of the navy. Except for a brief and unsuccessful bid for the Democratic nomination to the U.S. Senate in 1914—when a Tammany candidate beat him in the primary—Roosevelt held the naval post for eight years, learning the intricacies of the federal bureaucracy. He performed competently and won favorable notice as an administrator, although he had developed a disconcerting habit of throwing his head back and looking down his nose through his eyeglasses, a stance that struck some people as arrogant and condescending.

The Roosevelts had six children in their first ten years of marriage; one died in infancy. Eleanor also devoted much time to volunteer efforts for the Red Cross during World War I, not realizing that, in her absence, her husband had fallen in love with her attractive social secretary, Lucy Mercer. When Eleanor discovered evidence of the relationship, she offered Franklin a divorce. His mother would hear nothing of it, insisting that she would cut him off financially if he left his wife and children for another woman. Divorce would also have ruined his political chances. For the sake of the children, Eleanor agreed to continue the marriage, as long as he broke off the affair. The incident devastated Eleanor Roosevelt but also liberated her from the traditional role of an "ornamental" political wife, turning their marriage into more of a political partnership. Their cousin, the journalist Joseph Alsop, believed that Franklin's decision to give up the woman he loved to preserve his political career did much to lessen the "feather duster" aspect of his personality, toughening and maturing his character even before he was struck by serious illness.[73]

In 1919, Franklin Roosevelt addressed a Democratic banquet in Chicago, where he offered a liberal vision for the party. Since the McKinley-Bryan campaign of 1896, liberals and conservatives had battled each other over control of both political parties, and conservatism had triumphed in the Republican Party. Republicans had rejected their progressive ranks, said Roosevelt, so Democrats should embrace them to become the truly liberal party. "Perhaps there have been times when we appeared too liberal," he conceded. "Perhaps in 1896 we were a little too far ahead of the times." But he pointed out how much of what William Jennings Bryan had championed that year, ideas that had seemed so radical at the time, had since been enacted into law. The banquet crowd, which had cheered all references to Woodrow Wilson, grew noticeably cooler when Roosevelt mentioned Bryan, but the speech helped link FDR to his party's populist and progressive wing, and it inspired Democrats to nominate him for vice president in 1920. Campaigning on the ticket headed by Ohio governor James M. Cox, Roosevelt barnstormed the country, making the acquaintance of party leaders in nearly every state. He was realistic enough to know that the odds were slim for a Democratic victory that year, which helped him survive the defeat with an upbeat attitude and with an enhanced reputation. "Curiously enough, I do not feel in the least bit down-hearted," he commented.[74]

Roosevelt resumed his law practice and dabbled in business and charitable endeavors while biding his time before reentering politics. In July 1921, he toured a New York State Boy Scout encampment, where he was likely exposed to the polio virus. Soon after, while vacationing on Campobello Island, he was stricken with poliomyelitis, which destroyed his leg muscles. A sheltered childhood had left the adult Roosevelt unusually susceptible to childhood diseases, including polio—otherwise known as infantile paralysis. One of his relatives tried to disguise his condition as a severe rheumatic attack, considering it "too silly" for a grown man to have an infantile disease. Disabled at age thirty-nine, Roosevelt refused to withdraw from an active political life. Determined to recover, he underwent painful corrective surgery and exhaustive physical rehabilitation. He developed his upper body sufficiently to hoist himself onto crutches and walk short distances with the use of metal leg braces. His search for a cure took him to a dilapidated spa in Warm Springs, Georgia. Finding exercise in its therapeutic waters invigorating, he decided to use his own money to buy the spa and convert it into the Georgia

Warm Springs Foundation, for himself and other patients. Studies of polio survivors have found that many of them have been determined to excel despite adversity, becoming hard-driving overachievers. Polio may have weakened Roosevelt's legs, but it made him a stronger man.[75]

Eleanor Roosevelt believed that polio taught her husband to be more patient because he had to sit still and could not move around as much as he had in the past, and with that came "the discipline of once you made a decision, putting it out of your mind." Despite his disability, Franklin Roosevelt exhibited an exuberant cheerfulness that put others around him at ease. He showed little self-consciousness about being carried or moving in a wheelchair. Given his immobilization, Eleanor frequently served as his eyes and ears, traveling widely and reporting back to him about the people she met and the conditions she observed. Her absences left him lonely, however, and resentful over her reformer friends, whom he called the "uplifters." Despite having much in common and clearly caring for each other, Franklin and Eleanor always had trouble relaxing together, and they both sought other companionship.[76]

The social worker Frances Perkins had known Franklin Roosevelt for a decade before his bout with polio, and she believed that the illness resulted in a "spiritual transformation." Roosevelt no longer displayed the condescending attitude she had first noticed, literally looking down his nose at people, and he showed more concern about others. It required considerable confidence and stubbornness on his part to stay even minimally active in public life while undergoing arduous physical treatment. Yet during an era when the Democrats were torn by internal divisions, being sidelined offered some advantages. Illness kept Roosevelt out of the internecine fights and prevented him from entering races that might have pitted him against his fellow New Yorker Al Smith. Instead, he encouraged Smith to run for governor and for president. FDR returned to the spotlight in 1924 when Smith asked him to place his name in nomination at the Democratic convention. Rather than appear in a wheelchair, Roosevelt walked stiffly, leaning on the arm of his son James, and slowly proceeded to the podium. When he reached it, he threw back his head with a smile in a triumphant gesture that brought down the house. His rousing speech, which labeled Smith as the Happy Warrior, became the most memorable of the convention. In truth, Roosevelt hated the Happy Warrior reference, which Smith's aides had written, and he read it only because they insisted that he do so. Smith's campaign staff made him feel like little more than window dressing.[77]

Al Smith, a self-made man and hard-nosed politician, regarded Franklin Roosevelt as a dilettante, but he appreciated FDR's popularity among rural Democrats, as demonstrated in his campaigns in upstate New York and for the vice presidency. Smith tapped him to make nominating speeches in 1920, 1924, and 1928, causing the humorist Will Rogers to comment that Roosevelt could have gone far within the Democratic Party if he had not devoted his life to nominating Al Smith. Once Smith won the presidential nomination in 1928, he had to find a candidate to run for governor in his place, someone who could help him carry New York: Smith's circle identified Roosevelt as one of the few Democrats who was popular upstate. Meanwhile, Roosevelt had left for treatment in Warm Springs, more interested in getting his legs to move again than running for governor. He suspected what Smith wanted and avoided his phone calls. But Eleanor was then working for Smith's campaign and managed to get her husband on the phone. "I need you," Smith begged. "It's your duty to run." When Roosevelt mentioned his financial commitment to Warm Springs, John J. Raskob settled the matter by pledging a $50,000 personal contribution to the Georgia Warm Springs Foundation.[78]

The Democrats nominated Roosevelt for governor in October, giving him only five weeks to campaign against a popular Republican candidate—the state attorney general, Albert Ottinger. FDR made public ownership of hydroelectric power the centerpiece of his campaign, spending most of his time in upstate New York. Opposition newspapers feigned sympathy for his physical limitations as a subtle way of drawing public attention to them, which only stimulated Roosevelt to campaign harder. A steel bar mounted behind the driver's seat in an open car allowed him to stand before his audiences. In giving a speech, he would list the many towns he had visited that day, and he would get a laugh by adding, "Too bad about this unfortunate sick man, isn't it?" Still, his campaign organizers occasionally scheduled Roosevelt to make appearances in second-story halls, requiring him to be carried up back stairs or even to climb fire escapes using his muscular arms. On election night, the first returns indicated that both Smith and Roosevelt had gone down to defeat, but by the next morning, the upstate vote gave Roosevelt a narrow, 25,000-vote victory. Of the president-elect, the new governor said graciously, "Mr. Hoover is an old friend of mine and for the sake of the country, I hope that he will make good."[79]

Al Smith moved out of the governor's mansion and into a nearby hotel suite in Albany, expecting to stay on hand to run the state through

Roosevelt. The new governor, however, had other ideas. Roosevelt intended to continue Smith's programs and keep his cabinet, but he hated being patronized and made it clear he intended to govern in his own right. He dismissed Smith's two top aides, Belle Moskowitz and Robert Moses (who had treated him as a lightweight), and drafted his own legislative agenda. Stunned by the rebuff, Smith checked out of his hotel suite and returned to Manhattan, where he headed the company constructing the Empire State Building.

Roosevelt's longtime adviser Louis Howe took up residence in New York, living in the governor's Manhattan townhouse, planning political strategy, and seeing his own family in Fall River, Massachusetts, only on the weekends. Howe spent a good deal of time with reporters, giving them many stories but always keeping himself off the record. He followed all newspaper editorials on Roosevelt, favorable or unfavorable, and directed an extensive correspondence between the governor and Democratic leaders across the country. From Al Smith, Roosevelt had also acquired Samuel Rosenman as his speechwriter. The New York City–based Rosenman regarded the new governor as a country squire without much administrative ability, but he was surprised by Roosevelt's diligence during the campaign and in office and captivated by his genial informality. Another key addition to the administration was the Democratic leader of the Bronx, Ed Flynn, who advised Roosevelt on his prickly relations with Tammany Hall.[80]

Governor Roosevelt was no more alarmed by the stock market crash of 1929 than President Hoover was. Both regarded the downturn as a useful corrective to years of unchecked speculation. When Hoover telegraphed Roosevelt and other governors to ask them to expand their states' public works programs, FDR agreed to recommend construction work to the legislature, but he reminded the president that the state had limited financial resources. Roosevelt's industrial commissioner, Frances Perkins, began supplying him with reports of alarming levels of unemployment in the state. She believed that President Hoover was citing faulty unemployment data that did not reflect reality. Perkins regarded the manipulation of statistics as particularly heartless, since it suggested to the desperately unemployed that their inability to find jobs was their own fault rather than a massive breakdown of the system.[81]

The Democratic governor of New York had to contend with Republican majorities in both houses of the state legislature and an uneasy relationship with the New York City Democratic organization, Tammany Hall, but he managed to win enactment of relief programs that put his state ahead of the others. Roosevelt proposed minimum wages and maximum working hours, old-age insurance, public works, regulation of public utilities, stricter regulation of banks, farm relief, publicly developed waterpower, cheaper electricity, and reforestation. He opposed the so-called dole, however, and instead convinced the legislature to create the Temporary Emergency Relief Administration (TERA) to offer work programs instead of handouts. Headed by Harry Hopkins, TERA provided jobs to only about a tenth of the state's unemployed, but it still represented a significant step in helping the jobless.[82]

Governor Roosevelt expanded on Al Smith's plans to develop state-owned power sites and transmission facilities to bring electrical power into rural areas and cut the cost of electricity for consumers. When the Republican legislature crafted a more limited version of the program, confident that Roosevelt would oppose it, the governor surprised them by embracing their plan and claiming victory for having forced the opposition party to act. Socialist Party leader Norman Thomas protested that Roosevelt should have taken over all production and distribution of electrical power as a public operation, prompting FDR to respond that his chief interest was in "a better regulation of our public utilities and of securing cheaper electric rates," not government ownership. He had plans to develop waterpower on the St. Lawrence Seaway, which required a treaty between the United States and Canada. Hoover's administration declined to include New York State in the treaty negotiations, however, and moved too slowly to reach an agreement during Roosevelt's governorship.[83]

When he ran for reelection in 1930, Roosevelt tested national themes. He blamed President Hoover for not applying the brakes to the earlier stock market speculation, for concealing the seriousness of the economic situation with overly optimistic pronouncements, and for failing to take decisive action to counteract the Depression. Nettled by these charges, the president lent his top cabinet officers to campaign for the Republican gubernatorial candidate in New York. Roosevelt ignored their jabs until his last major speech of the campaign, when he mocked the federal government's efforts to influence the state election. Winning reelection by a record margin of 750,000 votes, he more than doubled Al Smith's mark.[84]

Immediately after the election, New York State Democratic chairman James Aloysius Farley met with Louis Howe to plan a presidential campaign. Farley, a former Al Smith protégé, took Smith at his word when he stated he would not run again. He was convinced that the Democrats would want a presidential candidate who had won as convincingly as Roosevelt had done in New York. "I do not see how Mr. Roosevelt can escape becoming the next presidential nominee of the party," Farley told reporters. Members of the Roosevelt team weighed two tactics: they could campaign for delegates in every state, or they could pick and choose their races to avoid challenging potential favorite-son candidates in state primaries. They chose the more the aggressive route. They would appeal to delegates from every region, tapping the contacts that Roosevelt had made during a decade of correspondence with Democratic leaders across the nation.[85]

Al Smith, preoccupied with renting out the largely empty Empire State Building, left politics to Raskob and Shouse. These men identified Prohibition as the most promising issue for the 1932 campaign. Raskob felt that the government had no right to curtail liberty in matters in which no moral wrong was involved, and he also believed that taxing the sale of liquor would avoid the need for raising income taxes. The Democratic Party chairman, who was also active in the Association against the Prohibition Amendment, lobbied the DNC to endorse the repeal of the constitutional amendment. The issue seemed tailor-made for a second Smith campaign, since Al Smith remained an overt wet, whereas Roosevelt was known as "damp" for having tried to straddle the wet-dry divide by advocating local option.[86]

Chairman Raskob convened a meeting of the DNC in Washington in March 1931 to advise the next year's convention team on a Prohibition plank. Drys protested that the DNC had no authority to make policy recommendations on controversial issues. Al Smith attended the Washington conference and offered an impassioned defense of Raskob and the wets, but the chairman's heavy-handed tactics offended too many of the committee members, and they voted down his proposal. Not giving up easily, Raskob sent each of the party's leading financial contributors a questionnaire: "Do you believe other economic issues will be so overwhelming in the 1932 campaign that the Democratic platform can successfully ignore the prohibition question *with its economic problems* by remaining silent or by adopting a mere law enforcement plank as was done in the 1928 convention?" A monumental battle for control of the party was developing between the Democrats' conservative and liberal wings, as well as between wets and drys, at a time when the deepening Depression was making it more likely that they could win back the presidency.[87]

3

A COUPLE OF CONVENTIONS IN CHICAGO

The newspaper columnist H. L. Mencken covered both the Republican and the Democratic National Conventions in 1932 and later judged them the most fateful in American history—except that "no one knew it at the time." In Chicago, where the two parties met that June within weeks of each other, the delegates walked past long lines of jobless, impoverished people waiting patiently for meals at soup kitchens. Most of the delegates held jobs, resided in better-off neighborhoods, and had not yet confronted the magnitude of the economic crisis, until they opened their hotel windows and looked out onto the homeless men and women living in Grant Park, sleeping in cardboard shacks, and washing in public fountains. Mencken, who had regarded distressing economic reports as exaggerated, conceded that the Depression "was making itself felt at last."[1]

Herbert Hoover entered the election year perplexed over the economy's failure to rebound but still confident he would win a second term. Hoover had gradually expanded government programs to fight the Depression without changing his argument that private charities and local governments, not the federal government, held the chief responsibility for providing relief to the needy. Time and again, he detected signs that the country was healing, only to have stock prices slump, banks fail, and businesses lay off more workers. He staked his reelection on an economic recovery by the fall. Republican editorial writers similarly greeted 1932 as a year of economic betterment, as long as members of Congress could put aside their partisan differences and enact Hoover's programs. Once business recovered, the commentators assumed that the political assault on the president would collapse. The columnist Frank Kent, a conservative Democrat, predicted that Hoover would once again "stand before the people as a strong, far-sighted, capable man who, silent under attack, wisely guided the nation through a period of Depression, averted a prolonged and painful panic, restored it to prosperity and contentment. The credit will, of course, go to him, his critics will be confounded, his popularity revived in a bound, and his triumphant renomination and re-election assured."[2]

ROOSEVELT'S MOMENTUM

Governor Franklin Roosevelt felt equally certain that the political cycle was swinging back to his party after so many years in the minority and that a Democratic president would be elected that fall. He considered himself the likely Democratic nominee because he occupied the governor's chair of the nation's largest state, whose forty-seven electoral votes would be critical to winning the White House. Roosevelt had received positive notice in the press for his innovative programs as governor, and he had the benefits of a familiar name and an attractive personality. Yet for all these assets, his critics declared him the weakest of the potential Democratic candidates, a group that included former governor Al Smith, House Speaker John Nance Garner, former secretary of war Newton D. Baker, industrialist Owen D. Young, and Maryland governor Albert C. Ritchie.[3]

Ending the Depression called for drastic remedies and robust leadership, but social and economic activists despaired that neither of the major parties, under the thumb of big business, would devise policies to aid farmers and wageworkers. It seemed possible that a larger share of the voters than usual would drift away from the Republicans and Democrats to the more radical third parties. To keep reformers from defecting, Roosevelt aspired to make the Democratic Party the truly liberal party, one that would unite urban liberals, southern populists, and western progressives. Since the Democrats had been out of power in the national government for a dozen years, he recognized that the party could win only by attracting disaffected voters from outside its core constituency, and he shaped his campaign accordingly.[4]

Roosevelt's political organization consisted principally of his strategist, Louis Howe; his political adviser, Edward Flynn; and his chief delegate-hunter, James Farley. The hundreds of letters that FDR had been exchanging with Democratic leaders around the nation over the preceding decade, including his frequent surveys of opinion within the party, enhanced his team's knowledge of the national political landscape. The replies helped Howe prepare state-by-state analyses of Democratic leaders and potential delegates. In January 1931, Howe opened a Manhattan office, where a staff of secretaries forged Roosevelt's signature onto thousands of personal letters. They sent out inconsequential booklets as feelers, and all who acknowledged receiving them would get friendly follow-up letters and have their names added to a massive card index.[5]

On January 23, 1932, a week before his fiftieth birthday, Roosevelt announced his presidential candidacy by consenting to have his name entered in the North Dakota Democratic primary. Long before then, political observers knew that Jim Farley had been touring the nation as his "traveling salesman," collecting pledges and delegates to make Roosevelt the clear front-runner. As a cover, Farley had made his annual pilgrimage to the Grand Lodge of the Benevolent and Protective Order of Elks, meeting in the summer of 1931 in Seattle. He, Howe, and Roosevelt spread out a map of the United States, a set of railroad timetables, and lists of all the local Democratic leaders to plan a route whereby he could visit as many potential delegates as possible. Farley traveled thirty thousand miles through the Midwest, Great Plains, and Rocky Mountains and down the Pacific coast, conferring with local party leaders. Roosevelt and Howe considered him "temperamentally and physically" the best man to send west, but they decided it would not be wise to send a Catholic into the South. Thus, to scout the southern states for delegates, they sent Marvin McIntyre, a former reporter from Kentucky who had handled publicity for Roosevelt's vice presidential campaign and was in need of a job during the Depression.[6]

A sunny smile, a ready handshake, and an unfailing memory for names and faces helped the big, burly Jim Farley charm the local party leaders he encountered. Expecting to meet a hard-boiled Tammany politician, the westerners were surprised to encounter a genial, churchgoing man who showed pictures of his family and did not smoke or drink (but never objected if anyone else did). At every stop, Farley would get off the train and walk around the station asking people at random who would make the best Democratic candidate. He sent back detailed lists of everyone he met, reporting an almost universal sentiment for Roosevelt among potential delegates (apart from a few Catholics still sentimentally attached to Al Smith). He also detected opposition from the "power crowd" of utility company executives who favored anyone other than the New York governor because of his support for public power projects. Farley advised that several senators and governors were considering running as favorite sons strictly so their names would be presented to the convention as presidential candidates "because they feel it is the only way they can be considered as a vice-presidential nominee." They all coveted the second spot on the ticket, for they felt sure Roosevelt would win. When a reporter later asked members of the Iowa delegation to the Democratic convention how they got into Roosevelt's camp, they told him, "Well, Jim Farley came out and asked us and nobody else did."[7]

Veteran party officials recalled Roosevelt's spirited campaign for vice president in 1920, as well as his electrifying appearance on crutches before the 1924 convention. Their generally favorable disposition toward the candidate helped Farley dissuade many of the state organizations from running favorite sons in the primaries and endorse Roosevelt instead. He played on the universal fear that another deadlocked convention might cost the party another election. Some of the potential delegates expressed concern about Roosevelt's health, because stories had been spreading about the nature of his disability and whether he could withstand a grueling national campaign. "We don't want a dead man on the ticket," Al Smith was telling Democrats. In response, the Roosevelt camp planted an article in *Liberty* magazine—"Is Franklin D. Roosevelt Physically Fit to Be President?" It asked whether a "cripple" could withstand the pressures of the presidency and answered with medical testimonials that FDR could meet all of the demands of public life. Farley felt that the article fully settled the question and would put to rest the concerns he had heard expressed on his western trip.[8]

Polls showed Roosevelt ahead of other potential Democratic candidates, but Louis Howe's surveys also alerted him to a stop-Roosevelt movement that John Raskob, Jouett Shouse, and Bernard Baruch had organized within the Democratic National Committee, promoting Smith, Ritchie, and Baker as candidates who would be safer on business issues. These were the same DNC leaders who had pledged cooperation with President Hoover to promote business recovery, a tactic that seemed aimed at removing economic issues from the political debate that year. Roosevelt stood alone among the potential Democratic candidates in staking an economic stance separate from the president's. Conditioned by the cultural politics of the 1920s, Democratic and Republican party leaders, along with much of the press, assumed that Prohibition would become the dominant issue in 1932, grossly misreading the public's concern about the economy. Although public sentiment had shifted against Prohibition, pocketbook issues determined how more people voted that year.[9]

Raskob's effort to center the Democratic campaign on the repeal of Prohibition was aimed at creating mischief for Roosevelt because of his so-called damp position—straddling the wet and dry camps by favoring local option. If Roosevelt could be compelled to side with the wets, he might alienate his supporters in the dry South. To that end, Raskob called an unusual meeting of the DNC in 1931 to commit the party in advance to a platform plank favoring repeal. The chairman collected sufficient proxies to give him a majority vote, but Roosevelt's supporters discovered his plans and alerted Tennessee representative Cordell Hull, a former national chairman and a leading dry. Hull denounced Raskob's tactics and accused him of trying to run the Democratic Party the way he ran General Motors. Roosevelt meanwhile had gathered his own proxies and persuaded a number of DNC members to revoke the proxies they had promised to the chairman. Despite a spirited defense by Al Smith, Raskob's proposals went down to defeat by a two-to-one margin. The meeting adjourned without adopting any policy on Prohibition.

By standing against a wet plank, Roosevelt enhanced his popularity among southern delegates, a critical step toward obtaining the nomination. As Cordell Hull noted, every Democrat opposed to Smith and Raskob gradually turned to FDR. Wanting to avoid an open division within the party, Roosevelt instructed his supporters to avoid any criticism of the defeated side. Meanwhile, although Raskob lost on Prohibition, he still ran the DNC and succeeded in scheduling the convention in Chicago rather than Kansas City, the friendlier location that Roosevelt had preferred. In Chicago, the stop-Roosevelt forces could count on Mayor Anton Cermak to pack the galleries with wets to demand repeal and boo FDR.[10]

Behind Raskob's maneuvers lay his hope of nominating Al Smith again, despite the Happy Warrior having traded politics for business. After living in the governor's mansion, Smith had shown no desire to return to his working-class roots on First Avenue and instead moved into a luxury apartment on the wealthiest end of Fifth Avenue; his old friends shook their heads when he took up golf. He spent the four years after his presidential race building and trying to rent out the vast and largely vacant Empire State Building—only its observation deck brought in much revenue at first. After the stock market crash in 1929, one of his chief financial backers, James Riordan, had committed suicide. Riordan's County Trust Fund had made large loans to Smith's presidential campaign that had not been repaid, and Smith, who served on its board, could not honor them. The wealthy Raskob sustained most of the loss himself. In 1930, when Ed Flynn questioned Smith about his future plans, the former governor assured him that he had no intention of running for office again. Pulling open his desk drawer, he took out a stack of bills and other debts and described himself as being "in an extremely bad position" financially.[11]

Even so, Al Smith seethed with resentment against his ungrateful successor in Albany, and he bristled at the thought of him becoming the Democratic candidate for president. Smith fought a state constitutional amendment that Roosevelt proposed for the purchase of marginal land to plant trees for conservation purposes, calling it socialistic because it put the state in the lumber business. FDR campaigned hard in favor of the amendment, winning passage comfortably. To mollify Smith, Roosevelt set up a luncheon meeting and made a show of soliciting his advice in front of a pack of press photographers, but Smith's wound was too deep to heal quickly. Roosevelt's supporters put pressure on Smith to win his endorsement. He could not possibly do otherwise, said Clark Howell, publisher of the *Atlanta Journal-Constitution*. "The hell I can't," Smith replied. Then, rising from his chair and stamping his foot angrily, he told Howell, "Do you know, by God, that he has never consulted me about a damn thing since he has been Governor? He has taken bad advice and from sources not friendly to me. He has ignored me!"[12]

Years later, Franklin Roosevelt had a sure measure for judging a politician's reliability: "Was he with us B.C.?" he would ask, meaning "before Chicago." He never forgot the opposition he encountered from many of the leaders of his party, who nearly denied him the nomination. His first obstacle down that road was the media baron William Randolph Hearst, an off-and-on-again Democrat who owned an influential chain of newspapers. In a New Year's radio broadcast, Hearst denounced all of the leading candidates for their Wilsonian internationalism, including Hoover, Roosevelt, Smith, and Newton Baker. Wanting a president who was unafraid to put "America first," he endorsed House Speaker John Nance Garner. Few outside of Texas regarded Garner as presidential timber, and the ruddy-faced, white-haired, cigar-smoking, bourbon-sipping

Many hats filled the Democratic ring as the primaries began in 1932, among them John Nance Garner's Stetson, Franklin Roosevelt's fedora, and Al Smith's derby, whereas President Hoover's homburg dominated the Republican ring.

Garner was entirely content to remain as Speaker. Since 1903, he had represented a district so safe that he never bothered to campaign, other than to host an annual barbecue. Having given few speeches in his thirty years in Congress, he had no intention of launching a speaking tour to win the nomination.[13]

"Cactus Jack" Garner had held the title of Speaker of the House for only a month at that point and was engaged entirely in turning the Democrats' three-vote majority into a cohesive legislative force. Although the Hoover administration had been picturing him as a radical, his politics were not far from the president's, and he expressed annoyance at Hoover's failure to seek a middle ground with congressional Democrats. "Hell's bells," said the Speaker. "If he wants to cooperate why don't he keep his secretaries from trying to block all our economy moves?" Hearst had sent his top Washington correspondent, George Rothwell Brown, to sound Garner out about running for president. The Speaker was flattered that Hearst considered him as a candidate but explained that he did not want to jeopardize his "tender majority of three." He refused to act like a candidate and resisted placing his name in the primaries until Hearst orchestrated a move to get him on the ballot in California, where the Hearst papers could boost Garner's chances.[14]

The unexpected candidacy of Speaker Garner hindered Roosevelt's delegate hunt in the Southwest, at the same time that Hearst's papers unleashed editorial fire on the front-runner. Jim Farley hastily arranged a meeting with a Hearst editor in New York and learned that the publisher wanted to hear from Roosevelt whether he still promoted U.S. membership in the League of Nations. Having lost one race because of the League issue in 1920, Roosevelt was unwilling to let it defeat him again. He responded with a speech on February 2, assuring his listeners that he no longer favored American entry into the League. This backtracking shocked his internationalist supporters, including his wife; in fact, Eleanor did not speak to her husband for days after the speech. Roosevelt tried to explain to his disappointed supporters that there was "a difference between ideals and the methods of obtaining them," but the speech also signaled that he intended to follow a nationalist course in finding a way out of the Depression. Retreat served his purposes, calming Hearst's editorial attacks and boosting his support among western progressives, who tended to be isolationists.[15]

As the Depression made the incumbent president increasingly vulnerable, Al Smith began to reconsider his own political status. He decided that it was his right to run again: who more than he deserved a chance at the White House? At a Democratic dinner early in 1932, Smith taunted the Republicans by asking, "What became of the old full dinner pail?" The economy had never been worse, with business almost paralyzed and millions of workers unemployed. Private charities could no longer handle a crisis of this proportion. It was time for the federal government to step in, Smith asserted. In February, he threw his derby into the ring with a terse announcement that he would accept the Democratic nomination for president. Some liberals cheered his entry into the race, finding him a more convincing reformer than Roosevelt, despite his growing ties with business. Others lamented that Smith's battle with Roosevelt could throw the nomination to a conservative candidate who would "out-Hoover" Hoover. Given Roosevelt's large lead among the delegates, Smith's only chance rested on using the convention's two-thirds rule to create a deadlock that would eventually compel the delegates to nominate him or a dark horse.[16]

Governor Roosevelt did not actively campaign during the primaries. He tended to state business and let his lieutenants represent him. Most of the speeches he gave dealt with state and local issues, although he made three strategically placed out-of-state talks in Minnesota, Virginia, and Georgia. Roosevelt wrote none of these speeches, but he did not simply parrot words that others had written. He preferred to "bat ideas around" with his staff and have them prepare a first draft. The speech might be the work of an individual or a composite from competing sources, but in each case, Roosevelt would put his stamp on the final version. He would go over every word, revising and rewriting the speech to the point where he could deliver it by heart. He wanted clarity and everyday vocabulary, heavily laced with homespun phrases and stories. He practiced his speeches by reading them aloud to get the sound right. No matter who wrote the words, Roosevelt's delivery gave them their ultimate personality and force.[17]

His gubernatorial speechwriter, Sam Rosenman, feeling inadequate to handle the big economic issues facing the country, urged Roosevelt to widen his circle of advisers. Rather than seek advice from industrialists, financiers, or other politicians, he turned to a group of academics. Raymond Moley, who taught political science at Barnard College, had been consulting with Roosevelt throughout his governorship. For the presidential campaign, Moley recruited two Columbia University professors, Rexford G. Tugwell, a specialist in agricultural economics, and Adolph

A. Berle Jr., who taught corporate law. Roosevelt referred to them as his "privy council," but a reporter dubbed them the "brains trust"—newspaper slang for experts; headline writers later shortened the name to "brain trust." Jim Farley devoted himself to collecting delegates and left the issues to the speechwriters, telling Moley, "You keep out of my business, and I'll keep out of yours." Together, Moley, Tugwell, and Berle mapped out campaign themes of governmental action to end the Depression and to counterbalance the concentration of corporate economic power. They did not simply write speeches: they generated ideas, and they convinced the candidate that the American people wanted a genuine alternative in 1932—a party of liberal thought and planned action.[18]

The brain trust produced Roosevelt's most sensational speech during the primary season. The *Lucky Strike Hour,* a popular radio program, offered each Democratic candidate ten minutes on its weekly broadcast. Roosevelt drew the April 7 slot, and Raymond Moley drafted his remarks for that program. The brief speech criticized Hoover's trickle-down policies of providing relief to banks and railroads but not to farmers and homeowners, and it called for the government to help "the forgotten man at the bottom of the economic pyramid." Ostensibly an attack on Hoover, the forgotten man speech challenged all of Roosevelt's more conservative rivals for the Democratic nomination to take a stand on the unemployed and the needy, and it established him as the Democrats' leading liberal advocate.[19]

The forgotten man speech touched a nerve with Al Smith. Having worked his way up from the bottom, he found it intolerable to have a country squire become the spokesman for the nation's poor and dispossessed. Smith responded at the DNC's Jefferson Day dinner in Washington. "This is no time for demagogues," he shouted, his face flushed and his eyes flashing, and he said he would take off his jacket and fight any candidate who appealed to class warfare. The intensity of his attack, which reporters called his "angry warrior" speech, startled Democrats, exploding their hope of having a harmonious convention. The diatribe invigorated Smith's supporters but also made him appear to stand with the old order, whereas Roosevelt represented the party's new hope.

Roosevelt responded a few days later in a speech in St. Paul, Minnesota, in which he tried to dampen the flames by denying that he advocated a "planned and regimented" economic life. Instead, he argued that a great fear had swept the country due to the Depression, causing people to turn to their national government for help. Hoover's response had been inadequate: "There are millions of people who cannot be helped merely by helping their employers," FDR insisted.[20]

Beyond his brain trust, Roosevelt tapped many other sources for speech drafts, even the reporters assigned to his campaign. Ernest K. Lindley, who covered Roosevelt for the Republican *New York Herald Tribune*, liked him well enough to write a sympathetic campaign biography. At Warm Springs, Lindley and others pressed the candidate to say what he thought, and Roosevelt replied that if the reporters did not like his speeches, they ought to draft one themselves. Lindley took up the challenge and prepared the commencement address that Roosevelt delivered at Oglethorpe University on May 22. "The country needs and, unless I mistake its temper, the country demands bold, persistent experimentation," Roosevelt proclaimed. "It is common sense to take a method and try it: If it fails, admit it and try another. But above all try something." The speech captured precisely Roosevelt's flexible approach to governing, contrasted to Hoover's commitment to an ideology that restricted his actions. But the speech infuriated Louis Howe, who warned the candidate that such "radical" talk would scare away voters.[21]

Except for the few favorite-son candidates, Roosevelt marched through the early state primaries without significant opposition, winning in Washington, New Hampshire, Minnesota, North Dakota, Georgia, Iowa, Maine, Arkansas, Wisconsin, Nebraska, Kentucky, and Michigan. State party conventions, run by the local party bosses, picked most of the delegates, and the voters participated in largely meaningless preferential primaries. But Roosevelt's solid victories in so many primaries demonstrated his popular support and convinced the bosses to hop on his bandwagon. Tammany Hall's boss, John F. Curry, however, was not among them. He arranged to send the New York State delegation to the convention uninstructed—knowing that most of the delegates would be loyal to Al Smith.

During his governorship, Roosevelt had tried to maintain civil relations with Tammany Hall, but the crooked administration of the debonair New York mayor James J. "Jimmy" Walker (also known as "Beau James") complicated these efforts. When charges of financial corruption surfaced against Walker, Tammany expected Governor Roosevelt to protect the mayor, even as reformers demanded that he throw Walker out of office. Roosevelt turned the matter over to the state legislature, which held a formal investigation. Accused by both sides of shirking his responsibility, Roosevelt insisted that he would not climb to power on the back of another man and that he would give Walker the full benefit of due process. Tammany chief Curry miscalculated that he could frighten Roosevelt into saving Walker by threatening to oppose him at the national convention. Although irrelevant to the economic issues of the Depression, the Walker case, by testing FDR's toughness as a leader, contributed significantly to the fight for the Democratic nomination.[22]

Roosevelt's string of primary victories was broken in April 1932 when Al Smith embarrassed him in the Massachusetts contest. Smith remained immensely popular in the Irish Catholic stronghold that he had carried against Hoover, but Boston's beguiling mayor James Michael Curley had enticed Roosevelt into the primary nevertheless. Fearing that backing away from the race would make him look weak, Roosevelt assigned his oldest son, James, to lead his campaign in the state's primary, assuring him that at least he would "learn a good deal about practical backroom politics from Brother Curley!" The primary developed into an internal fight between Mayor Curley, who wanted public works to put Boston's unemployed to work, and the Democratic governor, Joseph B. Ely, who wanted to cut spending and raise taxes to balance the state's budget. Other than Curley, the state Democratic organization stood behind Smith, enabling him to win by a three-to-one margin. Smith's big bounce from Massachusetts helped him triumph in Rhode Island and Connecticut and run strongly in Pennsylvania.[23]

Then, on May 3, Roosevelt and Smith both lost the California primary to Speaker Garner, who won handsomely with aggressive support from the Hearst newspapers. Garner's winning margin came entirely from Los Angeles, whose population included a large share of transplanted Texans. A leading California Democrat, William G. McAdoo, described the result as a "perhaps irreparable blow." to Roosevelt's candidacy. Although FDR continued to win primaries in the West and South, the Massachusetts and California defeats meant that he would go to the convention a hundred votes short of the two-thirds majority required for nomination.[24]

DARK HORSES

Aside from Roosevelt, Smith, and Garner, as well as a few favorite-son governors, the most serious Democratic candidates included a banker, a businessman, and a corporate attorney. These dark horses represented the "safe and sound," hard-money, probusiness, limited-government wing of the Democratic Party that dated back to the era of Grover Cleveland, as opposed to the inflationary, business-regulating, active-government faction that nominated William Jennings Bryan in 1896.

Among the favorite-son governors, from Virginia's conservative Harry Byrd to Oklahoma's populist William H. "Alfalfa Bill" Murray, the only one given a serious chance of winning the nomination was the aristocratic four-term governor of Maryland, Albert Cabell Ritchie. A Jeffersonian Democrat, Ritchie advocated states' rights and limited government, advising his audiences to "quit looking to Washington as much to police us and cure everything by piling law on law." Broad-minded on civil liberties, he declined to enforce Prohibition in his state and sent troops to arrest lynchers on Maryland's Eastern Shore. But narrow-minded on matters of taxes and spending, he resisted authorizing public works projects for fear of damaging the state's credit rating. Governor Ritchie dismissed the notion that anyone might be destitute in Maryland. "I do not know where you get the idea that anybody is starving in this State," he responded to one survey. "No such conditions as that exists here." Ritchie's greatest asset was his backing by the Democratic Party's largest campaign contributor, Bernard Baruch; during World War I, Ritchie had been Baruch's legal adviser on the War Industries Board. Southerners liked the courtly Ritchie, but others complained that no one west of the Mississippi had ever heard of him. Jim Farley offered Ritchie the vice presidential nomination, but the Maryland governor declined, feeling sure that Al Smith would throw the presidential nomination to him.[25]

Chicago mayor Anton Cermak pledged his support to Melvin Alvah Traylor, president of the First National Bank of Chicago. The mayor, exerting strong influence over both the Illinois and the Indiana delegations, could have played kingmaker by delivering those delegations to Roosevelt. But as a Czech Protestant who led an Irish Catholic political machine, Cermak could not afford to offend Al Smith. By backing the long-shot candidate, Traylor, the mayor gained some leeway to negotiate in the back rooms. The banker he chose had also caught the eye of the pioneer public relations specialist Ivy Lee, a conservative Democrat. Lee had conducted polls showing Democratic liberals coalescing behind Roosevelt and conservatives behind Garner. Since he doubted that Garner could be nominated, he thought there might be a chance that the Speaker would throw his support behind a sound-money Chicago banker who had kept his distance from Wall Street. Lee planted magazine articles that portrayed Traylor as the "new Abe Lincoln," calling him an

"Honest Mel" who understood the problems of the common people and could offer homespun ideas for handling the Depression. Lee's gift for publicity turned the unknown banker into a serious presidential candidate, beyond Traylor's wildest dreams.[26]

Another man to watch, however briefly, had been the chairman of General Electric (GE), Owen D. Young. He had won praise for fostering better cooperation between labor and management at GE and for his international negotiations to stabilize the precarious German economy. Young had served on one of President Hoover's unemployment committees, but he later grew frustrated with the president's stubborn resistance to federal relief. As a businessman, he was appealing to editors and feature writers, but the idea of nominating someone so closely connected with the so-called power trust during the Depression struck the party pros as very risky. Before the convention, Young dropped out of contention for personal reasons (his wife suffered from a heart ailment), but he kept delivering commencement addresses, suggesting that he was still available in case of a deadlock. He insisted that he was immune to a draft and candidly admitted that he lacked "the right kind of training to hold down that job in the White House."[27]

With Owen Young out of the race, Franklin Roosevelt predicted that "the Smith-Shouse-Raskob crowd" would turn to Newton D. Baker if Smith's candidacy faltered. The enthusiasm of his backers challenged Baker's own reluctance to become a candidate. Regarded as the true heir to Woodrow Wilson's legacy, he had been a student of the former president and had served as a reform mayor of Cleveland, Ohio, before joining Wilson's cabinet as secretary of war. Government service had impoverished Baker, however, and he left Washington to build his fortune as an attorney for utility companies and other big business entities. Popular in business circles and among military veterans, Baker held views of the world and of the domestic economy that largely matched the president's, and Hoover had appointed him to the Wickersham Commission.[28]

Newton Baker could move audiences to tears with his inspiring speeches, impressing listeners with his intelligent grasp of the issues. Yet he was a slight, frail man, guarded about his health due to the heart attack he had suffered. Having been close to Wilson and seeing how the presidency had ravaged him, Baker told friends that he could never crave the job for himself. Nor was he keen on assuming office during a massive economic crisis. Franklin Roosevelt had pegged Baker as extremely honest and capable but timid and unadventurous in economic matters.

Privately, Baker admitted he had no clear ideas about how to solve the unemployment problem, nor could he find anyone who could tell him "how long the present Depression is to last, or whether anybody in the Democratic Party has found an answer to our economic difficulties." Raskob and Shouse personally conferred with him, promising that he could count on Al Smith's support, but Baker refused to get into the primaries or otherwise campaign. He explained that he would take the nomination only if "every other possibility had been exhausted."[29]

The demise of the *New York World*, the nation's leading liberal Democratic newspaper, played a role in the Baker campaign. Financial difficulties due to the Depression caused its sale in 1931 to the Scripps-Howard chain, which folded it into the conservative Republican *World-Telegram and Sun*. The end of the *World* let loose its talented editorial page writers, Walter Lippmann being the most prominent of the group. Lippmann launched an influential column called "Today and Tomorrow" (known among journalists as TNT), which was syndicated by the Republican *New York Herald Tribune*. During the world war, Lippmann had worked for Baker in the War Department, and he joined with a fellow *World* alumnus, Ralph Hayes, to spearhead the Baker for President movement. Since Newton Baker himself found Franklin Roosevelt personally charming, with "a real desire to serve uprightly," Lippmann had to convince him of FDR's unfitness for the presidency and of his party's desperate need for his leadership. Lippmann described Roosevelt's record as governor as one of vacillation and evasion, particularly toward Tammany Hall. "[Roosevelt] just doesn't happen to have a very good mind," wrote Lippmann, dismissing the governor as an "amiable boy scout" who should never be president.[30]

A week into the election year, Walter Lippmann went public with these views in a column on FDR's candidacy that accused the governor of lacking either strong convictions or a firm grasp of public affairs. Franklin Roosevelt was no crusader, Lippmann asserted. "He is no enemy of entrenched privilege. He is a pleasant man who, without any important qualifications for the office, would very much like to be President." The nationally syndicated column—which Republicans reprinted and distributed even more widely—stunned Roosevelt, but he chose not to respond to it or anything else that Lippmann wrote through the spring. Lippmann had an editorial writer's desire for clear-cut stands on the issues, whereas Roosevelt had a politician's instinct for avoiding taking precise stands on polarizing topics. Instead, he positioned himself "just a little left of center." He considered Lippmann, for all his brilliance, politically unrealistic and out of touch with the nation beyond Manhattan.[31]

Lippmann's drumbeat of anti-Roosevelt and pro-Baker columns gradually fixed the attention of the conservative eastern press on Newton Baker. By doing nothing to promote his candidacy, Baker actually encouraged the press to churn out stories, editorials, and cartoons, speculating on his chances. Baker himself remained skeptical of this boom, worrying that a protracted Smith-Roosevelt battle could damage the party's credibility. He advised his supporters that Roosevelt's nomination would be infinitely better than having a divided party. He refused to join the stop-Roosevelt movement, to make any political speeches, or to give one of the *Lucky Strike* radio addresses. Explaining his reluctance to run, he claimed, "The upshot of it all is that I am trying to see what my real duty is and not to force the hand of Fate one way or the other."[32]

Talk about Newton Baker's presidential chances sent a shiver through the White House. The president and his staff saw Baker as a man of real presidential caliber, and they assumed that Franklin Roosevelt would be a much easier challenger to beat, especially once the public learned about his health. "I would prefer Roosevelt to almost any other leading Democrat for the President's opponent," presidential press secretary, Ted Joslin, recorded in his diary, since "the people would come to understand that he has not the ability nor the mentality to be President. As an unfortunate fact, too, he is a paralytic, depriving him of the strength to properly handle the duties of the President."[33]

In April 1932, the president invited the nation's governors to dine at the White House. Roosevelt sent word that he would need "a strong, sturdy chair" at the table where he would be sitting and a strong man to hold the chair. On the evening of the dinner, Franklin and Eleanor Roosevelt arrived early through the ground-level south entrance, as prearranged, and took the elevator to the hall leading to the state dining room. With one arm on his aide and a cane in his opposite hand, FDR walked slowly into the hall, to await the president and First Lady. Hoover knew of the elaborate preparations to facilitate Roosevelt's movements, but despite his own reputation for punctuality, he was inexplicably half an hour late that evening. Twice during the wait, White House personnel offered Roosevelt a chair, which he declined even though he was obviously in discomfort. The longer they stood, the more Eleanor Roosevelt

Franklin and Eleanor Roosevelt on the night they attended the White House reception for the nation's governors, April 28, 1932. Both believed that President Hoover deliberately kept them waiting that night to test Roosevelt's physical stamina.

became convinced that Hoover was deliberately putting her husband through an endurance test. Finally, the president arrived, shook hands down the line, and led the governors to dinner. The White House butler assigned to help Roosevelt watched as he literally fell into the sturdy chair provided for him. His legs shot straight out until he unlocked each brace and then discreetly arranged himself to face the table. The awkwardness of this effort made it clear why he had not taken a seat in full view of the other guests in the White House hall.[34]

At his fishing camp that weekend, Hoover reminisced with his inner circle about the days when he and Roosevelt had been neighbors during the Wilson administration, enjoying social evenings together. Roosevelt "was a pleasant fellow and well meaning," he commented, "but without a rudimentary grasp of the issues involved." The president asked the White House physician, Joel T. Boone, whether he was not afraid that Roosevelt would "collapse in office." Boone agreed that it would be impossible for a man in FDR's condition to run for president, and he insisted that the American people would never elect a "half-man." Justice Harlan Stone, however, warned the group against selling Roosevelt short. Stone had seen him stand and speak in public at length. "He has a magnificent torso, and he has a wonderful warm voice, and a gracious smile," he assured them, and since Roosevelt would be campaigning over the radio, the people were not going to realize his condition. "This man can be rather impressive," he said, "if they decide to nominate him."[35]

Hoover was not alone in questioning his rival's physical capabilities. Roosevelt's polio had been front-page news when he was stricken in 1921, and thousands of people had glimpsed his disability at political conventions and rallies. Yet he became adept at minimizing his condition by exercising regularly and building a strong upper body that enabled him to "walk" with braces, canes, and someone else's strong arm to lean on. Aides arranged for walkways with sturdy handrails and for strategically placed potted plants to mask his entrances. He often campaigned from the back seat of an open car. Reporters made only passing references to his awkward gait, and the press never photographed him in a wheelchair. As a result, Roosevelt appeared "young and vigorous" in his photographs and much healthier than Hoover in the newsreels' coverage of the governors' conference. The president's fatigued and aged appearance in the newsreel had made Lou Hoover cry, and Hoover complained that "they made me look as though I was 82 years old."[36]

WHO BUT HOOVER?

Time magazine confirmed that Herbert Hoover had aged twenty years since becoming president: "His hair is greyer. His shoulders seem to droop in discouragement. The lines about his eyes have cut in deeper and those around his mouth have hardened." Photographs showed a grim and solemn man, worn down by the burden of office. Rather than radiate a confidence that would match his optimistic reports on the economy, his portraits, political observers commented, "made one want to sell short, get the money in gold, and bury it."[37]

With the Republican primaries approaching, Hoover seemed indignant that anything should be required of him to be nominated: "I shall not turn a hand to get another term," he told his staff. "The convention can nominate me if it wants to or it can nominate someone else. It can do as it damn well pleases." He told the *New York Times*'s publisher, Adolph Ochs, that he "did not give a damn about being reelected" and would gladly be relieved of the problems placed upon him and "get out of the hell" in which he was living. Despite these disclaimers, however, his staff judged him "frantic for a second term." Feeling it undignified for a president to campaign, Hoover gave fewer speeches and held fewer press conferences during the half year before the conventions than he had during the same months of the previous year. Only two of his speeches focused on economic issues; the others dealt with ceremonial occasions. Yet Hoover held the advantage of incumbency, with the press and newsreels covering his every public movement. At a time when Americans were flocking to the movies for entertainment and escape, newsreels shown between the feature films offered nonpartisan images of Hoover placing a wreath on George Washington's tomb or hosting White House lawn parties, while at the same time they ignored the Democrats until their convention.[38]

Far from conceding the election, Hoover orchestrated a strategy tying him to other beleaguered but ultimately successful presidents. On Abraham Lincoln's birthday in February, the president addressed the nation by radio from the Lincoln Bedroom of the White House. The Republican National Committee sent messages to its precinct leaders, requesting that their followers listen in because "there is magic in the name of Lincoln." Republicans recalled Lincoln's campaign slogan from 1864, "Don't Change Horses in the Middle of the Stream," and urged voters not to desert the president in an economic crisis. For George Washington's bicentennial that same month, Hoover made his only appearance before a joint session of Congress. His supporters compared his burdens to Washington's at Valley Forge. Deciding that the country liked a fight and was looking for a little leadership to pull itself out of its troubles, Hoover called reporters to the White House to denounce the "swarm of lobbyists" patrolling the halls of Congress in search of "selfish privilege." He accused them of lobbying for increased federal spending rather than helping him balance the budget. Reporters commented that they had rarely seen Hoover looking so pleased and self-confident, seemingly convinced that the country was finally coming together behind him.[39]

Whatever the resistance within his party, Hoover knew that no opponent had any reasonable hope of gaining a majority of delegates at the convention. Most of the delegates were chosen by the local bosses, who were highly susceptible to federal patronage. California senator Hiram Johnson, a possible candidate himself, called on Hoover not to run again for the good of the party. Fellow progressives begged Johnson to get into the fight to keep Hoover from leading them to "a terrific licking in November," but Johnson concluded that even if he managed to beat Hoover, the bosses would likely nominate someone worse. Pennsylvania's governor, Gifford Pinchot, another progressive Republican, flirted with challenging the president, but his candidacy sparked little public interest. Press attention focused briefly on Dwight L. Morrow, a former diplomat and New Jersey senator, until he died unexpectedly. Hoover heard that prominent business leaders were supporting a draft-Coolidge movement, but the former president had no desire to run again and published an article endorsing Hoover's reelection. Coolidge's vice president, Charles Dawes, also surfaced as a possible nominee, until Hoover appointed him to head the Reconstruction Finance Corporation, effectively taking him out of consideration. Hoover's opponents eventually realized that the president had rounded up commitments from a majority of the delegates in advance of the primaries. Progressives such as Pinchot and Johnson, having conceded Hoover's renomination, would wait to see which man the Democrats nominated. If they picked a conservative, the progressives were ready to consider a third party.[40]

The only open challenge to the president came from a physician and former Republican senator from Maryland, Joseph Irwin France. Despite scant name recognition or popular support, France possessed the wealth to finance his own campaign. "The situation in Washington is rotten," he explained as his reason for running. His platform consisted of little more than his opposition to Hoover and Prohibition. France won several nonbinding, preferential primaries, garnering him only four delegates. Hoover retaliated by challenging France in his home state of Maryland, trouncing the senator soundly. Republicans met in Chicago without the possibility of nominating anyone but Hoover. The inevitability of his nomination made the campaign slogan "Who but Hoover?" sound fatalistic.[41]

The city of Chicago enticed both parties to hold their conventions at its brand-new, state-of-the-art arena, with the largest indoor seating capacity in the world. A product of the prosperous 1920s, the cavernous Chicago Stadium had opened just months before the stock market crashed. The stadium housed wrestling matches, hockey games, rodeos, and circuses, but its many boxing matches provided the most apt metaphors for the political conventions. Reporters described Herbert Hoover's uncontested renomination as little more than shadowboxing, and they declared Franklin Roosevelt, after his nomination, as the winner in the fourth round, with his opponents throwing in the towel.[42]

The two parties assembled in the same venue within two weeks of each other, but they were worlds apart in style. Republicans carefully planned their convention, stripping away passion and substance for a tightly orchestrated stage show. During the gathering, observers noted rows of empty seats in the stadium's balconies. On the floor below, the delegates complained about their candidates and their platform but stuck dutifully to the White House script. More than 400 of the 1,154 Republican delegates were federal officeholders, mostly postmasters whose dependence on patronage kept them in line. Noticeably absent were the members of Congress who usually exerted influence at the conventions. At President Hoover's insistence, Congress had remained in session, so few Republican senators or representatives traveled to Chicago. By contrast, members of Hoover's cabinet mingled prominently throughout the delegations, with Lawrence Richey serving as the president's field commander. At the White House, Hoover devoted "every spare minute" to preparing for the convention, keeping in close contact with his lieutenants in Chicago once the proceedings began.[43]

The drys had dominated the previous Republican convention, but this time, the talk was all wet. A *Literary Digest* poll revealed that 73.5 percent of Americans now favored ending Prohibition and that repeal would likely win in forty-six of the forty-eight states. The practical politicians realized that the noble experiment was doomed, arguing that Hoover's best chance of reelection lay in endorsing repeal. Massachusetts representative Joseph Martin, just beginning a career that would make him Speaker of the House, called on the president to endorse the legalization of alcohol, thus depriving the Democrats of both the issue and the millions of dollars of campaign contributions it would bring them. Hoover vacillated, not wanting to offend his dry supporters. "He wouldn't commit himself to the time of day from a hatful of watches," snapped the caustic columnist Westbrook Pegler.[44]

The Republican keynote speaker thundered for an hour without mentioning the only subject that the delegates were talking about, Prohibition. Hoover had urged speakers to avoid mentioning the issue in order to prevent stirring up the party's wet and dry factions. He adopted a "moist" strategy, personally drafting a platform plank calling for a national referendum to let the people decide for themselves whether to keep or repeal the Eighteenth Amendment. Still, many of the delegates thought that embracing repeal could save some Republican seats in Congress. "Vote Wet" buttons sold more briskly than did Hoover buttons at the convention hall. During the platform debate, Columbia University president Nicholas Murray Butler gave a rousing pitch in favor of outright repeal, but the drys threatened to walk out and nominate their own candidate if the platform went wet. Butler's repeal plank failed by a vote of 690 to 460, showing that a significant minority of the delegates were willing to buck their party's leadership. The Prohibition plank was so confusing that it took reporters several readings to grasp that it simply agreed to submit the issue to a popular vote, without taking sides. Its only virtue, wrote the passionately wet H. L. Mencken, was in "being quite unintelligible to simple folk."[45]

During the opening ceremonies, Senator France sat on the stage and conspicuously refused to join the standing ovations whenever a speaker mentioned President Hoover. From the press box, Mencken noted that France was being "watched carefully by the Hoover sleuth, Signor Richey." While Oregon delegate Lawritz B. Sandblast was delivering a nomination speech in favor of France, the sound system failed. France then strode across the stage, heading toward the podium. After the convention chairman, House minority leader Bertrand Snell, intercepted him, the two men engaged in a heated argument before the vast throng of delegates, with France explaining that he intended to withdraw his name and nominate Calvin Coolidge instead. Snell denied his right to speak, since France was not a delegate. As the senator tried to push past Snell, the police apprehended him and escorted him from the stage, followed by a gaggle of reporters and photographers trying to capture the convention's sole dramatic and unscripted moment.[46]

Metro-Goldwyn-Mayer (MGM) executive Louis B. Mayer, serving as a Republican delegate from California, produced some elaborate stagecraft when Hoover's name was placed in nomination. Moving picture images of the president appeared on giant screens at either end of the hall. At the podium, the convention chairman held up numbered placards to signal crews to let loose the balloons and begin the light displays, as well as alerting the bands about what to play. The delegates paraded to endless renditions of "California, Here I Come," and when the chairman held up his hand for silence, they stopped abruptly, suggesting there was very little spontaneity in their actions.[47]

In the absence of the president, the vice president, and most members of Congress, the convention turned into "a woman's show," with the vice president's formidable sister, Dolly Gann, conducting a personal crusade. She asserted that "Brother deserves the renomination." Hoover, however, wanted to replace "the old gentleman," seventy-two-year-old Charles Curtis, with a more politically attractive vice presidential candidate. They had never made a compatible team, as the publisher of the *Kansas City Star*, Roy Roberts, learned painfully when he sat between them at a Gridiron Club dinner. Whenever the skits lampooned Curtis, Hoover chuckled and kicked Roberts under the table; when they needled Hoover, Curtis laughed and kicked him. Curtis had drawn much negative publicity for getting carried away by the "lure of Washington society," particularly over the fuss his sister Dolly caused in exerting her social status as his official hostess. The 1932 Pulitzer Prize–winning musical satire, *Of Thee I Sing,* featured Vice President Alexander Throttlebottom, who could get into the White House only on public tours; the character was clearly based on Curtis. But Hoover failed to persuade former vice president Charles Dawes to run again, and he did not want to upset Curtis's friends in the Senate. As a result, political inertia kept Curtis on the ticket.[48]

The president instead dropped the resolutely dry chairman of the Republican National Committee, Simeon Fess, replacing him with Everett Sanders, an alumnus of the Coolidge White House. After being rejected by the "first-rate" men he had tried to recruit for the job, Hoover settled on the "second-string" Sanders, whose connection to Coolidge was his major asset. Nervous about a possible stampede to Coolidge by the delegates, the Hoover organizers had avoided making any formal salute to the nation's only living former president, and Coolidge had sent no greeting to the convention. Since leaving the White House, he had rarely mentioned his successor's name. The appointments of Sanders and Ted Clark, another Coolidge staff member who joined the White House staff that summer, seemed aimed at appeasing the Coolidge wing and enticing the former president to campaign for Hoover.[49]

In an atmosphere of gloom and loss, Republican delegates suppressed their uneasiness over Hoover's chances and nominated him again. They had no reasonable alternative, and their rejection of a sitting president would have hurt the party's candidates on all levels. Nor were they ready to count Hoover out, for all his liabilities. He had spent a dozen years learning the mechanics of politics, demonstrated by his carefully controlled convention, and he also held the advantage of incumbency. At the White House, the president listened to the convention over the radio. "Well, it wasn't exactly unexpected," he shrugged when he heard that he had won the nomination, and then he returned to work.[50]

HAPPY DAYS ARE HERE AGAIN

Two weeks later, the Democrats occupied Chicago Stadium, with the demand for tickets to the galleries running much higher than during the Republican gathering. The Democrats promised a more unpredictable spectacle and produced a true political cliff-hanger that kept delegates, spectators, and radio listeners up throughout the night. Democrats went to Chicago scenting victory. The best that Republicans could hope for was another splintering of the Democratic Party into factions. As Will Rogers had famously quipped in 1930, he was not a member of any organized political party—he was a Democrat.

The Republican convention barely mentioned the Depression, whereas the Democrats could talk about little else. Breadlines stretched for blocks near Chicago Stadium, the city had been unable to pay many of its employees (particularly schoolteachers), and twenty-five banks around the city closed their doors on the day the Democratic delegates arrived in town. Anxious depositors mobbed the larger downtown banks, threatening the solvency of those headed by former Vice President Dawes and Melvin Traylor. The dark-horse candidate Traylor stood in the lobby of his bank, imploring depositors not to withdraw their savings. On Monday, June 27, DNC chairman Raskob opened the convention by declaring that the Democrats were coming to rescue the country from "a pit of Depression that seems almost bottomless." Kentucky senator Alben Barkley, a longtime dry, followed, delivering a two-hour keynote address that set off a wild demonstration by calling for an understandable and unequivocal plank favoring the repeal of Prohibition. The next day, the convention moved to elect a permanent chairman. Jouett Shouse had passed up the opportunity to serve as temporary chairman, which carried the honor of delivering the keynote address, in order to run for permanent chairman, a role in which he could make the key procedural rulings. All of the stop-Roosevelt candidates backed Shouse, who thought that he had a commitment from Roosevelt too. But Roosevelt did not want a convention ringmaster working against his nomination and promised only to "commend" Shouse, not to "recommend" him for the post. FDR's supporters voted for Montana senator Thomas J. Walsh, who defeated Shouse, 626 to 528, in the first test of Roosevelt's strength.

The vote confirmed that Roosevelt had the support of a majority of the delegates but not the two-thirds needed for the nomination. A century earlier, when the first Democratic convention nominated Andrew Jackson, it established the two-thirds rule. The rule survived because it gave the South a veto over candidates it found objectionable, and over the years, it had eliminated some of the party's popular front-runners. In 1924, the worst deadlock ever resulted in the convention taking 103 ballots to pass over the front-runners William G. McAdoo and Al Smith and nominate the eminently forgettable John W. Davis. Now, in 1932, McAdoo and Smith met to put aside their old rivalry and plan on how to stop Roosevelt. The problem with the alliance was that neither man was willing to endorse the other. The specter of 1924 also haunted the convention chairman, Senator Tom Walsh, who worried that if the convention dragged out beyond five ballots, the Democrats' chances of winning the election would "wane with every succeeding ballot."[51]

Among Roosevelt's supporters, Louisiana's populist senator Huey Long urged fighting to abolish the two-thirds rule as undemocratic. Jim Farley sampled opinion among the delegates and concluded that the rule remained popular with most southern delegates, whom Roosevelt could not afford to offend; nor could he risk losing the first major vote of the convention. His lieutenants beat a strategic retreat, declining to challenge the rule. "It looks bad for Franklin," President Hoover remarked to his staff as they reviewed this news from Chicago. If Roosevelt had any boldness in him, the president conjectured, he could get control of the situation and ensure his nomination by announcing that he would put all of his Democratic rivals in the cabinet, to ensure their services to the nation. "It would turn the trick for him. But he hasn't it in him," said Hoover. (In fact, Roosevelt appointed none of his rivals to the cabinet.)[52]

As with the Republicans, liquor dominated the Democrats' platform debate. Their Platform Committee's report called for repeal of the Eighteenth Amendment; Cordell Hull presented a minority report that proposed straddling the issue by referendum. Speaking for outright repeal, Al Smith brought down the house with an ardent oration, touching off an exuberant demonstration that made clear the sentiments of the convention. Roosevelt got the message and released his delegates to vote their consciences on the issue. The repeal plank won 934¾ to 213¾, and even some of the driest state delegations went wet "with loud hallelujahs." Although Prohibition was pushed by FDR's opposition, the settlement of the issue worked to Roosevelt's advantage, since it was the one issue on which his rivals, all wetter than he was, might have united against him. At that point, Roosevelt simply discarded his earlier reservations and climbed aboard the popular repeal movement's bandwagon.[53]

The Democrats' repeal plank trumped the Republicans' referendum and swung the minority party in line with the majority of public opinion. Otherwise, the Democrats produced a short and tepid platform that called for a balanced budget, an expanded federal works programs, lower tariffs, regulation of the securities markets, and aid to farmers. An early draft had included support for federal unemployment relief, bank deposit insurance, and old-age pensions, but the Platform Committee worried that Republicans would denounce such economic proposals as socialism and denied them that ammunition.[54]

By Wednesday afternoon, the nominations began, kicking off ten hours of long-winded speeches, each followed by protracted demonstrations that were accompanied by the stadium's organist playing the candidates' signature songs, including "The Sidewalks of New York" for Smith and "The Old Gray Mare" for Garner. Chicago Stadium housed the world's largest organ, which, it was claimed, had the volume of a 2,500-piece brass band. Organist Al Melgard played for both conventions that year, and his repertoire at each included the popular melody "Happy Days Are Here Again." The song's bouncy rhythm seemed out of sync with the somber Republican proceedings and went unnoticed. But when Melgard played it for Franklin Roosevelt's parades, the tune meshed perfectly with the upbeat candidate. Roosevelt had requested "Anchors Away" for his theme song, but his campaign staff thought it sounded too funereal. Louis Howe's secretary convinced him to switch by singing and dancing to the new tune in his hotel room. "Happy Days Are Here Again" had started out as a slow ballad for an MGM movie musical, *Chasing Rainbows*. Studio executives rejected it as too mournful, so the songwriters picked up the beat and made it a rousing march. After the stock market crash, radio listeners began calling in to ask for the song to be played repeatedly as an anthem of restored hope. It remained Roosevelt's campaign song for the rest of his political career.[55]

An emaciated, asthmatic Louis Howe commanded Roosevelt's Chicago team from his hotel room. Howe lay propped up in bed between two fans, smoking cigarettes and wheezing, listening to the convention over the radio, and keeping in contact by phone with his floor lieutenants. He also had a direct line to Governor Roosevelt in Albany, and all orders from FDR went through him. On the convention floor, Jim Farley and Ed Flynn from New York and Arthur Mullen from Nebraska hunted down additional delegates. Flynn estimated that 90 percent of the operatives of Roosevelt's organization, from Farley down, were newcomers and amateurs, whereas those in the stop-Roosevelt ranks were "all the men of long experience in national politics who had run previous conventions."[56]

Farley, Flynn, and Mullen offered the vice presidency to any candidate who controlled enough votes to put Roosevelt over the top. They dangled it before Maryland's governor, Albert Ritchie, with visions of a "Roosevelt, Ritchie and Repeal" campaign, but he held out for the top spot on the ticket. The Roosevelt men looked desperately toward John Nance Garner's delegates from Texas and California. The Speaker had stayed back in Washington, and Texas representative Sam Rayburn served as his agent in Chicago. Garner gave no orders to his delegation, not even to Rayburn, who favored Roosevelt but stuck with the Speaker out of loyalty. The large and unruly Texas delegation was passionately devoted to the Speaker, which limited Rayburn's freedom to negotiate. The Texas congressman asked how long Roosevelt could hold his delegates. "Three ballots," said the downcast Farley, "four ballots, and maybe five."[57]

Al Smith commanded the stop-Roosevelt forces. Before the convention, Smith had received a glowing endorsement by the Scripps-Howard newspaper chain, which wrote off Roosevelt as "another Hoover."

Scripps-Howard's leading columnist, Heywood Broun, contributed a scathing attack on "Feather Duster Roosevelt: The Corkscrew Candidate," which the Smith camp gleefully distributed among the delegates. Energized, Smith allowed himself to believe that he might have a second chance at the White House. If he could hold back Roosevelt until the fourth ballot, many of the front-runner's delegates would likely peel away. Realistically though, most of the southern delegates would never switch to Smith. That meant his best option would be to throw his support to someone such as Newton Baker or Albert Ritchie. Yet Smith adamantly denied the rumors that he would withdraw in favor of some dark horse. "I am not only going to stick, but I am going to be nominated," he stated defiantly.[58]

Among the different stop-Roosevelt factions, Smith's supporters seemed the most determined to fight to the bitter end. Catholic delegates expressed a passion for vindicating their man. A delegate from Louisville, Kentucky, Patrick Callahan, assured reporters that if Franklin Roosevelt took the nomination from Smith, Catholic voters in the big cities would never forgive him and would cost him the election. Callahan predicted that Roosevelt would be beaten worse than Smith had been in 1928: "He won't carry a single big state." Massachusetts governor Joseph Ely put Smith's name into nomination, depicting his man as a straight-shooting, plainspoken, virile, and rugged personality, and he made veiled references to Roosevelt's physical debilities (which Roosevelt felt "overstepped the bounds of decency"). The demonstration that followed was the longest and most heartfelt of the convention, and the galleries were wildly enthusiastic for Smith, having gotten their tickets courtesy of Mayor Cermak. But the galleries could not vote.[59]

By 3:00 A.M., as the nominating speakers drew to a close, Roosevelt's team decided to seize the moment and try to rush the nomination through. They opposed all motions to adjourn and got the first vote going at 4:28 in the morning. Roosevelt received 666¼ votes, from thirty-six states and seven territories. That put him an impressive 464½ votes ahead of the second-place Smith but still 104 votes short of the two-thirds he needed. On the second ballot, Roosevelt's tally increased to 677¾, only because Farley had held back a few votes the first time to show some growth. Neither ballot caused a bandwagon effect, however, and Farley began to fear that two years of tireless work was heading toward oblivion. Having failed on the second ballot, Roosevelt's team moved to adjourn, only to be blocked by Smith's floor manager, Newark mayor

Frank Hague, and his team of "old-time, hard-boiled, season salted veterans" of past convention fights. Sure that the front-runner was about to stumble, the Smith forces launched a barrage of motions, protests, and parliamentary inquiries that turned the convention into an endurance match. Their tactic may have undone them. By forcing a third ballot, they gave Roosevelt's delegates no time to waver.[60]

The summer heat left everyone in the vast hall dripping with perspiration. Jim Farley had handed out fans bearing Roosevelt's picture, which even the stop-Roosevelt delegations waved. In the middle of the night, a thunderstorm dropped the temperature, and the police opened the large doors of the hall to let cool breezes sweep through. At dawn, the windows glowed with the morning light, and the draped flags gave them the look of stained glass. As the roll for the third ballot was called at 8 A.M., convention officials hunted down many of the delegates who had drifted away to nearby speakeasies. Arriving late was New York mayor Jimmy Walker, who took the microphone to ask that his vote be recorded for Al Smith, a defiant gesture considering that Governor Roosevelt was still weighing his removal from office for corruption. On the sly, the mayor's attorney approached Roosevelt's floor leader with a proposition: if Roosevelt promised to protect the mayor, Tammany's delegates would swing to his side. Roosevelt's men, considering Walker a liability, did not bother to relay the offer to Albany. Opposition from Tammany and to Wall Street had made Roosevelt's identification as a New Yorker much more palatable to Democrats from the South and the West.[61]

Across the country, 158 radio stations kept up continuous coverage throughout the night, and they reported enthusiastic telephone calls from listeners thanking them for broadcasting the suspenseful proceedings. On the third ballot, after Roosevelt gained just five additional votes, the exhausted delegates adjourned at 9:15 A.M. on July 1, staggering back to their rooms to get some sleep. Cleaning crews moved into the stadium and carted off tons of newspapers, telegraph blanks, banners, candidates' pictures, blank ballots, paper cups, cigarette packs, programs, fans, candy wrappers, and empty soda and liquor bottles. The work crews poured seventy-five gallons of disinfectant on the floor, spending all day getting the place ready for another session that night. They had never seen a prizefight audience do as much damage as the Democratic delegates had done.[62]

During the ten-hour recess before the convention reconvened, Roosevelt's team anxiously sought a breakthrough, while the stop-Roosevelt forces worked to wrest loose his shakiest supporters. Newton Baker's agents emerged from the shadows, searching openly for delegates. Walter Lippmann circulated a petition signed by eighty conservative internationalists who endorsed Baker for the nomination. The Mississippi delegation had split 10½ for Roosevelt to 9½ for Baker. Under the winner-take-all unit rule, all their votes went to FDR. The governor of Mississippi spent the day persuading them to switch to Baker. A similar shift was brewing in the North Carolina delegation. Maryland governor Ritchie seemed poised to give his state's delegation to Baker. One Baker lieutenant, a utility company executive named Wendell Willkie, worked his own persuasive powers on the southern delegations. Baker's campaign manager reported that Willkie "covered more territory and penetrated a greater diversity of groups than any of the others of your young Turks." The utility companies among Baker's clients were most likely the source of the thousands of telegrams that bombarded the delegates, urging his nomination.[63]

Franklin Roosevelt's last hope of winning the nomination lay with John Nance Garner's Texas and California delegations—which meant convincing William Randolph Hearst to cut those delegations loose. Joseph P. Kennedy, a Boston financier with Hollywood connections to Hearst and one of Roosevelt's most generous contributors, placed a call to Hearst at San Simeon, his palatial estate on the California coast. "W.R., do you want Baker?" Kennedy asked bluntly, explaining that unless Roosevelt won, Newton Baker would get the nomination. Hearst distrusted Baker as a Wilsonian and asked, "Can't I get Ritchie?" But Kennedy insisted that Baker would be the compromise candidate. Hearst heard a similar warning from Boston mayor Curley—and, surprisingly, from the White House. President Hoover fretted that Baker would emerge as the Democratic candidate if the convention deadlocked. "Our salvation lies largely in his nomination," Hoover said of Roosevelt. "I am afraid of Baker." Calculating that Hearst held the key to the nomination, Hoover directed Larry Richey to call MGM studio boss Louis Mayer and have him urge Hearst to get busy if he wanted to stop Newton Baker (MGM had Hearst's movie star girlfriend, Marion Davies, under contract).[64]

In Washington awaited the Hearst correspondent George Rothwell Brown, forgoing the convention—the only one he missed between 1908 and his death at the Republican convention in 1960—to be on hand for any dealings with Speaker Garner. On July 1, Brown received a telegram

from the Hearst organization: TELL GARNER THAT THE CHIEF BELIEVES NOTH-
ING CAN NOW SAVE THE COUNTRY BUT FOR HIM TO THROW HIS VOTES TO GOVER-
NOR ROOSEVELT. At 11:00 that morning, Brown visited the Speaker at the
Capitol and relayed the news. Garner agreed to release his delegates.
That afternoon, Hearst's *Chicago American* reversed its editorial line and
wrote favorably about Roosevelt's candidacy.[65]

Garner waited until 3:00 that afternoon to call Sam Rayburn, saying
it was time "to break this thing up." The Speaker said that Roosevelt
was the choice of the convention and should receive the nomination.
Rayburn replied that he could not swing Texas to Roosevelt unless Garner agreed to run as vice president: the die-hard Texas delegation would
accept nothing less. "All right," said Garner, "release my delegates and
see what you can do. Hell, I'll do anything to see the Democrats win one
more national election." Too late, he realized that his fling with presidential politics meant giving up one of the most powerful jobs in Washington, Speaker of the House, for one of the least powerful, as presiding
officer of the Senate. Standing before the Texas delegation at 6:00 P.M.,
Rayburn announced Garner's withdrawal, a disclosure met by tears,
shouts of protest, and accusations that he and others were deserting the
Speaker. They were not deserting Garner, Rayburn rebutted, since he
did not want the presidency. Even so, the vote within the delegation was
only 54 to 51 to support Roosevelt. In Washington, a reporter caught up
with Speaker Garner to ask whether it was true that he had gone over to
Roosevelt. "I'm a little older than you are, son," said the Speaker. "And
politics is funny."[66]

Hearing that Garner had released the Texans, William G. McAdoo
raced over to the California delegation, caucusing in the same hotel. Jim
Farley had tearfully solicited them. "Boys, Roosevelt is lost unless California comes over on the next ballot," he begged. But under California
law, only the primary victor, Speaker Garner, could release his delegates.
McAdoo went before the California delegation and announced Garner's
withdrawal. Since the delegates remained divided and angry, he declined
to poll them but instead created a steering committee to determine which
candidate they would support. Contacting Hearst, McAdoo made a last-
minute, self-serving effort to convince the publisher to support him for
president or, failing that, for vice president. Hearst had to remind him
that the presidential candidate made the vice presidential choice.[67]

At 5:20 that afternoon, just before the Texas and California delegations met, Franklin Roosevelt placed a phone call to Newton Baker. The

Chicago convention was in a jam, FDR said, and it appeared the delegates would turn to Baker. "I will do anything I can to bring that about if you want it," he stated. Baker thanked him but did not ask for Roosevelt's endorsement, still not wanting to "force the hand of Fate." He would accept a draft but would not seek it. Roosevelt possibly had anticipated Baker's response. Ralph Hayes, Baker's chief advocate in Chicago, said he had learned about the Garner deal more than an hour *before* Roosevelt placed his call. Whether FDR was sincere or was merely trying to shore up his support, Baker felt only "a deep sense of freedom and relief" when he lost the nomination.[68]

That evening, the delegates returned to the stadium, rested and ready for another voting marathon. The stop-Roosevelt forces were counting on Mississippi to break from Roosevelt and start a stampede against him. Before that could happen, McAdoo strode to the podium. The huge arena fell silent. "California came here to nominate a President of the United States," he began. "She did not come here to deadlock this convention." When it sank in that California was switching to Roosevelt, the pro-Smith galleries booed loudly. Mayor Cermak stepped forward and appealed to "friends in the gallery" to behave themselves, and McAdoo coolly remarked that he intended to have his say regardless of what the gallery thought. Then he announced that California would cast its forty-four votes for Franklin D. Roosevelt. A cheer rolled through the hall, and delegates jumped onto their chairs and waved their hats and state banners.[69]

Most delegates hastily climbed onto the Roosevelt bandwagon. Mayor Cermak released the Illinois delegates to vote for FDR, and Indiana followed their lead. Albert Ritchie announced that Maryland would vote for Roosevelt. Texas too came on board, despite its dejected delegates. By the end of the fourth ballot, Roosevelt had 945 votes and the Democratic nomination for president. Al Smith held on to 190½ votes from eight states, including the majority of the New York delegation. Roosevelt immediately telegraphed the convention, stating that he planned to fly to Chicago the next day to accept the nomination rather than follow tradition and wait for weeks for formal notification.

Al Smith had spent much of the day trying to telephone Speaker Garner to implore him to stand firm, but the Speaker would not take his calls. Smith realized what was coming and stayed away from the convention hall that night. "Haul that radio in here," he instructed the staff at his headquarters. As soon as he heard McAdoo's remarks, Smith signaled them to begin packing up his pamphlets, banners, and posters.

They were finished by the time Roosevelt had been nominated. When friends asked Smith to release his delegates so the nomination could be unanimous, he folded his arms petulantly and said, "I won't do it. I won't do it. I won't do it." Smith's admirers regretted that he could not overcome his disappointment and resentment. The convention would have warmly received a gracious gesture on his part after his defeat, wrote the veteran Democrat Claude Bowers, "and Smith would have gone forth better loved than ever before." Instead, he left Chicago before Roosevelt arrived. Had Al Smith thrown his support to another candidate, the convention would likely have followed his wishes, but because he coveted the nomination for himself, he prevented anyone else from emerging as the compromise candidate. The stop-Roosevelt coalition had confronted an old political truism: "You can't beat somebody with nobody."[70]

Franklin Roosevelt named Jim Farley to replace John J. Raskob as party chairman, while retaining the DNC's publicity chief, Charley Michelson. As pledged, the candidate invited John Nance Garner to run for vice president (had he declined, Roosevelt planned to ask either Albert Ritchie or Newton Baker). On Saturday, the delegates voted unanimously to nominate Garner and awaited Roosevelt's arrival. The lateness of his plane added to the suspense. People still perceived flying as dangerous and daring at that time, and the chartered American Airlines flight from Albany to Chicago took nine hours and two refueling stops, encountering strong headwinds and turbulence that made some of the passengers airsick. The candidate emerged at the Chicago airport smiling nonchalantly. The later-than-planned arrival allowed Roosevelt to address the convention during radio's prime time. With belated zeal, the Democratic convention greeted its candidate, taking his arduous effort to appear before them as proof, in the words of one columnist, "of his venturesome spirit and fine physical equipment for the office of President of the United States."[71]

Roosevelt carried with him an acceptance speech that Moley and Rosenman had written, but at the airport, Louis Howe handed him the text that he had drafted. Unwilling to offend his most loyal aide, Roosevelt read the first page of Howe's speech and the rest of the other version. This incident previewed how he would operate during the campaign when dealing with competing factions. In the stadium, he stood before the convention gripping the parallel bars of a stall specially made to aid him in public speaking, holding his shoulders high and throwing back his head in a gesture of challenge. As the party's presidential candidate, he thanked the delegates for waiting for him after six arduous days of meeting and reminded them that by appearing in person to accept the nomination, he was breaking with tradition because the times demanded unprecedented action. "Ours must be a party of liberal thought, of planned action," Roosevelt declared, "of enlightened international outlook, and of the greatest good to the greatest number of people." He congratulated them on voting to repeal Prohibition and embraced their position: "This convention wants repeal. Your candidate wants repeal. And I am confident that the United States of America wants repeal." He called for government programs for putting people back to work, overcoming the problem of farm surpluses, reducing the tariff burden on consumers, and cutting the administrative costs of government. Republicans blamed the Depression on economic laws that people could not alter, but Roosevelt insisted that economic laws were the products of human beings, not of nature, implying that through their government, people could take actions to prevent or mitigate depressions. He concluded by pledging "a new deal for the American people."[72]

Sam Rosenman had lifted that line from a series of articles then running in the *New Republic* under the collective heading "A New Deal." Their author, Stuart Chase, was a popular economist who called for greater governmental regulation of the economy. Rosenman had inserted the phase into the acceptance speech without imagining how it would take hold, but the old *New York World* cartoonist Rollin Kirby, then drawing for the Scripps-Howard syndicate, immediately grasped the slogan's utility. Kirby's cartoon the next day pictured a farmer looking up from his field at a plane flying high overhead, labeled New Deal. Other cartoonists, commentators, and headline writers picked up the term as a catchy shorthand for Roosevelt's proposals.[73]

Still, when Roosevelt arrived in Chicago, the journalist H. L. Mencken reported that "there were not many who thought he could beat Lord Hoover." The delegates whom Mencken interviewed expressed doubt that Roosevelt would be able to coax Al Smith back into the tent and worried that the party would go into the election divided. Chicago bookmakers offered five-to-one odds that Hoover would beat Roosevelt, and some liberals thought FDR could only win "by a kind of miracle." The *Nation*'s liberal editor, Oswald Garrison Villard, dismissed Roosevelt's flight to Chicago as a stunt and wrote that he had found a lack of real enthusiasm for the nominee at the convention. Echoing these sentiments from the right, the Democrats' 1924 standard-bearer, John W. Davis, commented,

"What a pity," as he watched the convention nominate Roosevelt. The remnants of the stop-Roosevelt movement lamented that the party had forfeited its chance of winning back the presidency that year.[74]

Reporters who covered both conventions detected little fervor for either candidate. Both Hoover and Roosevelt had collected most of their delegates early, before political passions had heated up, and the delegates for the most part operated under orders. Looking over the choice, the *Wall Street Journal* called it the first election since 1916 whose outcome was not readily apparent after the conventions. Counting the Solid South for the Democrats, newspapers calculated that Roosevelt would start the campaign with a base of 160 electoral votes to Hoover's 140, with the rest under contention. Most observers agreed that Roosevelt had made a good impression by flying to the convention, but they wondered whether the country would accept the Garner-McAdoo-Hearst deal that brought him the nomination, whether the Democratic Party could heal its rifts, and whether the voters would embrace repeal.[75]

The writer John Dos Passos walked out of Chicago Stadium and down West Madison Street, observing migratory workers, hoboes, and jobless men from all over the Midwest. He doubted that any of them knew or cared about the conventions that had decided who would run their government. "The convention is the sirens of police motorcycles, a new set of scare headlines, a new sensation over the radio," he wrote. "A man has got a job, or else he hasn't got a job, he's got jack in his pocket, or else he's broke, he's got a business, or else he's a bum. Way off some place headline events happen. Even if they're right on West Madison Street, they're way off. Roosevelt or Hoover? It'll be the same cops."[76]

THE ALTERNATIVES

The seeming dissatisfaction with the major party candidates raised expectations among the third parties. With capitalism foundering and fascism and communism on the rise abroad, if Americans were going to embrace radical alternatives, 1932 seemed the most likely year to do so. But minor parties in the United States faced daunting obstacles to getting onto the various state ballots, attracting publicity, or being assured of accurate vote counts. Poor financing, eccentric candidates, and factional squabbling further hindered their efforts.

The Socialists, the most politically potent of the third parties, had polled an impressive 6 percent of the national vote in 1912 for their magnetic labor leader, Eugene V. Debs. After Debs died in 1926, the party turned to an erudite and eloquent Presbyterian minister as its presidential candidate. Norman Thomas lacked Debs's working-class appeal, but he won the nomination in part because so many of the other Socialist leaders had been born outside the United States, making them constitutionally ineligible to run for president. In the 1930 elections, the size of the Socialist vote had increased from the party's showings over the previous decade, and Socialists had won several municipal races. In 1932, they held their national convention in Milwaukee at the invitation of its Socialist mayor, Daniel Hoan. There, the party condemned both the Hoover administration and the Democrats for the economic ruin. Socialists assailed middle-class liberalism as superficial and communism as dogmatic, offering their own platform as a reasonable middle path out of the Depression. The Socialist platform called for federal relief for the unemployed, public works programs, unemployment compensation, a six-hour workday, old-age pensions, health insurance, repeal of Prohibition, racial equality, increased inheritance taxes, and public ownership of basic industries, but the convention rejected a platform proposal for the confiscation of property.[77]

Socialists again chose Norman Thomas for president, with a Pennsylvania labor leader, James Maurer, for vice president. After nominating their candidates by acclamation, the delegates split into angry factions over the election of a national chairman. Thomas headed the party's younger, more militant "college men and white collar elements," and Morris Hillquit, counsel for the International Ladies' Garment Workers' Union, led the blue-collar, trade union, "orthodox" Socialists. They fought a pitched battle over formal U.S. recognition of the Soviet Union, which Thomas advocated and the anticommunist unions opposed. Mayor Hoan implored them to stop fighting over Russia and concentrate on building socialism in the United States.[78]

The more doctrinaire Marxist Socialist Labor Party had separated from the Socialists. Its thirty-three delegates held their convention in New York City, and on May Day, they nominated Verne L. Reynolds for president. An insurance agent, traveling salesman, and steam pipe fitter, Reynolds at the time was selling newspaper advertising. The Socialist Labor Party pronounced a "death sentence" upon the capitalist system and eagerly anticipated that its ranks would swell with the discontent of the working class.[79]

Thomas's Socialists drew support from an impressive array of scholars, including the philosopher John Dewey, the theologian Reinhold Niebuhr, and the African American historian W. E. B. DuBois. But others agreed with the writer John Dos Passos that joining the Socialists had the same effect "as drinking a bottle of near-beer." An impressive group of intellectuals, writers, poets, and artists endorsed the Communist Party ticket in 1932. The Communist convention in Chicago attracted between seven thousand and eight thousand people. Delegates needed no other credentials than membership in the party or a party-affiliated union. Some of them hitchhiked and rode the rails to attend the convention; others were detained by police and never made it to Chicago. The party's Central Committee selected as its presidential and vice presidential candidates a trade unionist, William Z. Foster, and an African American, James W. Ford, an organizer of the American Negro Labor Congress. Communist delegates ratified the choices and shouted down any mention of the Socialist Party as lustily as they hooted Herbert Hoover.[80]

The Communist Party had drained much of its energy in 1929 by purging "counterrevolutionaries" from its membership at the behest of the Soviet Union, which paid its bills. Expulsions debilitated the party and splintered the Far Left. Still hopeful of electoral gains in 1932 because of the economy's collapse, the Communists planned a vigorous petition drive to get on the ballots in each of the states (a generation later, during the McCarthy era, these petitions would serve as evidence that their signers had been either Communists or Communist sympathizers, causing them no end of trouble). At the time, the Communists devoted most of their attention to labor and civil rights organizing. Politically, they offered the unemployed little more than revolutionary rhetoric. An expelled party member, Max Shachtman, explained that at bottom, unemployed workers were only interested in finding work, but William Z. Foster preached revolution rather than jobs. Speaking at the University of Chicago soon after his nomination, he declared that overturning capitalism would require an open struggle of violence, since "the peaceful methods of the ballot will never win freedom for the working class." Foster could only count on mainstream press coverage when the police arrested him for holding rallies without permits.[81]

The Farmer-Labor Party, meeting in Omaha, Nebraska, nominated for president a California labor lawyer, Frank E. Webb, who wore pearl gray spats and carried a silver-headed cane. An odd choice to head a working-class movement, Webb refused to adhere to the party's platform, so its Executive Committee replaced him with the seventy-eight-year-old Jacob Coxey. Back in 1894, this man had led "Coxey's Army," an unemployment march on Washington. He had made a career out of losing elections since then, until the Depression turned his fortunes and helped him win office as mayor of Massillon, Ohio. The rejected Frank Webb traveled to St. Louis, where, on July 4, the Liberty and Unity Party nominated him for president—although he again dissented from its platform of government ownership of banks and industry. Webb's independence caused his opponents to accuse him of having been "hired by the Federal Reserve Bank to wreck all third parties."[82]

A Pittsburgh priest, the Reverend James Cox, had led an unemployment march on Washington in 1931, from which he created the Jobless Party. Its convention convened in St. Louis that August. Known as the Blue Shirts for the apparel Father Cox provided his followers, the Jobless Party pledged to be the voice of Main Street rather than Wall Street. Father Cox sought to merge with the Liberty Party followers of William Hope "Coin" Harvey, who had written a memorable pamphlet on free silver during the election of 1896. But neither the priest nor the eighty-one-year-old Harvey would step aside in favor of the other, so they ran separately. Father Cox eventually withdrew from the race and endorsed Franklin Roosevelt.

In contrast to the economic platforms offered by the parties on the left, the Prohibition Party cared mostly about protecting the Eighteenth Amendment. Meeting in Indianapolis, the drys failed to convince Senator William E. Borah to run as their candidate, choosing instead a former Democratic representative from Georgia, William D. Upshaw. He had lost his congressional seat after campaigning for Hoover and against Al Smith in 1928. A gaunt man with a look of perpetual disapproval, Upshaw resolutely predicted victory as long as all the "honest drys" were brave enough to vote for him. But for all their sound and fury, the alternative parties would collectively garner only 3 percent of the national vote in November, leaving the real race to Hoover and Roosevelt.[83]

A CAMPAIGN OF HOPE AND FEAR

Herbert Hoover smiled broadly at the news of Franklin Roosevelt's nomination, certain that the Democrats had selected their most vulnerable candidate, improving his own chances of reelection. Within days, however, Hoover's confidence waned. He began to suspect that he had not appreciated his opponent's appeal to "the radical elements of the West and South," where the hard times would help the Democratic candidate. As he mulled over the situation, he counted on four months of campaigning to reveal Roosevelt's dangerous flaws to the "business elements in the East." Hoover saw the 1932 election shaping up along the lines of the 1896 campaign between McKinley and Bryan—a conservative, hard-money Republican against a radical, inflationary Democrat, with himself as the triumphant McKinley. A nagging exception to this historical analogy was the fact that in 1896, the Democrats had been the incumbent party that took the blame for the depression of the decade. This time, the Republicans would bear that burden.[1]

Hoover counted on the economy recovering in time to assure his reelection, an assumption that seemed reasonable to others as well. Political commentators believed that the voters would forgive him for the two hard years of the Depression as long as things got better, especially since the Republican Party's majority in voter registration gave it a mathematical edge. The liberal journalist Elmer Davis predicted that "bread and business" would dominate the campaign and that if business was on the upswing, the Democrats could not beat Hoover. *Tough Luck—Hoover Again!* a short book by the journalist

John Heaton, warned of the likelihood of the president's reelection despite his unpopularity and lamented that liberals would need to wait until 1936 to place a "forward-looking man" in the White House. A similarly despondent Walter Lippmann confided in Newton Baker about the "exceedingly unpleasant" choice between candidates. He could not bear to vote for Hoover, but he had no confidence in Roosevelt and disagreed with Norman Thomas's Socialist program. "What I really want you to do," Lippmann appealed to Baker, "is to try and persuade me to vote for Roosevelt."[2]

As the incumbent president, Hoover intended to divorce himself publicly from the campaign and let party leaders carry the effort for him, the way they had for Calvin Coolidge in 1924. He would remain at the White House, tend to official business, and turn campaign management over to the RNC. Behind the scenes, he made Larry Richey his liaison to the national committee, keeping his finger on every move being made. The Republicans formally established their headquarters in Chicago, but so many party leaders crowded the White House anterooms that reporters described the West Wing as having "the unmistakable atmosphere of a campaign headquarters." Similarly, the real Democratic headquarters followed candidate Franklin Roosevelt wherever he went on the campaign trail. As a manager, Roosevelt surprised his closest lieutenants with his deft ordering of their various assignments. He delegated authority but maintained personal contact with each of his top strategists and speechwriters, avoiding most of the frictions and jealousies common in political campaigns. Raymond Moley judged the feat "a mark of superb administrative ability in the political field."[3]

ROUTING THE BONUS MARCHERS

In June 1932, an army of unemployed war veterans marched on Washington, disrupting Hoover's Rose Garden campaign. The so-called Bonus Expeditionary Force—some forty thousand World War I veterans and families—traveled from all parts of the country to demand early payment of their promised bonuses for wartime service. The bonus was an insurance policy, not due to be paid until 1944, but the unemployed veterans worried they might not survive the Depression to collect. Congress had passed a bill in 1931 enabling veterans to cash in their policies immediately, reasoning that that would pump money into the economy and stimulate consumer spending, but since the estimated cost equaled

President Hoover and First Lady Lou Henry Hoover greet a crowd at one of the many whistle-stops during the campaign of 1932. Her ease with audiences helped balance his stiffness.

an entire year's federal budget, Hoover had vetoed that bill. Now, the veterans came in person to lobby for another bill, marching through Washington and carrying signs with slogans such as "In Hoover We Trusted, Now We're Busted." They set up a makeshift camp on the Anacostia Flats, across the river from downtown Washington, and a smaller group occupied some vacant buildings scheduled for demolition to make way for the new Federal Triangle, a complex of office buildings between the White House and the Capitol.

Fearing for the public's safety and the administration's image, some of Hoover's advisers recommended stopping the bonus marchers at the District of Columbia border, but the president refused to take any action that might result in bloodshed. "Trouble must be avoided at any cost," Hoover insisted. He would be willing to meet with legitimate leaders of the Bonus March, he said, but not with any Communists among them. Unable to sort the radicals out, he met with no one. The Communist Party had been planning its own hunger march on Washington, until the bonus marchers upstaged it. Seeking to exploit the situation, Communist leaders sent several operatives to join the marchers. Army intelligence grossly overestimated the Communists' influence, putting the army in a state of readiness in case of insurrection. Hoover's own Secret Service agents infiltrated the Bonus Army and found little revolutionary fervor among the veterans. The Secret Service took the precaution of limiting the president's public appearances, and Hoover agreed, remarking, "There are too many assassins here now." On Capitol Hill, the House of Representatives passed the Bonus Bill on June 15. Protesters surrounded the Capitol during the Senate debate, and an anxious Vice President Curtis, on his own initiative, called in the marines for protection. On June 17, the senators rejected the bonus, adjourned, and hastily left town.[4]

Guards at the White House locked its gates, and the president remained safely inside. Hoover had persuaded Congress to appropriate funds to pay the veterans' fares home, and many of the marchers took the government up on the offer and left town. Others stayed behind, determined to maintain their vigil until they got their bonuses. Most of the remaining marchers were camped on the Anacostia Flats, but a problem developed with the squatters in the buildings along Pennsylvania Avenue. A contractor hired to tear down these structures threatened to sue the federal government if his work crews were delayed any longer. Hard-liners, fearing the danger of mob rule, criticized the administration for "coddling" the bonus marchers and wanted the military to drive them out of Washington, but Senate majority leader Watson cautioned Hoover about the political implications, warning that neither the bonus seekers nor their families and friends would ever forgive him for taking military action against them.[5]

The showdown came on July 28, when a skirmish broke out as the Washington police attempted to clear the downtown buildings. The marchers threw rocks, and the police opened fire, killing one of the protesters. Responding to an appeal from the District government, Hoover authorized the army to aid the police, but he insisted that the troops carry no guns. Instead, cavalry soldiers rode into the capital with sabers drawn. The Quaker president had instructed the army only to surround the downtown buildings and clear them without delay, not to take action against the camps on the Anacostia Flats. The army's chief of staff, General Douglas MacArthur (with his principal aide, Major Dwight D. Eisenhower), instituted more grandiose plans. After clearing the buildings on Pennsylvania Avenue, his troops crossed the Anacostia River; set off tear gas; and drove out the men, women, and children encamped there, burning down their shacks. The army claimed that the marchers set the fires before evacuating, but reporters had seen the troops carrying gasoline cans and matches.[6]

That night, President Hoover could see the flames from a White House window as General MacArthur and Secretary of War Patrick Hurley explained why they had exceeded his orders and used force against the main camp. Hoover accepted their argument that Communists, hoodlums, and ex-convicts had taken over the Bonus March, determined to start a disturbance. He never rebuked MacArthur's insubordination. "Well, that job's done," Hoover told his staff the next morning. But the military response had taken place in full view of the Washington press corps, and some of the reporters had been roughed up in the fracas. United Press reporter Tom Stokes, having been hit by a cavalryman's saber, recorded that he had "nothing but bitter feelings toward Herbert Hoover that night." Editorially, most newspapers supported the use of military force, but news photographs and newsreel footage of the rout shocked the public. Scenes of the army attacking American war veterans caused movie audiences to hiss when Hoover's image appeared on the screen.[7]

Reading the newspapers in bed the next morning, Franklin Roosevelt was astonished that the president had called out the troops. Like Hoover, he opposed an early payment of the bonus, but he could not understand why the president had not sent the veterans coffee and sandwiches instead of soldiers and tear gas. Spreading the papers out around him and pointing to the pictures of the burning shacks and fleeing people, Roosevelt said he might have to apologize for having suggested Herbert Hoover as a presidential candidate in 1920. Back then, Hoover had seemed to be just what the nation needed, an efficient administrator with an international reputation as a humanitarian. Either Hoover had been very different during the war, he reflected, or else he himself had not known the man as well as he had thought. The president's handling of the bonus marchers had turned him inside out, so that people could see there was "nothing left inside the man but jelly." With further reflection, he added, "Maybe there never *had* been anything." From that morning on, Roosevelt never doubted that he would win the election.[8]

The fiasco of the Bonus March shrank the proportions of Roosevelt's own problem that summer—deciding the fate of New York City mayor Jimmy Walker. In August, Governor Roosevelt summoned the mayor to Albany to question him about the corruption charges against his administration. For a presidential candidate to confront a popular Irish Catholic politician and the entire Tammany Hall political machine while trying to court urban, ethnic voters made for a potentially explosive situation. If Roosevelt reprimanded the mayor and left him in office, he would look weak. If he removed Walker, he might split the party and ruin his chance of carrying New York that November. "So you'd rather be right than President?" Louis Howe snapped when Roosevelt said he had decided against Walker. Then, unexpectedly, the defiant mayor resigned voluntarily. Al Smith, whose party loyalty overcame his hurt feelings, had told Walker to quit. (Smith further boosted the state Democratic ticket by supporting the nomination of the respectable lieutenant governor, Herbert Lehman, for governor, rather than a Tammany hack.) Roosevelt's patient and firm examination of Mayor Walker helped dispel his own image as a genial lightweight, making him look strong without having to take action. The Walker case provided the candidate with good press notices and editorial praise during the summer lull before the campaign officially opened.[9]

A QUIET SUMMER

Even after the Bonus March, political commentators were reluctant to declare the Democratic candidate a sure winner, and the oddsmakers were giving Hoover an even chance of winning reelection. The odds were pure speculation, however, since the magazines and newspapers would not conduct their straw polls until the fall. During the summer months, news reporters worried about the prospect of a dull presidential campaign, with neither candidate traveling extensively or delivering many speeches. An eclipse of the sun in August drew more publicity than the presidential campaign during that apathetic summer.[10]

Two young boys from Connecticut, Bill and Bub Marsh, self-published a little book on their handpress that summer. Entitled *Why You Should Vote for President Hoover,* it offered advice to adults. "The dark stormy-looking clouds which have been hanging over our Nation for the last year or so are passing over slowly but smoothly," the brothers wrote, capturing Hoover's basic campaign theme, "and we do not want an experiment by electing a new President now." Republican Party campaign posters and brochures reiterated that message, proclaiming "Vote for Hoover—Don't Change Now"; "It's an Elephant's Job—No Time for Donkey Business!"; and "The Dawn of Victory—Stand by Your President."[11]

President Hoover struck similar chords when he formally accepted his party's nomination for a second term on August 10. Amid encouraging reports of rising prices for stocks and commodities, he appeared at a colorful ceremony in the Daughters of the American Revolution's Constitution Hall, near the White House. Dapperly dressed in a blue blazer and white pants, the president greeted the crowd with the hint of a smile. Beside him stood Theodore Roosevelt's widow, Edith, to counteract the Democratic Roosevelt, whom many mistook for her son. The president had also hoped to have Theodore Roosevelt Jr., the territorial governor of the Philippines, stand on stage with him, but his sister, Alice Roosevelt Longworth, had telegraphed him not to bother coming back, since Hoover was bound to lose.[12]

Hoover's nationally broadcast acceptance speech drew its biggest headlines for his admission that he had doubts about Prohibition. Despite its virtues, Prohibition had fallen out of favor with Americans and was undermining law enforcement, which produced "degeneration and crime." Hoover said he could no longer continue to give his consent to a cause that had spawned disrespect for the law—a position designed to attract wet voters. Just a week later, however, Vice President Curtis, in his acceptance speech in Kansas, renewed his unwavering support for the Eighteenth Amendment. Critics accused the Republican ticket of straddling the wet-dry divide, but Hoover's staff had not seen copies of Curtis's speech until after its distribution to the press. The vice president would need to deliver the speech as written, Hoover said regretfully, "but it will undo a lot of the good that came from my handling of the question." Ultimately, the issue that worked for Hoover in 1928 worked against him in 1932. Wets enthusiastically endorsed Roosevelt and repeal, and the diminishing number of drys expressed unhappiness with both presidential candidates for backtracking on Prohibition. The steadfastly dry Methodist Church expressed support only for Vice President Curtis.[13]

Republican leaders advised Hoover to expect that he himself would become the major issue in the campaign. Political aide James H. MacLafferty explained that the people would have to decide "whether or not at this critical stage they were willing to trade him for Roosevelt." Republicans designed campaign themes to emphasize Hoover's principles rather than the nation's problems: he had done his best to meet the emergency and to protect the nation from the worldwide catastrophe, while preserving traditional American values of individualism and self-sufficiency. Republican speakers would repeat the "things could have been worse" motif relentlessly that fall. Yet the strategy also allowed his challenger to demonstrate that the president had not fulfilled the expansive promises of his first campaign. In calling attention to the incumbent's shortcomings, Roosevelt took care to attack the administration rather than the Republican Party. As the minority party candidate, he needed to convince a lot of Republican voters that he could accomplish what Hoover could not. In his own strategy sessions, Roosevelt spoke frequently about the man he remembered from the Wilson administration, and he pondered why that man became so inept as a national leader, with his isolation and aloofness and his contemptuous attitude toward Congress, the media, and public opinion. If anything, Hoover offered Roosevelt a model of how not to act as president.[14]

Democratic campaign banners projected such slogans as "Roosevelt and Repeal" and "Roosevelt and Prosperity" or just the image of a frosty beer mug positioned between their candidates. Optimistic Democrats talked of making a contest in every state, including the most rock-ribbed Republican bastions of New England, and they anticipated restoring the so-called Solid South to the Democratic column. Over the previous year, Jim Farley and Louis Howe had compiled the names of all the Democratic precinct committee leaders nationwide, and these people began submitting regular reports that gave the national headquarters knowledge of "the political currents in this campaign, the danger points, the sudden flares and local flaws that needed ironing out." Meanwhile, Roosevelt devoted much of the summer to meeting with his defeated Democratic rivals, mending fences, and turning the other cheek for party unity. He saw all except for the sulking Al Smith. In drafting campaign strategy, Roosevelt's aides debated about which approach would most effectively promote his policies as president. Some of them felt that he would be a more effective president having made no campaign promises. Others insisted that specific campaign commitments would be essential for convincing Congress to enact his legislation. As these arguments raged, Roosevelt had to remind them that he needed to be elected first.[15]

John Nance Garner made a pilgrimage to Hyde Park that summer. Roosevelt had laughed heartily at Garner's message: "Tell the Governor that he is the boss and we will all follow him to hell if we have to, but if he goes too far with some of these wild-eyed ideas we are going to have the stuffing kicked out of us." Unlike Vice President Curtis, who planned to make an extensive speaking tour, Garner saw no need for stumping himself. He had rarely given any campaign speeches during his thirty-year congressional career, and he was perfectly willing to let Roosevelt do the traveling and talking. (Nor was the Speaker taking any chances politically—Texas law allowed him to run for his House seat and the vice presidency simultaneously, and so he did.) Later, after Garner's reluctance to campaign had raised speculation about his unhappiness with the ticket, the Speaker agreed to deliver one radio address. The members of Roosevelt's brain trust found it a challenge to write for the crusty Texan, so they converted a speech they had originally drafted for Roosevelt, taking out most of the longer words. Garner delivered it with gusto.[16]

Despite Garner's reluctance to campaign, his reputation became an issue. In his Congress-bashing speeches, Hoover painted the Speaker as a radical, and Republican newspapers described him as a threat to the free enterprise system. With some amusement, Roosevelt realized that these attacks on the vice presidential candidate made him less of a liability among liberals and progressives, who regarded him as an archconservative. To counter the president's accusations, Speaker Garner met privately with Democratic business executives and financiers to assure them he was no extremist, recounting how he had opposed Bryan's free silver policies in 1896.[17]

Laying out their fall campaign plans, political leaders discovered that the usual wells of contributions had dried up during the Depression. The number of Democratic donors fell by a third between 1928 and 1932, and Republicans suffered an even more precipitous drop. Less than half of the manufacturers who contributed to the Republicans in 1928 gave anything in 1932. Instead, Republicans raised the bulk of their money from larger bankers in the Northeast, who were fearful of any change in government fiscal policy. Democrats, by contrast, drew from smaller bankers in the South and the West, hard hit by the farm depression and desperate for a change in policy. Democrats also solicited individual donations by asking people to become "Shareholders in America—organized to reclaim the equity of the Forgotten Man in America." Hoover's campaign raised only $1.8 million, far less than in 1928, causing a cutback in publicity and leaving the party in debt. Henry Allen, who again headed the Republicans' publicity effort, explained that the campaign would not operate with as large a staff as in the past because "we won't have the money for it." But Allen added that Hoover's record was "pretty well written already" and would not need such extensive selling.[18]

Roosevelt stayed in New York that summer and gave a few radio speeches (and sent instructions to the radio news broadcasters on how to pronounce his name: "Ro-se-velt, with the accent on the first of the three syllables. And the o pronounced as if there were only one, instead of two"). In a Saturday night radio talk, he endorsed the Democratic platform. Early the next morning, President Hoover, who was at Camp Rapidan, called his press secretary, Ted Joslin. Hoover had heard Roosevelt on the radio, regarded his speech as full of holes, and dictated a rebuttal. Rather than make a statement himself, the president wanted a half-dozen senators to issue statements under their own names. "The thing to do, Ted, is to carry the fight to Roosevelt," he said. "We've got to crack him every time he opens his mouth. Now's our chance." The press secretary was amused that Roosevelt would have no idea "who did the job on him when he reads the papers in the morning!" But FDR shrewdly ignored Hoover's surrogates, and their complaints attracted less press attention than a presidential statement would have received. The president's decision not to respond personally both weakened his arguments and left the impression that he had no answer to the charges Roosevelt was making.[19]

Hoover's silence made Roosevelt think that the president was getting ready to mount a massive offensive. His staff believed this analysis reflected Roosevelt's "exaggerated respect for his adversary," and they had a hard time convincing him that Hoover simply intended to stand on his record rather than go on the offensive by promising new programs. Stories about Hoover's scornful remarks in regard to his challenger began to drift into Democratic headquarters, causing Roosevelt to realize that the president did not respect him as a political rival, despite their earlier friendship. This awareness at first humiliated and then angered Roosevelt, making him determined to campaign at full throttle and hold nothing back. Although past incumbent presidents had made good use of party spokespeople during prosperous times, that approach no longer satisfied voters, who wanted to hear how the candidates themselves planned to deal with the Depression. New York County Republican chairman Samuel Koenig warned the White House that the Democratic candidate was making headway that summer because he encountered no opposition. "He hasn't advanced any concrete program. He hasn't had to," Koenig argued. "People have just said, 'Maybe this new doctor can cure us.'" Koenig insisted that President Hoover would need to lead his own campaign.[20]

With positive reports filtering back to Democratic headquarters from across the country, the party's elders advised a cautious campaign that would offer no surprises and make no mistakes. They worried about their candidate risking any physical or verbal missteps on the stump. Newsreel cameras might catch him falling down, or he might make an embarrassing gaffe during casual remarks on the back of a train. Louis Howe disliked taking any unnecessary chances, and he gave reporters the impression that Roosevelt would give no more than six or seven major speeches during the campaign, relying mostly on the radio to reach his audiences. But Franklin Roosevelt loved to campaign, and he intended to travel widely and engage crowds wherever possible to counter Hoover's reclusiveness and demonstrate his own stamina.[21]

Democratic leaders sent Jim Farley and Charley Michelson to Hyde Park to urge Roosevelt to stay home. "Jim, what do you think yourself?" Roosevelt asked. "I think you ought to go," Farley laughed, "and I know you are going anyway." The candidate, confident of his endurance, let party officials know that active campaigning would best answer any whispering campaign about his health. Democrats announced an initial campaign tour from the Atlantic to the Pacific coasts, covering some eight thousand miles through twenty-three states. Republicans took this as good news, since it increased the chances of Roosevelt making blunders. As William Allen White facetiously wrote to a Democratic friend, "How do you suppose Roosevelt is going to manage to elect Hoover?"[22]

Neither candidate spoke directly about Roosevelt's health, but it remained a central issue of the campaign. The Roosevelt camp prepared a booklet on the subject but never distributed it, since the Republicans did not make his disability an open issue. Instead, rumors spread that Roosevelt's condition was something other than polio—it was syphilis, a stroke, cancer, or mental illness, depending on the teller of the tale. Roosevelt deliberately minimized his infirmity, never using it to bid for sympathy. His press secretary, Steve Early, dismissed all questions on the subject by saying, "It's not a story." Some reporters wrote about his physical limitations but did not dwell on them. A *Time* magazine story, for instance, mentioned that Roosevelt could walk only with braces and canes and that while standing at public functions, "he still clings precariously to a friend's arm." The article concluded, "Never have his crippled legs deterred him from going where he would."[23]

Once during the campaign, Roosevelt's podium, improperly bolted to the floor, toppled over, carrying him with it. No reporter or photographer recorded the incident. The press honored his request not to depict him in ways that made him look helpless. Photographers on the campaign train bumped the arms of local press photographers who tried to snap Roosevelt being carried or seated in a wheelchair. In return, FDR always guaranteed them good pictures. He photographed well and willingly posed in attractive settings, unlike the president, whose expression could not hide his distaste for photographic sessions. Roosevelt's confidence and courage in dealing with his disability, no longer a detriment to his campaign, served as a metaphor for how he would confront the national economic paralysis. When asked at a public meeting whether her husband's illness had affected him, Eleanor Roosevelt responded that "anyone who has gone through great suffering is bound to have a greater sympathy and understanding of the problems of mankind."[24]

Photographs showed Roosevelt standing, and editorial cartoonists depicted him running and jumping. Newspapers credited his vigorous personal campaign with showing that "he was not a wheelchair invalid incapable of meeting the physical ordeals of the Presidential office." The public remained largely unaware of how little Roosevelt could walk, a strategic deception that focused public attention on his policies rather than his polio. His weak legs also limited his ability to gesture while speaking, since he needed to grip the podium or a railing tightly with at least one hand at all times. Instead of swinging his arms, he used vigorous head movements and varied facial expressions for emphasis. When he spoke from a train platform or on a stage, a railing or podium usually cut off sight of his lower body, and audiences saw instead a man with broad shoulders and an expansive chest who projected an impression of strength. Roosevelt would walk to the podium, one hand on the arm of his son for support, the other holding a cane. He would board and leave trains by gripping brass handrails and virtually swinging himself on his muscular arms. "He moves slowly, cautiously, but with great composure," wrote one columnist, adding that during this process, Roosevelt encountered very little heckling.[25]

Roosevelt somehow never looked fatigued. J. Fred Essary, who had covered every election since 1908 for the *Baltimore Sun,* said he had never traveled with a candidate who better endured the rigors of a presidential campaign. Ironically, Roosevelt appeared more robust than Hoover, who had worked himself to the point of visible exhaustion. Hoover's doctor could tell that he was under tremendous strain and showing signs of fatigue; he was "really under a sledgehammer of pressure on his whole body mechanism." Before leaving on one campaign trip, looking ashen, Hoover confided to his wife, "Lou, I do not know whether I will be able to weather this trip. I have reason to doubt that I will live through it." That was hardly the optimal attitude for conducting a campaign.[26]

SEPTEMBER: AS MAINE GOES

"The Roosevelt Special," a six-car campaign train, set out on September 12, with speaking stops scheduled for St. Louis, Kansas City, Topeka, Denver, Cheyenne, Salt Lake City, Butte, Spokane, Seattle, Portland, San Francisco, Los Angeles, Albuquerque, Omaha, Sioux City, Milwaukee, Chicago, and Detroit. Roosevelt called it a "look, listen and learn" tour to allow him to study conditions across the country firsthand and talk with the people. RNC chairman Everett Sanders assured the press that the Republican candidate did not intend to imitate the Democrat. "It is fairly definite that the President is not going to make a speaking tour," said Sanders. He would make two or three speeches, "not necessarily political speeches, either," confined to the discussion of governmental issues. Newspapers reported that Hoover considered the financial crisis over because economic indicators had risen and the stock market had rallied, making up the losses for the first half of the year. Republicans cited these conditions to express confidence that they would have a victory in Maine's early elections, on September 13.[27]

The Republican elephant suffered a setback with the Democratic victory in the Maine elections in September 1932. Here, Dr. Hoover prescribes strenuous treatment to two nurses, RNC chairman Everett Sanders and Vice President Charles Curtis.

"As Maine goes, so goes the Union" went the old political maxim. To avoid the winter weather, Maine held its state elections in September, becoming a barometer for forecasting the political winds. Ordinarily, Maine voted Republican, but in September 1932, Democrats unexpectedly elected a governor and two of the state's three congressmen—all of them "wringing wet" on Prohibition. On his way to connect with Roosevelt's transcontinental tour, Speaker Garner told a crowd in Oklahoma, "Maine's gone Democratic. You might as well make it unanimous." Almost everyone knew the significance of the slogan. At Roosevelt's stops, people in the crowd would shout, "As Maine goes, so goes the nation!" Maine buoyed Franklin Roosevelt's entourage and helped swell the crowds for the rest of his trip.[28]

The Maine results astonished Herbert Hoover. Aware that states in the West had been lost to him, he had counted on the East to stand firm. He trusted that the party faithful would recognize that he had done the best he could and let him continue his work. These assumptions reflected the insularity of the White House, leaving the president out of touch with shifting public opinion. Party officials tried to shrug off the Maine vote as a reflection of "local issues," but Republican newspapers acknowledged that the results had come as a "heavy jolt," showing what a real fight the party faced that fall. The White House faulted the RNC for weakly attacking the opposition, leaving the president alone to fight the battles, but the tight presidential control of the national committee had trained it to wait for the president to make the first moves. "It is a catastrophe for us," Hoover said of the Maine results. "It means that we have got to fight to the limit."[29]

Roosevelt's campaign train made one of its first stops in Topeka, Kansas, where the incumbent Democratic governor, Harry Woodring, was locked in a tight three-way race for reelection against a progressive Republican oil producer, Alfred M. "Alf" Landon, and a wealthy doctor, John R. Brinkley, whose medical license had been suspended after he used goat glands to restore male virility. Known as the "great promiser," Brinkley drew crowds by pledging to cut taxes and increase services for the state's poor farmers.[30]

In Topeka, Roosevelt scolded President Hoover for failing to do enough for farmers, denounced his Farm Board as useless, ridiculed his crop-control plan as a hardship, and promised a "tariff adjustment" to improve conditions. Twenty-five people had contributed to the Topeka speech, and they disagreed among themselves over endorsing higher tariff rates for agricultural products or reverting to the Democrats' traditional low-tariff philosophy. Faced with irreconcilable factions, Roosevelt simply instructed his staff to weave their arguments together. He was not going to solve the farm problem with a speech, but he could signal that he intended to make it a priority. Despite its inherent contradictions, the Topeka speech resonated in a region that had suffered grievously for so much longer than the rest of the country. Roosevelt even managed to draw a laugh with a self-deprecating remark that he had run a farm in Georgia for eight years "without profit."[31]

Officials at Republican headquarters listened on the radio to Roosevelt's Topeka address in "deep dejection." They could hear the crowd roar its approval of his attacks on the administration. At the White House, Hoover furiously dissected all of the inconsistencies in the farm speech. Certain that Roosevelt's views on the farm crisis were a vulnerable spot in the Democratic offense, he dispatched his agriculture secretary, Arthur M. Hyde, to belittle the Democratic candidate's effort. Once again, Roosevelt ignored attacks made by anyone other than the president. Urgent pleas from Republican leaders, along with the election returns from Maine, finally convinced Hoover that only he could adequately reply. He would need to scrap his Rose Garden strategy and take the stump himself.[32]

"The Roosevelt Special" stopped at the rural stations across the Republican plains states, and it was met by crowds of poorly clad people showing grim signs of the Depression's impact. Roosevelt appealed to the people's sense of idealism and tradition, especially the need for courage in the face of adversity. The American spirit remained undefeated, he insisted, and he intended to lead the nation out of the morass. He stressed cooperative themes in the western states, where Theodore Roosevelt's progressivism remained strong. At Portland, Oregon, FDR won cheers by advocating publicly owned and operated hydroelectric power developments. That issue put him at the furthest pole from Hoover, who had vetoed public power development at Muscle Shoals, Alabama, on the Tennessee River. Roosevelt argued that public power systems would benefit consumers through lower rates and more service to rural areas. Private electric companies still reached only 10 percent of the nation's farms. He did not call for government ownership of all utilities, but he believed that the government had a right to regulate private utilities and the rates they charged. President Hoover, who had approved some federal power-producing dams (including a project on the Colorado River that would

Franklin Roosevelt greeting the crowd from the rear of his campaign train.

be called the Hoover Dam), defended his veto of Muscle Shoals by insisting that the federal government should not compete with business. On this issue, progressive Republicans lined up solidly with Roosevelt, and the utility companies sided with Hoover. "Judge me by the enemies I have made," Roosevelt declared, meaning the utility company executives who had opposed his nomination.[33]

Roosevelt won endorsements from the most prominent progressive Republican senators, among them Wisconsin's Robert M. La Follette Jr., California's Hiram Johnson, and New Mexico's Bronson Cutting. "What this country needs is another Roosevelt in the White House," declared Nebraska's George Norris, and that became the slogan of their Progressive National Committee, which backed Roosevelt for president. Idaho senator William Borah remained a holdout, but he stayed neutral during the 1932 campaign, in marked contrast with his tireless stumping for Hoover in 1928. Roosevelt made it easier for the progressive Republicans to join his camp by his embrace of their core issues and their mutual admiration for Theodore Roosevelt. Except for Pennsylvania, every state that supported TR's Progressive Party candidacy in 1912 would cast its electoral votes for the Democratic Roosevelt in 1932.[34]

At the Commonwealth Club in San Francisco on September 23, Roosevelt continued his progressive themes and delivered a notable speech distancing himself from the Democratic Party's Jeffersonian, less-government past. Written by Adolph Berle, the speech reviewed American economic history from the colonial era through the Depression and reasoned that the increasing concentration of economic power in a few large corporations required a stronger central government to keep it in check. In the age of big business, equality of opportunity could exist only if government regulated powerful interests and protected the public welfare. The great issue before them, Roosevelt declared, was whether the people served an economic system or whether the system existed to serve the people. But rather than follow up on these ideas after leaving liberal San Francisco and traveling to the more conservative Los Angeles, he reverted to generalities.[35]

Straw polls showed the Democrats were well in front in the northern regions of the state, but conditions were more volatile in Southern California. There, the Prohibition issue dominated a three-way race for the U.S. Senate. The Democratic nominee, William G. McAdoo, had abandoned his longtime leadership of the dry movement to endorse his party's wet platform. Republicans had chosen a Napa Valley vintner, Tallant Tubbs, regarded as the "wettest of the wets." Against them both, the Prohibition Party had put up an evangelical radio minister from Los Angeles. A flamboyant stump speaker, the Reverend Robert Pierce Shuler promised farmers in the San Joaquin Valley that he would take a sack of their onions to Washington "and blow my breath all over the Senators until they pass laws to allow the growers to make money." The major parties could not afford to dismiss "Holy Bob" as inconsequential, since he threatened to drain away the drys and the populist protest vote (indeed, he collected a quarter of the statewide vote).[36]

When Roosevelt spoke to a vast throng at the Hollywood Bowl, he praised the city's sunny weather and otherwise "skated safely over all other recognized issues," noted the *Los Angeles Times*'s conservative political reporter Kyle Palmer. The young liberal journalist Carey McWilliams felt equally disappointed with the candidate's vague abstractions that day. These were tactics that Roosevelt employed throughout the campaign, skipping over local disputes and picking and choosing his themes from the conflicting input he was receiving from the planners, the trustbusters, the budget balancers, and the protective tariff and free trade advocates. He would try different approaches before different audiences.[37]

Other than mentioning the tariff and trade, Roosevelt made almost no reference to foreign policy during his campaign. He had backed away from the League of Nations to appease Hearst, had no major disagreements with Hoover's international policies, and believed that the voters' attention was fixed more on domestic economics. Roosevelt's speechwriters had drafted some remarks for him, knowing his interest in world affairs, but they decided that he was not anxious to discuss foreign policy during the campaign because "nothing said now will be listened to very much." The *New York Times* columnist Anne O'Hare McCormick also acted as a go-between on the matter when she interviewed the two candidates separately. She asked Hoover if he planned to speak about foreign affairs, and he replied that he would not until Roosevelt forced him to. She then asked whether she could tell this to Roosevelt, and the president said that he hoped she would. This was the only message, direct or indirect, that passed between the candidates before the election.[38]

On its journey back from the Pacific Coast, Roosevelt's train stopped in the industrial Midwest, where he encountered crowds of people who were out of work and feeling the full force of the Depression. The atmosphere was especially tense in Detroit. Michigan had not voted for a

Democratic presidential candidate since 1852, and state Republican officials were counting on the party faithful turning out at the polls for Hoover and for the incumbent Republican governor, William M. Brucker, a dry running against a wet Democrat, William Comstock. But mounting industrial unemployment had shaken partisan loyalties. For those whose wages had been cut and whose jobs were in jeopardy, Franklin Roosevelt was still "an unknown quantity, another candidate after a big job," his son James reflected, "and we were not certain how he would be received by people whose pants were ragged and whose belts were pulled in." The midwestern receptions, although sometimes muted, were always warm, and Roosevelt met with no unpleasant incidents. The tone of these gatherings indicated that even in traditionally Republican territory, people seemed ready to take a chance on the Democrats.[39]

With most of the progressive Republicans endorsing Roosevelt, the White House concluded that maintaining the party's conservative base would require former president Coolidge to get involved in the campaign. Hoover found a temporary White House staff position for Coolidge's former secretary, Ted Clark, whose primary mission was to recruit his old boss. Clark informed Coolidge that the president believed all that was necessary to ensure his reelection was to have the case for him presented by someone to whom the country would listen. Coolidge doubted that he was that person, since he no longer fit in with the times, he felt worn out, and he was not keen on reentering the political arena. But out of party loyalty, he finally agreed to address a campaign rally in October. Republicans begged him to do more, but Coolidge begged off, saying his throat was "in such shape" that he could make no more speeches. On the eve of the election, he relented and delivered a radio broadcast from his home in Massachusetts, endorsing the president's reelection as a matter of common sense in choosing known experience over "rash experiments."[40]

OCTOBER: THE CAMPAIGN TURNS PERSONAL

Hoover came out swinging in October. By then, the summer's rosy economic indicators had faded, Roosevelt's western trip had drawn rave reviews, and Hoover's surrogates had failed to rally public support. Republicans continued to predict the dawning of economic recovery, but the stock market had stagnated, and production, sales, and prices remained abysmally low. That fall, the furniture industry reported that a third of all furniture manufacturers had gone out of business since the beginning of the Depression and that 90 percent of the remaining companies were selling their output below cost. Across the country, municipalities were having trouble paying their employees. New York City grappled with cutting teachers' salaries. The mayor of Philadelphia warned that he might have to close its zoo. Hoover resented the Democrats' efforts to make him the scapegoat for all this bad news, and he intended to strike back. He chose his native state of Iowa for his first major campaign speech on the road, even though he knew it would not be friendly territory. By the fall of 1932, corn was selling at ten cents a bushel, so low a price that farmers were burning the crop for fuel. In Iowa, Milo Reno had organized the National Farmers' Holiday Association, which set up pickets to block the shipment of crops to market. Association members also poured milk (for which farmers were then getting two cents a quart) into the streets in a desperate effort to drive up prices. Iowa Republicans carefully selected an audience for Hoover that excluded demonstrators, but on the drive to the auditorium, he could not fail to notice the signs of hard times. "We are opposed by 10,000,000 unemployed, 10,000 bonus marchers, and 10-cent corn," he commented privately. "Is it any wonder that the prospects are dark?"[41]

In Des Moines, Hoover delivered his most personal speech, offering nostalgic memories of his childhood in West Branch during the depression of the 1870s in order to connect with his audience. He defended his efforts to combat the current depression and noted that he took pride in having kept the country on the gold standard, saving it from "complete disaster." Hoover blamed congressional Democrats for interfering with recovery by passing costly spending bills, which he had vetoed, and he dismissed his Democratic opponent for having not even a "remote understanding of the forces which confronted this country." Challenging Iowans' long-standing antitariff sentiments, Hoover insisted that the protective Smoot-Hawley tariff would restore markets for their farm goods. The Iowa Republican Henry A. Wallace, who edited *Wallace's Farmer*, shook his head over Hoover's defense of the tariff, which was not the issue on the minds of most Iowans. Thousands of these farmers had fallen behind on their taxes and mortgage payments. "They heard his suggestion that he was in favor of doing something about the mortgage situation," he said, "but they could not understand just what plan he had in mind." Rather than offering hope, Hoover's speech had been defensive and dogmatic in tone, reflecting his indignation over having his policies challenged.[42]

Roosevelt's brain trust met with the candidate to decide how he should respond to the charges Hoover had made in Des Moines. Advisers presented conflicting theories of monetary policy. Some advocated inflation as a means to fight the Depression, but as Adolph Berle noted, even in the Economics Department at Columbia, no agreement existed about how an inflationary program might work or whether inflation, once started, would be possible to control. The conservative sound-money men in Roosevelt's camp, led by Bernard Baruch, wanted him to take a firm stand against inflation. The liberals, led by Harvard Law School professor Felix Frankfurter, promoted the economic theories of John Maynard Keynes and wanted to remove from Roosevelt's speeches anything dealing with inflation. The brain trust worried about "the evils of inflation" but faced the reality that if the economic situation continued to deteriorate, inflation might be the only way out. Leaning toward ambiguity, Roosevelt decided not to refer to either inflation or the gold standard. "I do not want to be committed to the gold standard," the candidate informed the brain trust. "I haven't the faintest idea whether we will be on the gold standard on March 4th or not; nobody can foresee where we shall be."[43]

Hoover's assertion in Des Moines that the specter of a Roosevelt presidency had undermined business confidence and delayed any increases in production alerted FDR's team that the president intended to appeal more to voters' fears than to their hopes. They considered this tactic self-defeating. "What more could the millions of unemployed lose?" Roosevelt's aides wondered. "How much further into bankruptcy could farmers and businessmen fall?" As newspaper and magazine polls showed Roosevelt holding a lead, Hoover put the blame on what he regarded as Democratic misrepresentations of his policies. His bitterness made his attacks more personal than they had been during his 1928 campaign, when he had avoided mentioning Al Smith by name or responding to his charges. This anger turned the 1932 campaign into what reporter Anne O'Hare McCormick called "a duel between two men, two fronts, and two points of view, all plainly visible."[44]

On the way back to Washington from Iowa, Hoover encountered large but somber crowds at all the stops, reminding him of riding on President Harding's funeral train. As he pressed the campaign, however, the receptions grew warmer. Stumping helped him regain some momentum, but a severe lack of funding hindered his efforts. "We have turned the tide and we know now that we can win," he told his staff. "But what we need most of all is money." Business interests were hurting and business leaders thought that Hoover was licked, so they had not made their usual campaign contributions. The RNC reduced its staff and had no money to pay for the radio broadcasts of the president's speeches. Some cabinet members paid for their own radio time out of pocket. In mid-October, Hoover spent hours on the phone soliciting money. He finally solved the cash-flow problem by persuading the banker J. P. Morgan Jr. to guarantee a half-million dollars against moneys to be raised later. The campaign fund was still not equal to the sum the Republicans spent in 1928, but the consolation was that the Democrats had even less.[45]

Pleased with the president's Des Moines appearance, Republican leaders asked him to make more speeches. "Damn all of them, they lay down and think I should do everything," he stormed. He made seven additional political addresses, all broadcast coast to coast over the radio. Hoover labored for an excessive amount of time over each of these speeches, losing sleep, wearing himself out, and growing irritable, all of which showed in his press photographs. But he took great pride in writing his own remarks, and he condemned Roosevelt for reading ghostwritten texts. The writing of any Hoover speech was an elaborate scissors-and-paste affair. He would read through the data his staff had compiled, dictate his thoughts, and then cut apart the first rough draft, spread the paragraphs out, and clip connected themes together. Sometimes, he boarded the campaign train with just an envelope filled with clippings that he and the staff would glue together as they rode. He would dictate it all over again to smooth it out and improve its sequences. A single speech might go through this process several times—his staff counted fourteen versions of one speech—squandering the candidate's time and energy. The end result was a series of formal addresses consistent in theme but heavily laden with facts and argument, delivered in a wooden manner that made them an ordeal for both the speaker and his audiences.[46]

Only once during the campaign did Franklin Roosevelt try his hand at drafting a speech, and after his wife and other advisers judged it dull, he tossed it in the wastebasket. He relied instead on numerous speechwriters, who often strongly disagreed over policy. He found this approach useful in bridging the divisions within the Democratic ranks. His core speechwriters, besides Sam Rosenman, were the brain trust academics, Moley, Tugwell, and Berle. They admired his political skills but hoped to influence his thinking on policy through their speech drafts. Other contributors came and went during the campaign, and all had to contend with the protective Louis Howe. Roosevelt's campaign speeches were "of major importance to his advisers," his New York industrial commissioner Frances Perkins observed, because they all wanted him to reflect their own special concerns to their own audiences and because they all were conscious of what those groups wanted to hear from the candidate. Perkins felt that their "affection and jealousy for him and his reputation" were what caused so much sparring over each speech. After laboring over many drafts, the speechwriters would meet with Roosevelt, and he would quiz them on what they had produced and present his own suggestions. The candidate showed a great capacity for absorbing attractive ideas and a knack for avoiding political pitfalls. He patiently explained to his academic collaborators that a political campaign was a fight for office, not a program for adult education. Once elected, he could try to enlighten the public, but as a candidate, he "had to accept people's prejudices and turn them to good use."[47]

In offering himself as an alternative to a failed incumbent, Roosevelt delivered a mix of speeches that presented some new ideas along with broad generalities and a fair share of inconsistencies that nonetheless helped him appeal to a broad coalition of liberal and conservative Democrats and progressive Republicans. He presented general themes that audiences found readily understandable. He scattered enough clues about where he would lead that his speechwriters later insisted he had outlined almost every program of the essential New Deal. At least his openness to fresh ideas indicated he would conduct an experimental administration. Rather than provide specifics, his speeches revealed his basic instincts and the likely ways in which he might react to the type of events that presidents must confront. In place of Hoover's cold statistics, Roosevelt's speeches dealt with the human side of the Depression, depicting him as the national doctor, ready to care for the people's ills.[48]

Despite extensive newspaper and radio coverage of the candidates' major campaign speeches, the commentator Will Rogers made the obvious point that there was "not a voter in America that twenty-four hours after any speech was made would remember two sentences in it." What mattered was less the details than the general impression that the orator had made. Roosevelt employed an active and vigorous campaign rhetoric, adopting a positive, forward-looking attitude, mixed with humor and banter. He accused Hoover of offering excuses and empty promises, presenting himself as the man to turn things around. Hoover gave speeches that were more carefully argued but humorless and defensive. Senate Republican leader Watson despaired over the president's uninspiring oratory and regarded his lack of humor as a severe political handicap. "When a man cannot see the humorous phases of human life or take advantage of them either in private conversation or public speech to impress some point of his own," he commented, "well, in my judgment, he is most unfortunately constituted."[49]

The candidates delivered many more rear-platform, "tank-stop" remarks than formal addresses. Hoover's trip from Washington to Indianapolis, for instance, took forty-one hours, during which he gave one major speech and seventeen shorter, rear-platform speeches. The presidential train consisted of twenty sleeping cars, a couple of lounge cars, and a dining car in order to accommodate an entourage that included Secret Service agents, reporters, photographers, newsreel camera operators, stenographers, mimeograph and telegraph operators, party officials, and high-level railroad executives, with the last car being reserved for the president.[50]

Each tank stop followed the same pattern. The train would pull into a station, a band would play, and the newspaper correspondents and photographers would get off to gather on the station platform with the local onlookers. A local dignitary would climb aboard and give welcoming remarks that invariably took too long. Little girls would present the candidate's wife with a bouquet. The exuberant Roosevelt loved a crowd and excelled as a rear-platform speaker, whereas Hoover usually looked like he would rather have been somewhere else. Even with amplifiers, the soft-spoken president was hard to understand, but audiences could easily hear Franklin Roosevelt's booming voice. Hoover usually recited a set speech, but Roosevelt tailored his remarks to each locale, offering personal anecdotes about the trip or observations about local crops he had seen from the train window. He would introduce his family, ending with his "little boy, Jimmy," who towered inches above him and whose strong arm he gripped for support. The atmosphere reminded the reporters of a family party, and at some point, Roosevelt would toss back his head and roar with laughter over something, the crowd joining in heartily. The brief remarks completed, the candidate would wave goodbye, the engineer would sound the whistle, the correspondents and photographers would scramble back on the train, and they would all roll on toward the next stop, to repeat the process again and again. Despite the seemingly spontaneous nature of these rear-platform appearances, both candidates took pains to avoid careless statements that might be used against them, and neither made any embarrassing slips.[51]

Beside the candidates on the rear platform stood their wives. Lou Henry Hoover dutifully accompanied her husband on his campaign tours, although she limited her role to waving at the crowd and chatting with dignitaries who joined them on the platform. Always a crowd pleaser, she elicited warm applause but made no speeches and followed the unwritten rule that First Ladies granted no interviews. On the Roosevelt train, the Associated Press reporter Lorena Hickok freely talked with Eleanor Roosevelt, giving the candidate's wife generous publicity. In response, Lou Hoover summoned AP reporter Bess Furman to her private car. "She said she thought I might be interested in some facts that she would tell me," Furman recalled, "but I was not to quote her directly—I was just to set them down as though I'd read them in a library." Lou Hoover's reticence provided little news to the women reporters assigned to cover her.[52]

From the start, Eleanor Roosevelt signaled that she would be an unconventional First Lady. She gave her own speeches, her views occasionally differing from her husband's. Although he supported repeal, for instance, she did not. Eleanor disliked riding on smoke-filled campaign trains and standing mutely on the rear platform. She preferred going off alone to gather political intelligence, later providing Franklin with her observations. She was ambivalent about what his election might mean for her independence. In mid-October, she left his campaign train to return to New York City. "Why, I have to teach school tomorrow," she explained about the classes she gave in history and current events at a private, progressive school in Manhattan.[53]

To deflect Republican efforts to paint him as a radical, Franklin Roosevelt shifted to the center in October, toning down the rhetoric of change and stressing such traditional Democratic doctrines as balanced budgets and restraint on government spending. Some of his advisers began to worry that he would not be radical enough to meet the national crisis. Rexford Tugwell, in particular, argued that the candidate should endorse "collectivized progressivism" and government planning, terms that Roosevelt avoided during the last weeks of the campaign. Leery of venturing too far out ahead of public opinion, the candidate reminded the professors in his brain trust that he was "a teacher on another campus." The campaign showed him to be a flexible politician with few fixed opinions. He believed that the modern state had to regulate the economy to protect the public interest and to ensure economic stability, making him receptive to a greater degree of planning, but he was also unsympathetic to the ruthless centralization that characterized totalitarian regimes abroad.[54]

As he played down his own progressivism, Roosevelt accused Hoover of having centralized the government and caused budget deficits through excessive spending. Marriner Eccles, whom Roosevelt later appointed to the Federal Reserve Board, commented that some of these campaign speeches read like "a giant misprint" in which Roosevelt delivered Hoover's lines. This was particularly true of Roosevelt's speech in Pittsburgh on October 19. Louis Howe, fretting that the brain trust's speeches were alienating the business community, pressed FDR to let Bernard Baruch draft something reassuring to business. Baruch and his aide Hugh Johnson wrote the speech that Roosevelt delivered in Pittsburgh, which blasted Hoover's fiscal excesses and embraced economy in government. But Roosevelt added the caveat that he would not practice economy "at the expense of starving people."[55]

Roosevelt's liberal advisers gritted their teeth at the conservative financier Baruch's prominent role in the campaign, but he was the party's top financial contributor and an asset in making their candidate palatable to business. Most leading industrialists, such as the automaker Henry Ford, had endorsed Hoover's reelection. Ford went as far as to place notices in all his plants advising employees that any break in the president's program would hurt industry and employment: "To prevent times from getting worse and to help them to get better, President Hoover must be elected." The Democratic camp could also claim some prominent businesspeople among its supporters, including Jesse Isadore Strauss, head of Macy's department store; Owen D. Young, chairman of General Electric; and the archconservative Pierre Du Pont, who supported Roosevelt because of his stand on repealing Prohibition. Yet newspaper reporters found that the taxi drivers, porters, elevator operators, and other laborers they interviewed inevitably rooted for Roosevelt's election, whereas the businesspeople and bankers usually said the country would do better by not changing. Baruch sought to reassure a nervous business community that the Democratic candidate was "safe," and the *New York Times* picked up his cue in an editorial that reminded business leaders that it would be better for the millions of unemployed to turn toward Roosevelt's liberalism rather than "destructive radicalism."[56]

In industrial Pittsburgh, a Republican stronghold hit hard by the Depression, Roosevelt openly blamed Hoover for the nation's economic ills. He charged that the president had not done enough to slow down the overheated stock markets in the 1920s and had not responded promptly once the crash occurred. The brain trust suspected that Roosevelt still harbored a high regard for Hoover and would accept such harsh rhetoric only from Baruch, not from his academic advisers. FDR also accused Hoover of campaigning on a "gospel of fear." Democrats charged that some businesses were threatening their employees that Roosevelt's election would cost them their jobs. Such efforts would surely fail, the former Democratic nominee James M. Cox asserted, because "you can't scare a man who has been sleeping on the floor by telling him that he is going to fall out of bed."[57]

Four years later, when Roosevelt returned to campaign in Pittsburgh, he asked Sam Rosenman to read his 1932 speech and reconcile its pledges of a balanced budget and fiscal economizing with the reality of New Deal deficit spending for relief and public works. Rosenman reported back that the best advice he could offer was for Roosevelt to deny categorically he had ever made the speech. The brain trust, too, lamented the compromises that crept into Roosevelt's speeches, but decades later when Rexford Tugwell read them over again, he saw that their discussions of public utilities, farm credits, tariff revision, and government spending all gave the impression that the candidate was on top of economic matters, on par with the formidable Herbert Hoover.[58]

Hoover's campaign train headed to Springfield, Illinois, where he visited Abraham Lincoln's tomb and drew comparisons between Lincoln's reelection in 1864 and his own in 1932. He reiterated the Civil War theme about not changing horses in the middle of the stream. "Change horses or drown!" Democrats responded. The historical analogy to which Hoover most frequently returned was the McKinley-Bryan contest of 1896. The economic crisis of the 1930s was a much larger version of the crisis of the 1890s, and people sought government help on a larger scale. Industrial workers, drawn to McKinley and the Republicans in 1896, now found Roosevelt and the Democrats more attractive. Hoover referred to his opponent's New Deal as "Bryanism under new words and methods," but he did not mention that Republican policies had changed considerably since the days of McKinley. Seeing anarchy as the chief threat to freedom in the 1890s, Republicans had advocated a strong state—in both domestic and foreign policy—as the solution. During the Coolidge and Hoover era, conservatives began to view the state itself as a threat rather than a solution. Hoover's belief in equal opportunity and enterprise free from government interference made him viscerally opposed to big government. Throughout his campaign, he extolled the virtues of individualism and local, voluntary, private economic efforts, as opposed to any form of state regimentation. Contradicting this message, however, was the public memory that the president had been willing to use troops against the bonus marchers.[59]

Roosevelt headed into the South, where the Depression had dragged down both the agricultural economy and the cotton mills, causing the nation's highest jobless rate. The writer W. J. Cash observed that by 1932, the Depression had either ruined southerners beyond their wildest fears or threatened to do so, for which they "blamed the Yankee in the shape of Wall Street." In Atlanta, Roosevelt addressed a tumultuous crowd and criticized Hoover for preaching a "doctrine of despair" over fallen farm prices and unemployment. He promised that the nation would "march to a better day." In Kentucky, he described Hoover's efforts to pin the Depression on foreign causes as an alibi, and he blamed the Smoot-Hawley tariff for the worsening conditions, leveling responsibility at the president for failing to veto it. In rear-platform speeches, Roosevelt liked to share a story he had heard about a hitchhiker who traveled across the country in record time by holding up a sign reading "If you don't give me a ride, I'll vote for Hoover."[60]

The best news for Roosevelt was Al Smith's willingness to swallow his pride and embrace him. After refusing to make Roosevelt's nomination unanimous and stalking out of Chicago, Smith had cooled down sufficiently to endorse the whole Democratic ticket. Yet he avoided any contact with Roosevelt for three months. Smith's supporters and detractors waited anxiously to see what he would do. In October, the two men met on the stage of the New York State Democratic convention in Albany. Smith walked over and greeted the seated Roosevelt, "Hello, Frank, I'm glad to see you." Roosevelt replied, "Hello, Al, I'm glad to see you too— and that's from the heart." Although reporters in the press section sat too far away to hear this brief exchange, Fred Storm of the United Press guessed that Smith had used his familiar greeting, "Hello, you old potato." He had not, but Storm took the liberty of putting the words in his mouth. The old potato reference went out over the wires to newspapers across the country, making the reunion seem warmer than Smith likely intended.[61]

Al Smith's blessing made it easier for Catholics to vote for Roosevelt. Even though Smith barely mentioned Roosevelt in his speeches, he always drew large and joyful crowds in the northeastern cities that Roosevelt needed to carry. Moreover, Smith's very presence on the campaign trail spoke louder than the speeches he delivered. In late October, Roosevelt invited him for a chat at the governor's mansion. "If we were a couple of Frenchmen, we'd kiss each other," Smith told the press. Another influential Catholic was the "radio priest," Father Charles Coughlin, whose broadcast sermons called for compassion for the helpless and needy. Father Coughlin warned his radio flock that they faced a choice between "Roosevelt or ruin!" The National Catholic Welfare Conference also opened fire on Hoover and called for an administration more responsive to the unemployed.[62]

The stronger Roosevelt looked, the more desperately local Republican leaders urged their candidate to campaign in person. On October 22, the president opened a concerted drive for reelection, sending out his cabinet officers and a barrage of lesser officials as he boarded the campaign train himself once again. The farther that the president ventured from the White House, the more vigilant the Secret Service became. Hoover had received an unusually high number of crank letters and threats, and protestors occasionally pelted his train with tomatoes and eggs. When his entourage reached Detroit, he confronted an angry mob for the first time. As the president and First Lady walked to the motorcade, they heard loud jeers from members of the Workers Ex-servicemen's League gathered across the street from the station, holding banners reading "Down with Hoover" and "Hoover Murdered the Bonus Marchers." The police held the demonstrators back, but one man climbed a telephone pole to drop leaflets on the crowd. "For the first time in my long experience on the Detail I heard the President of the United States booed," recalled Secret Service agent Edmund Starling. The agent thought the president looked bewildered and stricken. Ahead of them lay a four-mile drive to the Olympia Arena, where Hoover would speak. Republican officials had handpicked the audience in the hall to exclude troublemakers, but the motorcade passed block after block of grim-looking men and women standing along the curbs. Their silence had a more powerful effect on those in the motorcade than the radicals' catcalls.[63]

Upset by his reception, Hoover delivered his speech that night in an uncharacteristically angry tone. He accused his opponent of distorting his record and making frivolous promises of federal jobs for the unemployed. He claimed that business was recovering because he had stopped the pork-barrel relief proposals of the Democratic House. "I can well understand that my countrymen are weary and sore and tired," said Hoover, but they had to persevere. There could be no interruption in the battle, no change in strategy, no change in the leadership. The outcome in November would "determine the permanent course of the country." After making the Detroit speech, Hoover insisted that even though he had not wanted to campaign originally, he now intended to carry his case to the people. This resoluteness in the face of defeat, wrote Anne O'Hare McCormick, "revealed the last-ditch fighter, the strong-willed, pertinacious, emotional man Hoover really is." But when McCormick left her interview with the president, her cab driver assured her: "I tell you, lady, the day Roosevelt is elected will be a national holiday—like Armistice Day, you know. I figure out that if we get rid of Old Gloom and put in a feller that can laugh and act human, the Depression will be half over."[64]

Late in October, Roosevelt made the sole verbal slip of his campaign. In Baltimore, he delivered a partisan attack drafted by some of his Democratic supporters in Congress. Intended as a reply to Hoover's criticism of both Congress and the candidate, it became known as the "Four Horsemen speech" for its portrayal of the Hoover administration as the Four Horsemen of the Apocalypse—Destruction, Delay, Deceit, and Despair. Roosevelt pointed out that at the time of the market crash, the Republicans had held complete control of the federal government. He then ad-libbed, adding "the Legislature, with the Senate and Congress, and the executive departments, and, I might add for good measure, the Supreme Court as well." This last remark, broadcast over the radio, suggested that the Supreme Court was a political body. Republicans quickly jumped on what they called a slur on the high court. Roosevelt realized that he had made a mistake but decided that any response would only perpetuate it, so he let their complaints go unanswered.[65]

Speaking in Indianapolis, Hoover assailed the notion that the Republicans held any political influence over the Supreme Court, reminding his audience that he had appointed Benjamin Cardozo, a Democrat, as a justice. (His press secretary had earlier recorded in his diary that Hoover appointed Cardozo out of "political considerations" because the judge was popular in the eastern states considered key to Hoover's reelection.) A fired-up Hoover declared that if he had the time, he could drive Roosevelt "from every solitary position he has taken in the campaign. They are all equally untenable." Regarding FDR as an opportunist who changed his positions to suit his audiences, Hoover referred to him as a "chameleon on plaid." The more bitter Hoover's attacks grew, the more deftly his Democrat opponent responded. Roosevelt recalled that the president had first "sought to create the impression that there was no campaign just as he had sought to create the impression that all was well with the United States." Roosevelt's care in showing deference to the office of president made Hoover's attacks sound less than presidential. Hoover took heart at the large crowds that greeted him in Indianapolis, but Indiana senator James Watson burst his bubble. "They are only here to see a President of the United States," Watson informed an incredulous Hoover. "We are all going out on the ash heap together." As he predicted, Senator Watson would be defeated in November as well.[66]

Democrats staged a counterrally in Indianapolis the same night that Hoover spoke there, complete with a torchlight parade featuring empty beer kegs under the banner "Happy Days Are Coming." Their speaker, Maryland governor Albert C. Ritchie, mocked charges that the Democrats would jeopardize the future of the country, reminding his audience that Hoover had held his first national job in a Democratic administration. His allegiance to the Republicans and his fear of the Democrats dated back only a dozen years. The president's blanket attack on the Democrats helped unify that historically fragmented party.[67]

Anxious to reverse public opinion with a dramatic gesture, Hoover contemplated advocating the outright repeal of Prohibition instead of a referendum. On the night before he left for a major rally in New York, he gathered some of his top advisers at the White House and read them a draft of his speech, which included his intention to ask Congress to repeal "that experiment noble in purpose" because "sometimes experiments fail." The next day, he made no mention of Prohibition in the speech. When asked about it later, Hoover shrugged, "I'm no politician." On the train to New York, he had decided that he could not break faith with the Republican platform and his dry supporters, despite polls showing the nation was overwhelmingly in favor of repeal.[68]

On October 31, 1932, at Madison Square Garden—where, four years earlier, he had accused Al Smith of promoting socialism—Hoover warned that Franklin Roosevelt's "inchoate new deal" would "crack the timbers of the Constitution." The election was more than a contest between two men or two parties, Hoover insisted; it was a contest between two philosophies of government. Voters should beware of the "glitter of promise" and resist those who would lead them down the path to regimentation. He went on to charge that if the Democrats succeeded in repealing the Smoot-Hawley tariff, "grass will grow in a hundred cities . . . the weeds will overrun the fields of millions of farms . . . churches and school houses will decay." (The imagery recalled William Jennings Bryan's warning in 1896: "Destroy our farms and the grass will grow in the streets of every city in the country.") Hearing the speech over the radio in Boston, Roosevelt grew livid at Hoover's attempt to portray him as a revolutionary. He swore that he would not allow anyone to challenge his Americanism, and it took several members of his staff to talk him out of making an angry rebuttal. In his own address that night, he adopted the calm and confident tone of a leader. Later on, he brushed off Hoover's apocalyptic vision with the comment: "Well, the grass has little chance to grow in the streets of our cities now. It would be trampled into the ground by the feet of the men who wander these streets in search of employment."[69]

Roosevelt's Boston speech, broadcast immediately after Hoover's, offered a program for unemployment relief and a pledge that "no one shall be permitted to starve." He contended that the federal government should provide temporary work and expedite public works programs. Roosevelt pointed out to his listeners the change that had occurred in Hoover's speeches as the public shifted to the Democrats. "First, they were plaintively apologetic. Then they were indignant at Congress. Finally, in desperation, they have resorted to the breeding of fear." Roosevelt refused to accept economic conditions as either inevitable or beyond control. It was not enough to say things might have been worse: "Here is the difference between the President and myself—I go on to pledge action to make things better."[70]

The back-to-back radio addresses were the closest thing to a debate that the two candidates would have during the campaign, attesting to the political influence of the new medium. The costliest campaign expenditure for either party was for radio airtime. By 1932, half of all American households owned radios, and the National Broadcasting Company (NBC) and Columbia Broadcasting System (CBS) networks broadcast speeches nationwide. Hoover had spoken on the radio occasionally as president, but in the spring of 1932, he turned down an offer to deliver a series of ten-minute weekly addresses, at no cost, because he found it difficult "to deal with anything over the radio except generalities." Roosevelt showed no such reticence as governor and had logged many hours of airtime presenting his ideas to the public. During the campaign, he spoke nationally twelve times on NBC and nine times on CBS. Hoover's midwestern tone had scored well against Al Smith's New York accent, but it was no competition for Franklin Roosevelt's highly cultivated and appealing voice. A CBS radio production manager rated Hoover's voice as heavy and showing signs of strain—the voice of a man "who does not like to talk"—whereas Roosevelt's voice was "a well-trained instrument" that convinced listeners "that he was sincere in utterance and good natured even in attack."[71]

Nor did Hoover's press relations help his chances of reelection. He held fewer press conferences in 1932 than before, and those he held often amounted to little more than a reading of an announcement, with no questions taken. Not surprisingly, attendance at the conferences fell off, causing Hoover to grumble about a press corps boycott. After September 17, he held no press conferences for the duration of the campaign. Washington observers speculated that the correspondents' daily dispatches about Hoover did as much to defeat him as all of the DNC's propaganda. Some of the press photographers competed with each other in taking unflattering pictures of the camera-shy president. On the editorial pages, Hoover won a bare majority of press support, which represented a significant reversal for him, considering that Republicans predominantly owned U.S. newspapers. Normally, the Republican candidate would have been able to count on two-thirds to three-quarters of the press endorsements. Now, however, some prominent Republican newspapers such as the *Springfield Republican* in Massachusetts supported Roosevelt on the grounds that Hoover had "exhausted his capacity to serve effectively." The Hearst and Scripps-Howard newspaper chains, which had sided with Hoover in 1928, opposed him in 1932.[72]

With the straw polls showing Roosevelt's lead widening, some of the earlier skeptics changed their minds about him. The nationally syndicated columnist Walter Lippmann informed his readers that he had become convinced of Roosevelt's abilities—or at least his capacity for growth. The Democrat's speeches had allayed his fears, and he concluded that a new president would have an easier time than the incumbent in instituting needed changes in economic policy, so Lippmann indicated he would "vote cheerfully for Governor Roosevelt." His conversion offended some of the Republican papers that carried his column, and several either refused to print it or cut offending paragraphs for the duration of the campaign.[73]

The third parties received less publicity from the mainstream media than the Democrats and Republicans did, but they were hurt even more by the apparent lack of mass appeal for radical change. Most of the public wanted the economic system restored to its prior health, not overturned. Both Hoover and Roosevelt recognized and responded to this public attitude, Hoover by trying to portray Roosevelt as a radical and Roosevelt by avoiding extremist rhetoric and emphasizing his traditional values. Roosevelt saw his mission as clearing away the wreckage of the Depression, not causing more by fomenting revolution. He twitted speechwriter Rexford Tugwell about his literary friends who had issued an open letter aligning themselves with "the party of revolution." Among those who signed this Communist manifesto were John Dos Passos, Edmund Wilson, Malcolm Cowley, Granville Hicks, Sidney Hook, Lincoln Steffens, Matthew Josephson, and Lewis Mumford, whom Roosevelt predicted would all have a "morning-after" feeling when they sobered up. Although many of the intellectuals who endorsed the Communists did not join the party, they admired what they saw as the Communists' self-sacrificing devotion to their cause and found attractive the promise of national economic planning, modeled after the Soviet Union's Five-Year Plan, along with governmental control of finance and industry. Matthew Josephson recalled the impatience of his colleagues at the *New Republic* for the coming of the revolution: "They talked of it, dreamed of it." Idealists estranged by the defects of capitalism, social injustice, and government ineffectiveness, they desired to march in the vanguard of a new order.[74]

The Communists conducted their most extensive campaign since the party's founding in 1919. Their leaders talked of winning a million votes in 1932, but they polled only a tenth of that amount. Anti-Communist sentiments kept the party off the ballot in many states, and the police often broke up the party's political rallies. The Communist presidential candidate, William Z. Foster—whom observers found strangely quiet and gentle in manner for a revolutionary—was arrested in Lawrence, Massachusetts, and knocked to the pavement when he attempted to speak in Los Angeles. California police jailed him under the state's World War I–era criminal syndicalism law, which made it a crime to advocate violence to achieve political ends. After giving some seventy speeches, Foster suffered a heart attack and was bedridden for weeks prior to the election. Although attacking the established order, the Communists spent most of their energy trying to discredit the Socialists for their deviant brand of Marxism.[75]

Of all the third parties, the Socialists came closest to playing the spoiler, serving as a magnet for those most alarmed over the mainstream parties' inability to stop the breakdown of the economy and threatening to drain votes from Roosevelt. Socialists confidently predicted that they would more than double their prior high vote of 920,000, in 1920. Some employers reported to the Republican National Committee that their workers had become so dissatisfied with Hoover they planned to vote Socialist as a protest, and both Democrats and Republicans counted every vote for the Socialists as one lost to Roosevelt.[76]

"Everybody agrees that this year is a year of Socialist opportunity," presidential candidate Norman Thomas boasted after his nomination. Thomas attracted the support of a number of prominent liberals, including the philosopher John Dewey and the economist Paul Douglas, who had failed to unite the "leaderless progressive groups" into an independent liberal party. Thomas also received more newspaper and magazine coverage than any other third-party candidate, and he aimed his radio addresses more at Roosevelt than at Hoover. He advised his audiences not to attribute responsibility for the Depression to Hoover, since no one man was big enough to cause such a calamity. The Socialist candidate avoided class-conflict rhetoric, presenting himself more as a reformer by proposing higher taxes on land values, inheritance, and upper incomes to pay for emergency relief and social welfare programs. Thomas played his own fear card when he warned that unless the United States adopted the Socialists' relief program, the nation would face starvation and riots during the next winter. He attracted large crowds to his rallies, culminating in a mass meeting at Madison Square Garden—with the Communists outside distributing anti-Socialist literature. Inside, young Socialists in the balcony hung a banner that read: "Columbia professors write Roosevelt's speeches, but the students vote for Thomas."[77]

The *Nation* advised its readers that the only vote worth casting was a vote for Norman Thomas. However, Walter Lippmann, a former Socialist, questioned whether it did any good to treat the party as "a kind of a trash basket by people who did not know how to cast their votes." American Socialists lacked the strong union support that their European counterparts enjoyed. The American Federation of Labor (AFL), for instance, endorsed Roosevelt's labor record (although not his candidacy, given its tradition of nonpartisanship). AFL president William Green had submitted a program to the presidential candidates that called for higher wages, fewer working hours, and unemployment insurance. All of the political parties responded positively, but Roosevelt embraced the job insurance plan more completely than did Hoover. Organized labor played only a limited role in the campaign, since the treasuries of individual unions had shrunk due to the Depression and could only supply a fraction of the campaign contributions they had provided in the past.[78]

When his aides expressed concern about the vote going to Norman Thomas, Roosevelt commented that intellectuals never gave politicians much leeway. They did not appreciate that he needed to be practical in order to win the election. He trusted that at least the attacks upon him from the Left would convince voters he was no dangerous radical. Unlike the minor party candidates, who stood no chance of winning, Roosevelt offered a real opportunity for movement and change. Jerry Voorhis had voted for the Socialists in 1928, and when he saw a newspaper headline that the Democrats had nominated Roosevelt, he felt a "poignant sense of being left out of the main stream of American life." Voorhis switched party allegiance and four years later was elected to Congress as a Democrat. Others leaning toward the Socialists as a protest vote had second thoughts when Hoover began campaigning more aggressively and Republican leaders predicted that the tide was turning in his favor. The wavering protest voters switched back to the Democrats, fearful that Hoover might somehow win again. Despite Thomas's arduous campaign, his share of the vote dwindled far below what he and the pundits expected. The disappointed candidate blamed the results on election officials' failure to count all the Socialist ballots, yet he ran behind many of his party's candidates for lower offices, indicating there was considerable ticket splitting on Roosevelt's behalf.[79]

NOVEMBER: A CRUSHING DEFEAT

As the election approached, a few polls showed a rise in Hoover's popularity, suggesting that the president still had a long-shot chance. Republican officials claimed that his aggressive campaign had swung voters back to the party. By this strategy of releasing optimistic statements about the tide turning, party officials aimed to create the impression that the president would be reelected, and they counted on voters wanting to side with the winner and on party members still on the fence deciding to return to the Republican ranks. Running contrary to these upbeat public pronouncements, however, local Republican organizations largely abandoned Hoover and concentrated their funds and energies behind their candidates for governor and Congress.[80]

Political polling in 1932 remained in its infancy—George Gallup's organization did not get under way until 1935, and Elmo Roper began polling during the 1936 elections. Instead, the Republican National Committee polled everyone listed in *Who's Who*, to demonstrate that this compendium of upper-income professionals and high achievers substantially supported Hoover. Although hardly representative of popular sentiment, the opinion of the *Who's Who* elite sounded impressive and helped the RNC identify potential campaign contributors. Around the country, various newspapers also conducted straw polls to test the local voter sentiment, with results that sometimes contradicted the paper's editorial endorsements. Though the *Des Moines Register* strongly supported Hoover and the statewide Republican ticket, for instance, the paper's poll accurately predicted that the president would lose the state by a wide margin, with Iowa's Republican governor, Dan Turner, and Republican senatorial candidate, Henry Field, going down to defeat as well. Most of these straw polls depended simply on the number of people who were contacted at random as their measure of accuracy, but scientific pollsters insisted that only by identifying a representative cross section of opinion could a poll serve as a "faithful replica" of the electorate at large.[81]

In those days, a weekly magazine, the *Literary Digest*, conducted the most credible national poll, one whose results were widely reprinted in the press. Primarily to push circulation, the magazine compiled a mailing list from telephone directories and car registrations. By ignoring those who had neither a phone nor a car during the Depression, the sample missed most of the "great wage-earning class." It relied instead on the sheer size of its operations. The *Digest* mailed out 20 million ballots and got back about 15 percent. Its editors pointed with pride to their polls' "uncanny accuracy" in the 1924 and 1928 elections. They hired some 2,500 men and women to sit at rows of long tables, hand addressing envelopes, inserting paper ballots that listed seven presidential candidates (Hoover, Roosevelt, Thomas, Foster, Reynolds, Coxey, and Upshaw, with space for write-ins as well), and tabulating the results as the ballots were returned beginning in mid-September. Each week throughout the campaign, the *Digest* published updates on the results until the data from all forty-eight states and the District of Columbia were recorded.[82]

At the end of September 1932, the first results of the *Literary Digest* poll gave President Hoover a slight lead, but the magazine cautioned readers against making too much of the preliminary data. The first tabulation showed Hoover leading in New York and Indiana and Roosevelt ahead in Pennsylvania—exactly opposite to the way those states would go in November. Far more significant was the poll's comparison of voters' current preferences with their choices four years earlier. The returns showed barely any drift from the Democrats to the Republicans, but of the first 27,654 ballots marked for Roosevelt, 10,927 had voted for Hoover in 1928. The stampede across party lines became more pronounced each week. In its October 1 issue, the *Literary Digest* reported that the Republican candidate had suffered a loss of 28 percent of those who voted for him in the last election. By the October 8 issue, the Democrat had attracted 32 percent of Hoover's previous supporters, and by October 15, that figure had climbed to 36 percent.[83]

Roosevelt took the lead in the second week of balloting, although the gap between himself and Hoover remained close, and the Socialist Norman Thomas registered a strong third-place tally. From then on, Roosevelt's majority expanded each week of the campaign, until the final *Literary Digest* poll on November 5 gave him 56.2 percent to Hoover's 37.3 percent and Norman Thomas's 4.8 percent. (The actual results of the election put Roosevelt at 57.4 percent, Hoover at 39.7 percent, and Thomas at 2.2 percent.) The *Digest* poll correctly called forty-four of the state races, missing Pennsylvania, which it gave to Roosevelt, and Massachusetts, Rhode Island, and New Jersey, all three erroneously awarded to Hoover. In addition to the seven candidates on the ballot, the largest write-in vote went to Al Smith, with others for Father James Cox, William Borah, Newton Baker, Huey Long, and Mickey Mouse.[84]

Jim Farley, who had been predicting since August that Roosevelt would prevail with some 20 million votes, happily pointed to his candidate's lead in the *Literary Digest* poll and similar polls in the Hearst newspapers as convincing evidence of voter sentiment. Not so, said radio newsman William Hard, who reported on his program that 35,000 of those who had voted for Roosevelt in the *Literary Digest* poll had asked to switch to Hoover. The *Digest* denied that it had received a single letter asking to change a vote, however, and Hard admitted that his information had come from the Republican National Committee. RNC chairman Everett Sanders dismissed the *Literary Digest* poll as having little value, since "those opposed to the party in power vote more regularly than others."

Republicans also asserted that many of the *Digest* votes had been mailed in before the president began his personal campaign.[85]

Hoover scored best in the straw polls taken on college campuses, where the majority of the students came from upper-income families. Harvard went for Hoover by 1,741 to Roosevelt's 620 and Norman Thomas's 484. At Yale, Hoover took 1,415 to 370 for Roosevelt and 347 for Thomas. Hoover also won at Wellesley with 376, and Thomas beat Roosevelt 83 to 48. Colgate students went 5 to 1 for Hoover, with 11 of its fraternity houses for Hoover and 1 each for Roosevelt and Thomas. At Rutgers, political science students predicted Roosevelt's victory but personally voted for Hoover. The president prevailed on college campuses in every region except the South. He also scored well among northern clergy. A straw poll taken at a meeting of the Greater Federation of Churches in New York gave Hoover 177 votes to 3 for Roosevelt, 25 for Thomas, and 1 for the Prohibition candidate, William Upshaw.

The disappointing economic data that fall flattened whatever bounce the president might have derived from these polls. To stave off inflationary legislation by Congress, the Federal Reserve Board had loosened credit early in 1932, which boosted the economy. As soon as Congress adjourned in July, the board's governors tightened credit again. The stock market stagnated, banks failed, production slowed, and many of those who had gone back to work were laid off again. Faced with such dismal economic news, Hoover made the protective tariff the centerpiece of the last week of his campaign. Newton Baker, the opponent Hoover had feared the most, fired back that the Smoot-Hawley tariff had ruined international trade and isolated the United States. "I want a change!" Baker declared. He and all the other Democrats in the stop-Roosevelt movement returned to the Democratic fold by the election; most of them delivered campaign speeches in Roosevelt's behalf. Al Smith's endorsement was less than wholehearted, however, leading the Socialist Norman Thomas to assert that only "the hate of Hoover" held the Democrats together.[86]

Wanting Hoover to end his campaign with a dramatic speaking tour to California, Republican strategists floated a suggestion that he fly across the nation in an airplane piloted by Colonel Charles A. Lindbergh, one of his supporters. Hoover's White House staff ruled out plane travel as too dangerous and too reminiscent of Roosevelt's flight to the Democratic convention. Hoover expressed doubts about returning to the West Coast, where public opinion had turned strongly against him, but he agreed to make the trip by train. On his way west, he delivered his last major campaign address in St. Paul, Minnesota, where protesters held "Ex-President Hoover" signs. Deeply fatigued, Hoover grew short of breath and his vision blurred while delivering his speech, causing him to lose his place repeatedly in the text. A Secret Service agent positioned a chair behind him in case he collapsed on the stage. During that speech, the president referred to a Democratic orator who had suggested that mob rule would result if the Republicans won, and he ad-libbed, "Thank God, we still have a government in Washington that knows how to deal with a mob." This reference to the bonus marchers drew some audible gasps, and a party official asked the head of the president's Secret Service detail, "Why don't they make him quit? He's not doing himself or the party any good. It's turning into a farce." Red-eyed and exhausted, Hoover ended the campaign with one last radio address to the nation from Elko, Nevada. The next day, he cast his vote at Stanford University. The trip marked his first visit back to California in four years.[87]

By midafternoon on November 8, 1932, election day, Hoover heard that early reports from the East indicated his chances did not look good. At dinner that night, he was handed a note that he had lost New York, and he knew that meant the election. He left the table without a word. Back in Washington, his press secretary dictated a telegram conceding the election, which he recommended that the president send immediately. Hoover delayed a little longer, so Roosevelt did not get his congratulatory telegram until 2:00 A.M. With that news, the doors to his room at New York City's Biltmore Hotel flew open, and campaign workers and party faithful streamed in to celebrate, among them Al Smith and John J. Raskob. That night, Roosevelt paid special tribute to the two people who more than anyone else had been responsible for his victory, Louis Howe and Jim Farley. When it was over, Ed Flynn enthused that they had run a "nearly perfect campaign."[88]

To broadcast the returns, the budding Columbia Broadcasting System scrapped its entire Tuesday evening schedule. Radio lacked its own news gatherers, so CBS contracted to purchase United Press wire service reports. Newspapers that subscribed to the UP howled that radio would steal the thunder from their headlines, which forced the UP to cancel the contract at the last moment. The Associated Press, unaware that its rival had backed out of the deal, offered its own news dispatches to the radio broadcasters for free. CBS and NBC were therefore able to provide the most extensive election night coverage that Americans had

Democratic National Committee chairman Jim Farley answers the phone on election night, as New York governor Franklin Roosevelt awaits the results at his headquarters at the Biltmore Hotel in New York City.

ever heard. CBS correspondent Robert Trout announced that the results of the election appeared certain: "The ticket of Roosevelt and Garner has won a clear-cut majority over the ticket of Hoover and Curtis. And so the United States has a new president."[89]

Franklin D. Roosevelt won the presidency with 22,829,501 votes to Herbert Hoover's 15,760,684. Running far behind, the Socialist Norman Thomas drew 884,649, and the Communist William Z. Foster 103,253. The rest of the vote was scattered among the Prohibitionist William Upshaw, 81,869; the Liberty Party's Coin Harvey, 53,425; the Socialist-Labor candidate Verne Reynolds, 33,276; and the Farmer-Labor Party's Jacob Coxey, with 7,309. Roosevelt became the first Democrat in eighty years to win the presidency by a majority rather than a plurality of the popular vote. Until then, the nation had witnessed only narrow Democratic presidential victories, the newspapers noted, whereas Republicans had held "a monopoly on landslides." RNC chairman Everett Sanders privately blamed this staggering defeat on "the block of unemployed, dissatisfied farmers, and dissatisfied formerly rich who had lost their imaginary wealth by speculation." The only consolation for Hoover's staff was that the vote against them had been so large that nothing they could have done would have changed the result. Hoover conceded that "General Prosperity" had elected him in 1928, but "General Depression" had now defeated him.[90]

Maine, whose defection in the state elections in September had rocked the Republicans, wound up voting for Hoover. Maine Democrats had so exhausted themselves in the earlier campaign that they failed to press their advantage. Hoover carried five other northeastern and mid-Atlantic states: Vermont, New Hampshire, Connecticut, Delaware, and Pennsylvania. Together, they gave him 59 electoral votes to Roosevelt's 472. Even in the states he carried, Hoover's winning margin dropped precipitously from four years earlier—for example, his Pennsylvania vote fell from 65 percent to 50.8 percent. His overall popular vote was only three-quarters of what he had received four years earlier. Hoover's appeal remained strongest among Protestants, the college-educated, middle- and upper-class professionals, large business and banking interests, and rural voters in the Northeast.[91]

Only 52.5 percent of the eligible voters nationwide cast ballots, but 3 million more people voted than in 1928. Why had so many potential voters stayed home at the depth of the Depression? Some were too beaten down by the hard times to cast a ballot; some were on the road; some were apathetic or indifferent. Those higher up on the economic scale were more likely to vote than those at the bottom, but nonvoting was not simply a matter of wealth or education. The distinguished physicist J. Robert Oppenheimer, for example, had been too preoccupied with his scientific research at Berkeley to bother to vote in 1932.[92]

Roosevelt's detractors argued that he did not win the election so much as Hoover lost it. Yet the national vote in 1932 represented a sweeping party victory that suggested more than an impulse to oust an incumbent president. Roosevelt united the Democrats and drew in substantial numbers of Republicans, independents, and previously inactive voters. The majority of women's votes, which had gone to Republicans since the suffrage amendment, now went to the Democrats. Roosevelt gained support among all economic classes, particularly from those in the middle-to-lower-income brackets, farmers, industrial workers, members of organized labor, and individuals in small businesses and banking interests. He drew equally from southern Protestants and northern Catholics and attracted a significant number of Jewish voters into the Democratic ranks. Roosevelt especially appealed to younger, first-time voters, most of whom would stay Democratic for the rest of their lives. The South overwhelmingly restored its Democratic ties. For example, Hoover's share in Alabama between 1928 and 1932 fell from 48.5 to 14.1 percent. Roosevelt ran strongly in the Northwest and on the Great Plains, where Democrats had rarely done well. He took Hoover's birth state of Iowa, his childhood state of Oregon, and his adopted state of California—but Roosevelt lost his own Dutchess County and never carried it in subsequent elections.[93]

African Americans, despite their uneasy relations with the Hoover administration, remained loyal to the party of Lincoln. Democrats had made little effort to compete for their votes. Blacks viewed Franklin Roosevelt suspiciously for having depended on southern white delegates to win the nomination and for choosing a segregationist as his running mate. During the campaign that fall, the NAACP magazine, the *Crisis*, failed to locate a single prominent black Democrat who would endorse Roosevelt. Republicans denounced those blacks who switched to the Democrats as "race traitors" and warned of the terrible consequences that would follow a Democratic victory. As a result, Roosevelt received only about a quarter of the black vote in the northern cities. By contrast, black Democrats scored well in state and local races amid the Democratic sweep. The *Chicago Defender* observed that "as Democrats they floated along on the wave of protest against state and national G.O.P. policies." Ambitious African American politicians would see electoral advantages in switching party affiliation, and they would find the New Deal more welcoming than previously suspected.[94]

Roosevelt's coattails provided ample pull for Democratic congressional candidates, who won more seats than anyone had dared predict. During Hoover's presidency, Republicans fell from 62 to 27 percent of the U.S. House of Representatives and from 56 to 36 of the 96 senators. But in 1932, Democrats added 97 seats in the House, expanding their margin to 313 to 117 during Roosevelt's first two years in office. The large class of incoming freshmen was filled with liberals who would faithfully support Roosevelt's New Deal legislation—and win plaudits for their serious attention to the issues and absence of corruption—but the individuals among them who would last the longest and stand out the most prominently were such conservatives as the Democratic senators Richard Russell of Georgia, Harry F. Byrd of Virginia, and Pat McCarran of Nevada and the Republican representative Everett M. Dirksen of Illinois. Democratic congressional candidates swept the South, much of the Midwest, the Great Plains, the Rocky Mountains, and the Pacific Coast. Only in the northeastern states from Pennsylvania to New Hampshire did House Republicans retain a bloc of rural districts.[95]

Republicans lost their tenuous grip on the Senate's majority and with it their majority leader and most powerful committee chairmen. Most stunning was the defeat of Utah senator Reed Smoot, an apostle of both the Mormon Church and protective tariffs. Oregon voters had already defeated Willis Hawley in a primary, eliminating both authors of the Smoot-Hawley Tariff Act. Two progressive Republican senators, South Dakota's Peter Norbeck and North Dakota's Gerald P. Nye, won reelection despite the fact that their states had gone for Roosevelt. But across the nation, nine incumbent Republicans fell to Democratic challengers, from William G. McAdoo in California to Augustine Lonergan in Connecticut. (Traditionally Republican Connecticut narrowly stayed in Hoover's column but sent a Democratic delegation to Congress to work with Roosevelt.) The winning Democrats were largely wet on Prohibition and thereby gained assistance from the repeal forces that had concentrated their efforts on congressional races and state referenda. By commanding leads, voters struck down state Prohibition laws in Arizona, California, Colorado, Louisiana, Michigan, New Jersey, North Dakota, Oregon, and Washington. Congress got the message and in February

1933, even before the newly elected members took office, sent to the states the Twenty-first Amendment to repeal Prohibition.[96]

Of the thirty-four states that elected governors in 1932, eight Democrats and seven Republicans were running for reelection. At the polls, Democrats nearly swept the field, electing governors in thirty of these states. The four they lost went to a Farmer-Labor candidate in Minnesota and three Republicans, including the incumbent governors of Vermont and New Hampshire. Only Alf Landon managed to defeat a sitting Democratic governor, Harry Woodring, and he also beat the goat-gland doctor, John Brinkley, in Kansas' three-way race. Franklin Roosevelt ran ahead of most of these Democratic gubernatorial candidates and near enough to the others to demonstrate that his popularity had aided their victories. He became the first Democrat since the Civil War to win Michigan, carrying along with him the Democratic candidate for governor, William Comstock (who had lost a similar race two years earlier), and most of the statewide Democratic ticket. In Illinois, Roosevelt's lead closely matched that of the Chicago Democrat judge Henry Horner, who became the state's first Jewish governor. In Texas, where conservative Democrats had threatened to boycott the candidacy of former governor Miriam "Ma" Ferguson—whom they viewed as radical and "unsafe"—the Roosevelt-Garner landslide helped sweep Ferguson back into office. The election put legislative state houses and governor's mansions across the nation largely under Democratic control.[97]

Like so many other Americans, Herbert Hoover lost his job to the Depression. Despite the signs of impending defeat, he had not anticipated a rejection of such devastating proportions. After the election, returning to Washington, he telegraphed his old friend Roy Roberts, publisher of the *Kansas City Star,* and invited him to board the presidential train as it passed through Kansas and Missouri. Roberts found the defeated president crushed by the election results and reported that Hoover "could ask but one question: 'Why?'"[98]

5

THE NEW DEAL EXPERIMENT

The votes were counted, and the winning margin was decisive. But a constitutional glitch prevented Franklin D. Roosevelt from assuming the presidency for another four months. During the long interregnum between the election on November 8, 1932, and the inauguration on March 4, 1933, the "President-reject," as *Time* magazine called Herbert Hoover, and a lame-duck Congress remained in charge. As unemployment rose and banks failed at an alarming rate, Hoover reached out for cooperation from the man who had defeated him, but their mutual suspicion and accumulated antagonism undermined any chance of a joint effort. Relations between the two former friends had become strained during the campaign, and they grew more so in the months immediately after the election.

The old system of electing presidents in November and inaugurating them in March fit the horse-and-carriage era, giving incoming administrations time to organize. After the inauguration, the new president enjoyed nine months in office before Congress convened on the first Monday in December—unless the president called Congress back earlier in a special session. By the twentieth century, this leisurely arrangement was obsolete. The second session of every two-year Congress did not convene until after the next election took place, meaning that members who had lost or not run continued to serve for another session, and these lame-duck legislators proved especially susceptible to lobbyists. Nebraska senator George Norris argued for years that the system needed reform, eventually persuading Congress to amend the Constitution by moving the opening of Congress to January 3 and the inauguration of the president to January 20. Congress sent the Twentieth Amendment to the states in March 1932, but not until February 1933 did the necessary three-quarters of the states ratify it, too late for Roosevelt's inauguration.

After voting in California, President Hoover had planned a postelection vacation in Hawaii until word came that the British and French wanted to extend the moratorium on war debts and were threatening to default on future payments. Hoover believed he would need to educate Roosevelt on the matter. "I am going to return to Washington just as rapidly as possible to give myself freely to my incoming successor, if he wants my services," he told his doctor, who begged him to rest after the exhausting campaign. "I'd love to do it—I need it—I need it badly—but we just can't do other than return to Washington."[1]

Traveling east, Hoover detoured to see the gigantic dam being built across the Colorado River. His secretary of the interior, Ray Lyman Wilbur, had named it the Hoover Dam, but humorists jested that this designation would be subject to the election returns. (Two months after Hoover left office, Roosevelt's secretary of the interior, Harold Ickes, renamed it the Boulder Dam, an act that Hoover considered "a public defamation." It grated on him until 1947, when a Republican Congress—prodded by Lawrence Richey—restored the Hoover Dam name.) Florence Boyer, who accompanied her father when he escorted the president on his visit to the construction site, later recalled that she had never seen a man "look so worn out and so completely defeated." Hoover spent just an hour and a half touring the facility. He gave a short speech that extolled the engineering wonders of the dam but made little reference to the workers who had risked their lives to build it. Nor did the work crews hold their visitor in high esteem. When Hoover entered the mess hall, some workers kept on eating rather than stand in his honor.[2]

Back on the train, Hoover drafted a long telegram to his successor, asking to meet for a discussion of the war debt issue. The invitation caught Roosevelt by surprise. Collaboration between outgoing and incoming presidents of opposite parties was unprecedented, and the war debts were not a subject on which the two men were likely to agree. During the campaign, Roosevelt placed his emphasis on internal rather than external priorities, accusing Hoover of using world conditions as an alibi for his domestic failures. Roosevelt believed ending the Depression required that foreign affairs take a back seat to domestic policy. And he could not forget that he owed his nomination to William Randolph Hearst, an implacable foe of any extension of the war debt moratorium.[3]

Hoover was seeking cooperation, not a coalition. Roosevelt reasoned that if the president wanted him to take charge sooner rather than later, he could appoint him secretary of state and then resign along with the vice president, giving FDR the job constitutionally. Under the law of presidential succession at that time, the secretary of state stood next in line after the vice president; a later law inserted the House Speaker and Senate president pro tem ahead in the line. Otherwise, Roosevelt felt that he lacked authority to assume any responsibility for government policies before he took office. He had neither a cabinet for advice nor access to government records to assist him in shaping policy. Also, senior Democrats in Congress were warning him not to commit himself to the defeated president's policies.[4]

Roosevelt met Hoover at the White House on November 22, in the more accessible Red Room for his convenience. Thousands had lined the streets from the train station to the gates of the White House, greeting and cheering the president-elect. Those inside the mansion heard his triumphant arrival. Hoover did not trust Roosevelt to keep his word and wanted Treasury Secretary Ogden Mills to join them as a witness. Over the phone, he had invited Roosevelt to bring someone with him—"a secretary or somebody" to take notes for issues to be decided later—and he was surprised when Roosevelt readily agreed. (He chose to bring Raymond Moley.) "I hooked him the first time," Hoover commented with satisfaction, employing a fishing metaphor. Throughout the interregnum, he acted the fisherman, casting lures and waiting for the fish to bite.[5]

Greeting his guests uneasily, Hoover delivered an hour-long monologue on the war debts. He stared at the carpet or glanced at Moley, avoiding eye contact with the man who had defeated him. Hoover wanted to reactivate the War Debt Commission, despite strong opposition in Congress to any further reduction in the debts. He argued that if both he and Roosevelt named negotiators to serve on the commission, they could win congressional support and establish continuity between their administrations. Roosevelt replied that the president could negotiate with foreign nations without approval from Congress. He resisted naming any members to the debt commission or issuing a joint statement on the matter, explaining that he had attended the meeting simply to be informed about pending matters, not to reach any decisions. After an hour, Mills and Moley left, and Hoover and Roosevelt spent another seventeen minutes talking together in private. From this reasonably cordial encounter, the two men came to a mutual misunderstanding: Hoover felt sure they had agreed on reconstituting the debt commission, and Roosevelt felt equally sure they had not. When he heard that Roosevelt later told reporters that the debt problem was not his baby, Hoover grumbled that the baby would be on his doorstep whatever happened.[6]

In December, Hoover delivered a farewell address to the Gridiron Club, the annual dinner where the capital's journalists entertained and spoofed the movers and shakers. "Well, as nearly as I can learn, we did not have enough votes on our side," he said with the kind of self-deprecating humor the occasion required. A return to prosperity would require dealing with the foreign situation, Hoover insisted, and it would take cooperation with other nations to ensure economic recovery and prevent a relapse. Aiming his message at Roosevelt, he added that foreign policy required a level of cooperation and party responsibility at home that "rises above partisanship."[7]

After the election, Roosevelt spent his time wrapping up his service as governor, recruiting a cabinet, planning a legislative agenda, and taking a postelection vacation, under the assumption that it remained Hoover's job, not his, to run the government until March. His team of advisers drafted programs, all the while aware that by March 4, they could have anything on their hands from a recovery to a revolution. "The chance is about even either way," Adolph Berle estimated. In the face of such menacing uncertainty, Roosevelt's composure impressed those around him. He seemed tireless, conducting conferences, making decisions, and showing not the slightest strain. His outward cheerfulness in the face of ever-bleaker economic news perplexed others less familiar with the Roosevelt style. "It's incredible," said Henry Wallace, his designated secretary of agriculture, after a chat that revealed little about what the new president intended to do about the farm crisis. "The country is in ruins; and we seem to be on a kind of Sunday picnic."[8]

Roosevelt received another telegram from Hoover on December 17, this time asking for a joint decision on the upcoming World Economic Conference. Once again, the president-elect declined to commit himself in advance on foreign policy matters, explaining that he did not want to send the wrong signals to other nations. Hoover spent a sleepless night after getting this response. "That was a nasty telegram Roosevelt sent last night," he complained the next morning, but he added, "I have given him a reply now that will make him do some more sidestepping." Hoover released their correspondence to the press with a statement reflecting his displeasure over Roosevelt's unwillingness to follow his lead. In response, Roosevelt instructed Raymond Moley to meet with Secretary of State Henry Stimson to work out some common action and to announce that he had agreed to meet with Hoover again.[9]

Former president Coolidge doubted that the president-elect could afford to wait, feeling that the emergency required immediate action. In Northampton, Massachusetts, where Coolidge had retired, the failure of the local bank had plunged the town into gloom. The rich men whom he admired were shrinking in public esteem, and the world that he knew was crumbling. Coolidge admitted that he had not expected the Republicans to lose so badly but commented that "since it had to be, it is just as well that the Democrats have it lock, stock and barrel." He remained pessimistic about the government's ability to respond to economic issues, expecting that people would have to find a way out for themselves. In January 1933, he died of a heart attack while shaving.[10]

After Coolidge's funeral, Hoover renewed his efforts to commit Roosevelt to his policies or else blame him for not cooperating. "From the day I sent that first telegram from the train the main thing I wanted to do was get this debt matter off my doorstep and put it onto Roosevelt's and I have done it," he told his staff, using another fishing metaphor: "He has swallowed my bait." Hoover reasoned that if he had not made the move, he would have had the British hounding him, but now they would have to wait for Roosevelt to take office. For Roosevelt, the president's insistence on joint action suggested his failure to grasp how differently the new administration planned to operate. Hoover considered settlement of the war debts essential for maintaining the international gold standard; Roosevelt regarded the debts as largely irrelevant for rebuilding the American economy. (The United States would abandon the gold standard in 1933, and most of the European nations would default on their war debts in 1934.)

At Roosevelt's suggestion, they next met at the White House when he visited Washington on January 20, 1933—the date that future inaugurations would take place under the Twentieth Amendment. Their second encounter went no better than the first, and Hoover dismissed their conversation as "piffle." The president refused to allow photographers to record the scene, telling his press secretary, "I will never be photographed with him. I have too much respect for myself." However, he assured his staff, "I'll have my way with Roosevelt yet."[11]

The incoming administration almost ended before it began. On February 15, Franklin Roosevelt disembarked in Miami, Florida, after vacationing on Vincent Astor's yacht. The Miami city government had erected grandstands in Bayfront Park to enable the president-elect to address a crowd of about 20,000 well-wishers while perched in his open car. In the front row of the stands sat Chicago's mayor, Anton Cermak, there to make amends for opposing Roosevelt at the convention. During the campaign, Cermak had spoken repeatedly for the Democratic ticket and organized the Czechoslovakian Friends of Roosevelt Society. For eight months, Chicago had been unable to pay its schoolteachers, and the mayor traveled hat in hand to Miami to appeal to the incoming president for federal funds. A few rows behind Cermak sat a young Italian immigrant, Giuseppe Zangara, who was carrying a pistol that he had purchased with the idea of shooting President Hoover, until he read about the president-elect's visit to Miami. Roosevelt sat on the trunk of his car to address the crowd, making an easy target, but when Zangara aimed his pistol, the crowd stood to applaud and the five-foot-one anarchist could not see over it.

Roosevelt completed his remarks and slid down into the back seat of the car. Mayor Cermak walked forward to talk with him as the crowd in the bleachers dispersed. Not far away, Zangara opened fire, but a woman near him grabbed his arm. His deflected shots missed Roosevelt while striking five other people, including Cermak, who was wounded in the chest. Secret Service agents tried to speed the president-elect away, but Roosevelt insisted that the car back up to retrieve the mayor. They rushed Cermak to the hospital, cradled in Roosevelt's arms. The next day, FDR visited and told the press that all the mayor wanted to talk about was Chicago's unpaid schoolteachers. Cermak lingered for weeks, dying shortly after Roosevelt's inauguration. His funeral took place in Chicago Stadium, where the two national conventions had met. Had Zangara assassinated Roosevelt, the vice president–elect, John Nance Garner, would have taken the oath as president according to the rules of constitutional succession, and a dramatically different administration would have followed. Instead, Roosevelt's calm response to the attempt on his life bolstered his public appeal. American justice moved swiftly in 1933, and the state of Florida executed Zangara just thirty-three days after the shooting.

LAME-DUCK LEADERSHIP

Herbert Hoover wanted to do as much as possible in his remaining months to leave a positive legacy, yet he found there was little that he could accomplish "while handcuffed by a hostile Congress and an uncooperative President-elect." The last session of the 72nd Congress (elected in 1930) convened on December 5, 1932. Republicans, having lost 101 seats in the House and 12 in the Senate, blamed Hoover for their plight. Until the next Congress convened, Democrats still held only a three-vote majority in the House, neither fully in charge nor likely to follow the rejected president's lead. National unity seemed urgently needed to meet the economic crisis, but both sides in Congress viewed every issue from a partisan standpoint, unwilling to give each other the slightest credit. Hoover had only the negative power of the veto to keep the unruly Congress in line.[12]

Unsure how his legislative initiatives might fare, Hoover repeatedly sought some sort of alliance with Roosevelt. Within his own party, he faced strong opposition to any further moratorium on the European debts. Twice during the lame-duck session, the former Republican chairman of the House Banking Committee, Louis McFadden, introduced resolutions to impeach the president for capitulating to "international bankers" and depriving Americans of the money they were owed And both times, the House defeated these resolutions, with more Democrats than Republicans voting against the impeachment. The Senate, still technically under a Republican majority, stopped confirming Hoover's nominations. Louisiana's populist senator Huey Long conducted a filibuster against the administration's banking bill. The president and Congress also clashed over a bill granting independence to the Philippines. Worried that Congress might override his veto, the president called in the *New York Times*'s Washington bureau chief, Arthur Krock, and asked that he deliver a private message urging Roosevelt to let congressional Democrats know that he shared Hoover's opposition to Philippine independence. Roosevelt listened to Krock without comment, taking no action. Congress went ahead and overrode Hoover's veto.[13]

Determined to balance the federal budget, Hoover appealed to Congress to enact a national sales tax, despite the burden it would place on consumers. Democratic congressional leaders supported him, believing that it would be politically safer to impose the disagreeable tax before the Democratic administration took office. But Roosevelt surprised them by opposing a sales tax as deflationary. Speaker Garner and other Democrats withdrew their support, and Hoover's sales tax and balanced budget proposals evaporated.[14]

About all the outgoing Congress accomplished was to repeal Prohibition. The voters had spoken loudly and clearly against the law; those drys left in Congress were now mostly lame ducks, having no incentive for opposing repeal. In February, both the House and the Senate gave the necessary two-thirds vote to repeal the Eighteenth Amendment. Hoover, although astonished that the drys failed to filibuster repeal in the Senate, accepted its demise as inevitable (and after maintaining total abstinence during his presidency, he reinstituted his own cocktail hour). Conservatives had come to see Prohibition as an affront to states' rights and individual liberties, and liberals had grown suspicious of any attempt at legislating morality. By December 1933, the states had ratified the repeal of the noble experiment.[15]

The lame-duck Congress also shaped public opinion through a revival of the Senate Banking Committee's investigation into Wall Street banking and stock exchange practices. Its hearings providing stunning revelations about the financial irresponsibility of some of the nation's most prominent bankers and brokers, which would prove to be a boon to Roosevelt's efforts to reform the financial system—an unintended political gift from his predecessor. Republicans had suspected a conspiracy among Democratic financiers to use the stock market to embarrass the administration. Senator Simeon Fess felt this explained why "every time an Administration official gives out an optimistic statement about business conditions, the market immediately drops." Back in March 1932, President Hoover had received a tip that "short sellers" and "bear raiders" were planning massive stock sales to drive down the markets and sabotage his reelection chances. He believed that John J. Raskob and Bernard Baruch were behind the stock manipulation. "I want the shorts investigated and the quicker the better!" he ordered the Republican chairman of the Senate Banking Committee. The investigation would establish that none of the leading Democrats had engaged in bear raiding, although it turned out that short sellers had indeed timed their sales to follow Hoover's optimistic speeches, having learned that investor distrust inevitably pushed down the market whenever the president predicted recovery.[16]

As the Banking Committee prepared to wrap up its investigation in January 1933, its chairman hired a New York prosecutor, Ferdinand Pecora, to write the final report. The document was not due until March, and he took advantage of the extra time to hold a few more hearings. These hearings got under way just as the nation's governors began declaring bank holidays, and they offered bewildered depositors a timely education in financial malfeasance. Pecora selected the president of the National City Bank, Charles E. Mitchell, for his first inquiry, and he sent staff investigators to Mitchell's bank, armed with subpoenas. The tall, tanned, stately banker, an adviser to Harding, Coolidge, and Hoover, swept confidently into the Senate hearing room, surrounded by a retinue of bank officials. But his confidence waned (and his retinue disappeared) when the committee began producing evidence against him. Despite earning a high salary and receiving generous bonuses from the bank, Mitchell had paid no income taxes during the Depression, and under his leadership, the National City Bank had unloaded poor stocks onto unwary investors. The investigation earned banner headlines, and Mitchell resigned as president of the bank. (Fortunately for Roosevelt, his brain trust had blocked Bernard Baruch's efforts to recruit Mitchell as an economic adviser to the Democratic campaign.)[17]

The president-elect encouraged the Banking Committee to continue the investigation into the next Congress, and over the coming months, Pecora would call bankers of the stature of J. P. Morgan Jr. to the witness stand. By personalizing the causes of the Depression through creating a string of villains, thus translating complex economic problems into moral terms, Pecora's investigations contributed to the reforming, rather than revolutionary, nature of the New Deal. The banking and securities systems, it followed, needed only a change in personnel and stricter governmental regulation to prevent a reoccurrence of past abuses, rather than public ownership of the banks and stock exchanges. Launched by Hoover, the Senate Banking Committee hearings helped push through Roosevelt's banking and stock market regulations, including the Federal Securities Act of 1933, the Securities and Exchange Act of 1934, and the Public Utilities Holding Company Act of 1935.[18]

Three days after Roosevelt survived the assassination attempt in Florida, a Secret Service agent delivered to him a ten-page, handwritten letter from the president. Faced with a collapsing banking system, Hoover sought cooperation with the president-elect while simultaneously blaming the crisis on his election. Roosevelt dismissed this argument as "cheeky." He resisted letting Hoover tie his hands before his administration had considered all the options on how to restore confidence in the financial system. It seemed absurd to believe that the nation that had just elected him somehow feared him, and he had no intention of assuming responsibility for measures he could not control. Roosevelt composed a letter of response but waited eleven days to send it to Hoover, blaming the delay on a secretarial error. Meanwhile, he went about conducting his prepresidential activities on the assumption that Hoover could carry on without his concurrence.[19]

Bank failures spread alarmingly. Since 1929, more than 5,000 banks had closed their doors permanently, beginning in the rural South and West and spreading into the cities of the Northeast and Midwest. The collapse of the New York–based Bank of the United States in December 1931 represented the largest bank failure in American history. The Federal Reserve's efforts to raise the discount rate exacerbated the deflation without restoring depositor confidence. Hoover's Reconstruction Finance Corporation saved a number of larger banks but failed to stem the crisis. Every bank failure triggered a contagious fear among depositors, who panicked and withdrew their savings. In February, the RFC fought with the auto manufacturer Henry Ford over how much money he needed to put up to support two Detroit banks he controlled. The RFC refused to grant loans to the banks, and the ensuing panic caused the governor of Michigan to declare a bank holiday, shutting down the banks throughout the state. Other states followed suit, and the governors of the Federal Reserve Board asked Hoover to consider a national bank holiday.[20]

"There is nothing we can do," Hoover said of the bank failures. "The American people are writing off 'the new deal.'" He attributed the depositors' jitters to Roosevelt's failure to state publicly that he opposed inflation. Roosevelt's policies did not "square with what the country wants," he asserted, ignoring the election returns. Uncertainty about the legality of suspending national banking made Hoover reluctant to act alone. And once again, he thought he could persuade Roosevelt to endorse his economic policies. As he explained candidly to Senator David A. Reed, a Pennsylvania Republican, Hoover realized that he was asking the president-elect to ratify the economic policies of the Republican administration, meaning that Roosevelt would have to abandon "ninety per cent of the so-called new deal." Otherwise, the New Dealers would run the risk of precipitating a complete financial debacle. "If it is precipitated, the responsibility lies squarely with them for they have had ample warning—unless, of course, such a debacle is part of the 'new deal.'"[21]

Roosevelt would not allow Hoover to preempt his presidency any more than he would let Al Smith dictate his governorship. Like Smith, Hoover erred in treating Roosevelt with condescension, which only aroused his stubbornness. James H. Rand Jr., of Remington Rand, added a more sinister interpretation. Late in February, Rand reported to the president that over lunch, Rexford Tugwell had told him Roosevelt expected the banks to collapse but planned to do nothing until he took office, laying the responsibility "in the lap of President Hoover." To Hoover, this explained why Roosevelt had not responded to his appeals. The talkative Tugwell admitted saying as much but explained that Rand had been snooping around for information and that he had tried to be evasive in answering, adopting a flip tone that Rand took more seriously than Tugwell intended. A year later, the conspiratorially minded Rand spread charges that Tugwell and other left-wing New Dealers were plotting to overthrow Roosevelt and replace him with a Stalin. Congress investigated those accusations and found them groundless.[22]

While Hoover vacillated, the governors of New York and Illinois declared bank holidays, and the rippling effect closed most of the nation's banks by the inauguration. Members of the incoming Roosevelt administration could not cash checks when they arrived at the capital. Roosevelt got to Washington on March 2, and the next day, he went with his family to pay a social call on the president and First Lady. As they entered the White House, the chief usher whispered to Roosevelt that Ogden Mills, the secretary of the treasury, and Eugene Meyer, the Federal Reserve Board governor, would also be present. Roosevelt quickly called Raymond Moley, who managed to join them as the meeting began. Moley surmised that Hoover had decided he could persuade Roosevelt to change his mind if he separated him from his advisers. There was little chance of that happening, however, given the depth of their animosity. Roosevelt flatly refused Hoover's request that he sign a joint proclamation closing all the banks. If Hoover was unwilling to act, Roosevelt said he would wait until he became president the next day. As Secretary of State Henry Stimson recorded, Hoover simply could not bring himself "to make his last days in office an admission of bankruptcy." Eugene Meyer judged both men at fault, Hoover for asking Roosevelt to do more than he should have and Roosevelt for not finding some room for cooperation. Whatever their personal feelings toward each other were, the four-month stalemate hardly served the national interest.[23]

As the meeting broke up, Roosevelt mentioned that it was difficult for him to move in a hurry and that the president should not feel he had to wait for him. Hoover looked at him bleakly and said in a flat voice, "Mr. Roosevelt, after you have been President for a while, you will learn that the President of the United States waits for no one." Hoover then turned abruptly and left the room. Roosevelt returned to his hotel suite angrier than his staff had ever seen him.[24]

The tense interregnum left a stain on both men's memories. In later years, Roosevelt often referred to it, showing his resentment at Hoover for having treated him like a schoolboy. At the same time that he refused Hoover's request to sign a joint proclamation closing the banks, Roosevelt accepted an offer from the president's top Treasury Department officials to remain on the job to draft emergency legislation for the new administration. Under that plan, Roosevelt declared a bank holiday, closed the banks, and then reopened them following government scrutiny of their books. Hoover could have issued the same proclamation if he had not exhausted his political will and credibility. For the rest of his life, he revisited these events, alternately arguing that the banking crisis had not been severe enough to justify the bank closures and accusing Roosevelt of deliberately prolonging the crisis to worsen the emergency, justifying a drastic response. Hoover's indecisiveness handed his successor a distinct triumph at the start of his presidency. The New Dealers regarded the bank holiday as the turning point of the Depression, as public confidence rebounded with the reopening of the banks in sound condition.[25]

ROOSEVELT TAKES COMMAND

On a bleak March 4, Roosevelt and Hoover rode together in an open car from the White House to the inaugural ceremonies at the Capitol. Their only conversation concerned the fate of Hoover's secretary, Walter Newton, who needed a job, since the Senate had refused to confirm his nomination to a federal judgeship. Roosevelt agreed to help and later appointed Newton to the Federal Home Loan Bank Board. That transaction completed, Hoover sank into silence while Roosevelt chatted amiably without response. As they passed the new Commerce Department building under construction, Roosevelt heard himself commenting on the fine quality of its steel girders. Realizing the hopelessness of any further conversation, he turned away from Hoover and waved his top hat to

President Hoover and President-Elect Roosevelt barely spoke to each other on their ride from the White House to the Capitol for the inauguration on March 4, 1933.

Eleanor and Franklin Roosevelt arrive at the Capitol for his inauguration. Roosevelt walked with the aid of leg braces, a cane, and the strong arm of his oldest son, James.

the crowds. The contrast between the stone-faced Hoover and the cheery Roosevelt struck onlookers as a positive omen.

After taking the oath of office, Roosevelt delivered his eagerly awaited inaugural address. He had to avoid any hint of hollow optimism while at the same time offering the troubled nation some sense of encouragement. The address, a collaborative effort between FDR and Raymond Moley, managed to strike the right chord, but Louis Howe inserted its most memorable line: "The only thing we have to fear is fear itself—nameless, unreasoning, unjustified terror which paralyzes needed efforts to convert retreat into advance." Howe had probably lifted the phrase from a Chamber of Commerce report published a year earlier, which read, "In a condition of this kind, the thing to be feared is fear itself." Herbert Hoover's staunch ally Julius H. Barnes headed the chamber and issued the report. Hoover had been groping to express that same sentiment but had never found the right words.[26]

The nation faced not a natural disaster, Roosevelt insisted, but one brought about by the failure of the "rulers of the exchange of mankind's goods." Government had to put people back to work in the same way that it would prepare for war, by national planning and strict supervision of the economy. He would call the Congress into special session to address these needs. If Congress failed to meet the challenge, he would seek "broad Executive power to wage a war against the emergency, as great as the power that would be given to me if we were in fact invaded by a foreign foe." It was stirring rhetoric, but the nation was waiting to see what he would do, not just what he said. A North Carolina minister who attended the inauguration returned to tell his congregation that "as I stood up there in that vast throng watchin' Hoover go out and Mr. and Mrs. Roosevelt come in, I felt like weepin.' I thought, one man of big promises goes out and another comes in, and like always the people go on in need."[27]

Roosevelt returned to the White House to review the inaugural parade from a special seat that gave the illusion he was standing. Hoover headed to Union Station, where he learned that his successor had not authorized the Secret Service to accompany him any farther, despite numerous threats against his life. (Not until 1965, after Hoover's death, did Congress finally provide Secret Service protection for former presidents.) Hoover had been planning to sail to California via Panama, but he decided to wait in New York City for a few days. The Depression had hurt him economically as well as politically, and he needed to put his own financial house in order. He also wanted to stay within easy distance of Washington in case Roosevelt summoned him back to help with the banking crisis. When no call came, he took the train to Palo Alto, California, at the end of the month. He intended to stay silent on economic and political matters for the time being. Bitter over his defeat, he had to be coaxed by friends into signing autographs and speaking to schools and various civic groups; they assured him that the requests came because people respected him as a former president of the United States.[28]

In Washington, the first days of the new administration obliterated all traces of Herbert Hoover. "If swift decision and action, vast political power and willingness to use it are the chief prerequisites in the pilot, Franklin D. Roosevelt in a week has displayed them," Arthur Krock wrote admiringly in the *New York Times*. "Gone is the fortress that was the White House; the formal uneasy place that was the Executive Office; the wild-cat cage that was Congress." Roosevelt promptly proclaimed a moratorium on all banking and called Congress into special session on March 9. By the time that session adjourned three months later, on June 15, 1933, the "first hundred days" of the New Deal had achieved an unprecedented legislative record. Eagerly receptive to the new president, the equally new Congress passed his emergency banking bill without taking the time to read it. Roosevelt signed the bill that night and went on the radio the following Sunday evening to give his first "fireside chat" to an audience estimated at 60 million people. He explained that only those banks the government had decided were stable and solvent could reopen and that, acting together, the people and the government could restore the financial system. The public responded overwhelmingly and unconditionally. Where Hoover's White House had averaged 600 letters a day, Roosevelt received 450,000 in his first week alone. A letter from a woman in Oklahoma assured him that "in your ten minute radio talk Sunday Night you said more than Mr. Hoover did in four years." The bank holiday served as a national catharsis. The banks reopened with no further runs on deposits, and the New Dealers breathed easier.[29]

Next on his legislative list was the Economy Act that cut federal salaries and veterans' benefits. The act fulfilled Roosevelt's campaign pledge to reduce government costs, but its effect was deflationary at the very moment when the economy needed inflating. The Economy Act displayed Roosevelt's ambiguity on fiscal policy. He had sided with his conservative budget chief, Lewis Douglas, but almost immediately afterward, he endorsed expanded federal spending for work relief through the Civilian Conservation Corps (CCC), sending unemployed youths from the city into rural areas to plant forests and prevent soil erosion, and the Federal Emergency Relief Act (FERA), which provided federal grants to local governments to run relief programs. His budget chief caught the drift and resigned. Roosevelt further shook orthodox economic thinking by taking the United States off the gold standard and allowing the dollar to float. Freed from the gold standard's constraints, the United States could pursue more expansionary monetary policies. The rise in the money supply lifted prices and began an economic revival.[30]

During the first hundred days, the president and Congress created such a profusion of new programs and agencies, usually known by triple-letter acronyms, that the press dubbed them an alphabet soup. For those who favored greater government planning, Roosevelt's programs included the Agricultural Adjustment Administration (AAA) to pay farmers to eliminate crop surpluses, thus raising prices; the Tennessee Valley Authority (TVA) for public power development; and the National Recovery Administration (NRA) to enable trade associations to set competitive codes on hours, wages, and prices and guarantee labor's right to bargain collectively. To reform the financial system, Roosevelt backed the Federal Securities Act, which required disclosure of accurate stock information to investors, and the Glass-Stegall Banking Act, which separated banks from stock brokerages and created federal deposit insurance for bank accounts. Unlike Hoover, Roosevelt encouraged legislators to take the initiative, and he regularly shared credit for their legislative proposals. His performance gained praise from all quarters, and some of those who had underrated him earlier had to eat their words. The Republican editor William Allen White was amazed at how quickly Roosevelt had "developed magnitude and poise, more than all, power!"[31]

The New Deal appealed widely to farmers and workers, producers and consumers, and the middle class and the unemployed, with their often conflicting needs. Roosevelt played the juggler, balancing one interest against another, just as he had handled his squabbling advisers during the campaign. As different groups vied for his attention, he rotated his focus between the planners, the reformers, and those promoting monetary policies to combat the Depression. His frustrated advisers could never be sure which policy direction he would choose, but those who tried to steer Roosevelt eventually grasped that he intended to be his own manager, in government as in politics. Rexford Tugwell recalled the president telling him to see someone, to prepare some data, or to make an inquiry without Tugwell always knowing what it was for: "Roosevelt regarded it as his own responsibility to put things together, and he never delegated it."[32]

Roosevelt's administrative style was reflected in his farm program. He asked for a plan to increase the value of farm products, noting that "if the darn thing doesn't work, we can say so quite frankly, but at least try." The agricultural economists he tapped recognized they were dealing with a capitalistic democratic system containing millions of farmers who were unaccustomed to following orders from the central government. The resulting Agricultural Adjustment Act authorized the Department of Agriculture to follow several different directions at the same time and let its various bureaus hammer out policy over production controls, price supports, and credit relief, in order to encourage farmers to reduce the acreage they planted and raise prices for their goods. Federal money enabled farmers to pay their debts and taxes and to spend more on consumer goods. Urban relief programs helped the unemployed to buy more food. Despite their imperfections, these programs kept thousands of farmers from bankruptcy and fed the hungry.[33]

To reform the stock markets, Roosevelt recruited some talented young lawyers who drafted a tough new law requiring corporate honesty in issuing stock. Corporate executives, expecting a Hoover-like trade association arrangement to emerge, were caught off guard by the Security Act's liability provisions, which held corporate directors responsible for misleading stock registrations and allowed investors to sue to recover their losses. The law put a damper on the issuance of new stock, however, making it harder for industry to raise funds for new operations and hiring. Hearing reports about a "strike" of capital against the securities law, Roosevelt authorized new regulatory legislation that created the Securities and Exchange Commission (SEC) as a watchdog over the financial markets, with the authority to issue rules and punish transgressors. SEC regulations turned the stock exchanges from private clubs into public institutions and restored investor confidence in the markets.[34]

The Depression persisted and Hoovervilles remained visible in many cities, yet Roosevelt managed to maintain a climate of hope. Joseph Alsop, who reported on Roosevelt for the *New York Herald Tribune*, believed that the president never gave the country time to lose faith in the New Deal. Rather than withdraw into the White House like his predecessor had done, Roosevelt remained out front, selling his programs to the public. Through his regular radio broadcasts, addressing his audiences as "my friends," he mobilized public support to keep Congress behind

Franklin Roosevelt delivers a fireside chat to a national radio audience in 1937. As president, Roosevelt made far more effective use of the media than did his predecessor.

him. The composer Alec Wilder found it fascinating that Roosevelt had such a highly cultured voice, one that people mocked; he imitated FDR's "my friends" but marveled that at the moment Roosevelt said it, "bang!—you were home." Roosevelt also dominated the headlines, even in newspapers that were editorially opposed to him, by carefully cultivating the Washington reporters. He did away with Hoover's requirement that reporters submit questions in advance and engaged in direct exchanges with them. His twice-weekly press conferences became genuine sources of news, and the working press rewarded him with generally favorable treatment of New Deal initiatives.[35]

Roosevelt doubled the size of Hoover's White House staff and further expanded the West Wing, adding a new and larger Oval Office. He retained Hoover's system of three secretaries, appointing Marvin McIntyre as appointments secretary, Steve Early as press secretary, and Louis Howe as political troubleshooter. All three had been loyal to him since his service in the Navy Department, and they still wore the FDR-engraved cuff links he had given them after his failed vice presidential campaign. The members of the brain trust found themselves excluded from the White House staff and "scattered ambiguously," as Rexford Tugwell put it, throughout various government agencies. Roosevelt resisted delegating presidential authority to his subordinates and acted as his own chief of staff, coordinating between the cabinet and agency heads, pitting conflicting advisers against each other by blurring responsibilities among them, and playing the umpire. He preferred dramatic actions, novel ideas, and the kind of advisers who thought of them. He attracted a cadre of "legal realists," a generation of young lawyers from some of the most prestigious law schools who had adopted a flexible approach to law and administration. They would provide creative solutions to the problems Roosevelt faced. At the same time, he concentrated on issues that he thought solvable and steered around those that seemed intractable, particularly avoiding fights over civil rights legislation. Despite the urging of his wife and African American leaders, he refrained from engaging the southern Democrats, who chaired most of the major congressional committees, on antilynching legislation they were sure to bottle up in committee or filibuster.[36]

Those in Hoover's inner circle had followed his urges and woven a cocoon around him; by contrast, Roosevelt opened himself to a wide circle of political associates, and the extended Roosevelt clan peppered him with different opinions. His personal secretary, Grace Tully, claimed that no previous president saw as many visitors or listened more carefully and fruitfully than did Roosevelt, "when he felt there was something and somebody worth listening to." The president spent hours absorbing information from an array of sources, but he was also deft at dodging their multiple problems. James M. Landis, who chaired the Securities and Exchange Commission, described a typical meeting with "the Skipper." Landis would sit in a crowded anteroom for an hour and a half past the time of his scheduled appointment. Ushered into the Oval Office, he would find Roosevelt seated at his desk, with his coat off. The president would wave him to take a seat, offer him a cigarette, and proceed to let him in on what his last guest had been saying. When the allotted time was up, the president would hold him for a few more minutes to find out what was on his mind. Roosevelt might not have helped at all, Landis recounted: "He might have just thrown the problem back at you. But you went out of there as if you were walking on air. The feeling of joviality that he gave you, the stimulation . . . then you'd go back and solve the damn problem yourself."[37]

Roosevelt's thinking tended to take on the coloration of those closest to him at the moment. Because he relished unconventional approaches, his staff sometimes worried that he might be too amenable to dubious ideas, but he exhibited a good sense of what might work and what was inadvisable. Roosevelt was more than open-minded, the British writer H. G. Wells recorded after spending an evening with him. "My impression of both him and Mrs. Roosevelt is that they are *unlimited* people, entirely modern in the openness of their minds and the logic of their actions." The president combined a receptivity to new ideas with a capability for implementing them. However, some of his associates failed to realize that he nodded his head to signal he heard them, not necessarily that he agreed with them. Thomas Eliot, as a young member of Congress, attended a White House dinner party where he heard Secretary of the Navy Frank Knox propose an abominably misguided plan. "That's an idea, Frank, that's an idea," President Roosevelt responded ambiguously, to which Eleanor Roosevelt added: "It's a *terrible* idea."[38]

Eleanor Roosevelt's rectitude balanced her husband's compromising tendencies. She broke all conventions as First Lady. Traveling almost constantly, observing, lecturing, and meeting with various groups, she served as an extension of her disabled husband, making sure that people's concerns got back to him. Secretary of Labor Frances Perkins observed that much of what Eleanor learned about the life of average citizens during the Depression rubbed off on Franklin: "Her mere reporting of the facts was full of a sensitive quality that could never be escaped." Nor could the public escape her radio broadcasts or newspaper column, "My Day." She was the first president's wife to hold press conferences, limiting attendance to women reporters only, a practice that forced Washington news bureaus to hire more females. She advocated the inclusion of women and minorities in government programs. She drew national attention to racial injustices. Her appeals for her husband to do things he considered politically unfeasible raised his blood pressure, but her frequent absences left him lonely. "He might have been happier with a wife who was completely uncritical," she later reflected. "That I was never able to be, and he had to find it in other people."[39]

The New Deal offered citizens greater protection from financial insecurity, yet it never went as far as progressives and radicals had wished. Despite Roosevelt's fiscally conservative campaign pledges, they held out the hope that he would turn out as radical as Hoover had predicted. Some reformers felt that the bank crisis had so damaged American finances that the government should have nationalized the entire banking and credit system. Others regretted that Roosevelt did not impose a greater degree of centralized planning on the economy. Instead of overturning the market system, he intended to save it from its worst excesses. His administration also helped usher in a modern, pluralistic nation. Urban ethnic groups provided much of the voting base of the New Deal coalition, and some of their members played pivotal roles in the administration. As president, Roosevelt appointed fifty-nine Catholic and Jewish federal judges, compared with the sixteen appointed by his three predecessors combined. The journalist Joseph Alsop, a scion of the old white Anglo-Saxon Protestant establishment, rated Roosevelt's real achievement not in the number of agencies he created or programs he launched but in the fact that he "included the excluded." The New Deal shook the social as well as the economic system, and the anxiety of those who felt threatened by the changes accounted for much of the fury directed against Roosevelt as a "traitor to his class." (The New Deal's higher taxes on the wealthy contributed to their ire.)[40]

Having gone abroad in 1933, the writer Matthew Josephson was astonished at the changed political landscape on his return the next year. The Washington he knew during the Hoover administration had seemed a

provincial town filled with courthouse politicians smoking cigars in hotel lobbies. On his return, he found the capital crowded with "a bustling
sort of people," young academics, lawyers, social workers, and others
humming with excited talk about new ideas the administration was going to try. The entire government had adopted Roosevelt's exuberance.
One night during the first hundred days, a group of reporters hovered
outside the White House waiting for a conference to break up. When it
started to rain, a presidential aide invited them to stand under the White
House portico. Before long, they organized a quartet and were singing to
pass the time away. One of them exclaimed, "Imagine doing this in the
Hoover administration!"[41]

RATIFYING THE NEW DEAL

As the congressional elections approached in 1934, Herbert Hoover
felt frustrated that congressional Republicans had neither countered the
New Deal nor defended his administration from political slurs. Fifty-
eight years old at the time of his defeat, Hoover felt young enough to
make a political comeback. He took up residence in Palo Alto and left the
loyal Lawrence Richey in Washington to keep him informed of political
developments. Walter Newton worked on an official history of Hoover's
presidency as the first step toward his public rehabilitation. The former
president planned to keep silent for a year and then raise hell, by writing and giving speeches as he pleased. Being an ex-president gave him
drawing power, he said, "and I'm going to make use of it. I'm going to
get into the thick of things." He regarded the New Deal as a dangerous
gamble with the nation's future, insisting that its effects had proven all
of his campaign warnings accurate.[42]

Congressional Republicans, reduced to a tiny minority, remained divided and unable to find common ground on which their conservative
and progressive wings could unite. The progressives mostly voted with
the New Deal, and the conservatives were too demoralized to register
much opposition. The RNC deepened the schism when it urged its congressional candidates to turn the campaign into an assault on the New
Deal. Rhode Island Republican senator Felix Hébert explained to Hoover
that "politically, we here in this part of the country feel it is not wise to
attack the Chief Executive." Some Republicans admired what Roosevelt
was trying to do and felt it unpatriotic to oppose his efforts to lead the
nation out of the Depression.[43]

Hoover broke his silence in September 1934 with the publication of *The Challenge to Liberty*, a book that articulated his thesis that Roosevelt's election had dashed the economic recovery under way during his administration and that the New Deal posed the danger of totalitarianism, since government could not intrude itself into daily life without "making it the master of people's souls and thoughts." Hoover received a respectful hearing, although conservative allies such as Robert Taft regarded his interpretation as "extreme" and friendly reviewers such as Arthur Krock called the book a brooding tome. On the eve of the congressional elections, Hoover released a public letter urging voters to support the Republican opposition in Congress "if our institutions are to survive." Delighted to have the former president resurface, Democrats used him to remind voters of the bad old days. The Republican congressional campaign committees considered him a liability.[44]

Nearly always, the opposition party increases its ranks during a midterm congressional election. In 1934, political observers gave the Democrats a chance of gaining seats in the Senate—where the Republicans who had swept in with Hoover six years earlier were up for reelection—but predicted they would lose as many as fifty seats in the House. Speaker Henry T. Rainey advised House Democrats from marginal districts that their best hope for reelection was to "preach the Roosevelt philosophy and stand behind the President." They did, and the election confounded the pundits' expectations. Democrats gained ten seats in the Senate and eleven in the House, giving them two-thirds of the membership of both bodies. Reliably Republican Pennsylvania, one of the half-dozen states Hoover had carried, defeated Republican old guard senator David A. Reed. Indiana pitched out its anti–New Deal senator Arthur Robinson. Ohio dismissed Senator Simeon D. Fess, Hoover's RNC chairman. Missouri voters ousted incumbent Republican senator Roscoe Patterson in favor of a little-known Kansas City functionary, Harry Truman. The sole African American representative, the Chicago Republican Oscar De Priest, lost to a black Democrat, Arthur Mitchell. Democrats who sided with the president triumphed, whereas those whom the president kept at arm's length went down to defeat, from the radical gubernatorial candidate Upton Sinclair in California to the conservative governor Albert Ritchie in Maryland. Marylanders split their vote, ousting Ritchie while electing to the Senate a New Deal Democrat, George Radcliffe, who defeated Joseph France, Hoover's sole opponent at the Republican convention. France knew what had hit him and issued a brief statement that "the President has won."[45]

After 1934, the New Dealers stepped farther to the left. Some said, "Do nothing," and others said, "Do everything," as Roosevelt told a Young Democrats gathering. "I say to you: 'Do something,' and when you have done something, if it works, do it more; and if it does not work, then do something else." In 1935, the Supreme Court declared the NRA and parts of the AAA unconstitutional, forcing Roosevelt to try something else. Populist critics opened fire at the New Deal. Louisiana senator Huey Long promoted an income-redistribution plan to "share our wealth" by taxing the wealthy and making "every man a king." The radio priest Father Charles Coughlin advocated a guaranteed annual wage, and Francis Townsend crusaded for old-age pensions. All three threatened to join their forces in a third party to block Roosevelt's reelection. The president responded with a second barrage of New Deal legislation that created the Works Progress Administration (WPA), a huge and creative unemployment relief program; supported labor's right to organize; levied higher taxes on the wealthy; and established the Social Security system to provide old-age pensions, unemployment compensation, and aid to the disabled and to dependent children. The Second New Deal's social insurance provisions, creating a vast safety net for those who could not support themselves, became the signal accomplishment of Roosevelt's presidency.[46]

Such legislative bursts inspired New Dealers to talk about a "Roosevelt revolution," but Europeans described what was happening more realistically as a "Roosevelt experiment." Political leaders in Britain and France, virtually paralyzed over their inability to find a middle way between state socialism and laissez-faire capitalism, carefully watched FDR's efforts to rein in, regulate, and reform the capitalist system without overturning it. When the Socialist premier of France, Léon Blum, introduced his own reform programs in 1936, he compared them to the New Deal. "What has been most remarkable about the Roosevelt experiment," Blum commented, "has been the courage of President Roosevelt to try one method after another, to refuse to take a stubborn stand against experience, to try something else until he at last he found the method that succeeded." The Europeans admired the U.S. president for his immense curiosity and pragmatic temperament rather than for a constant philosophy.[47]

Roosevelt's policy shifts served his political needs as well. Registered Republicans still outnumbered Democrats by about 2 million. As he prepared to run for reelection in 1936, Roosevelt sought to attract lower-income men and women in the North and West who until then had been indifferent to both parties, considering the Republican party beholden to big business and the Democrats dominated by the conservative South. The social and economic reforms of the Second New Deal, aimed at helping the working class, marked a change in Roosevelt's focus from the largely agrarian strategy he had employed in 1932, when he campaigned hardest in the South and West (which Louis Howe had advocated), to making peace with the Democratic organizations in the larger cities, including New York's Tammany Hall. Howe's death in 1936 coincided with Roosevelt's urban liberal political shift.[48]

Roosevelt rebuilt his party, abolishing the Democratic convention's two-thirds rule and forging a coalition of populist agrarians, progressives, urban poor, northern blacks, and southern whites, all of whom were united by economic discontent and the demand for social welfare reform. New Deal liberalism included economic security for citizens of all classes and a tolerance for ethnic and cultural variety. The enemies that Roosevelt made further strengthened his coalition. Having pre-empted the assault from the Left, Roosevelt became the target of the Right. The country's wealthiest citizens came to hate "that Man," unable even to utter his name. "It is a passion, a fury, that is wholly unreasoning," wrote the journalist Marquis Childs in 1936. If Charley Michelson had harassed Hoover, Roosevelt's opponents escalated the propaganda war to new heights, as exemplified by a Republican National Committee pamphlet, entitled *Tories, Chiselers, Dead Cats, Witch Doctors, Bank Wreckers, Traitors,* that rebuked every aspect of Roosevelt's recovery efforts. Such stridency embarrassed congressional Republicans running for reelection, prompting many of them to distance their campaigns from the national committee. Angry assaults also came from the media baron William Randolph Hearst, who regretted having helped Roosevelt win the Democratic nomination. Higher taxes and expanded government regulation caused Hearst to insist that all of his newspapers refer only to the "Raw Deal." More virulent opposition came from homegrown fascist organizations such as William Dudley Pelley's Silver Shirts, which denounced the prominence of Roosevelt's Jewish advisers as the "Jew Deal."[49]

With Republicans in disarray, conservative opposition to the New Deal emerged from the Democratic Party's right wing. In 1934, John J. Raskob and Jouett Shouse formed the American Liberty League as a bipartisan, probusiness, antiadministration lobby. Al Smith, Newton Baker, and other Democratic exiles joined the Liberty League, feeling that the Roosevelt administration had abandoned the party's 1932 platform and was promoting class warfare against the rich. Roosevelt could not understand why Al Smith turned on him, since the New Deal, to his thinking, represented a national expansion of many things Smith had begun as governor, and he never lost his own affection for Smith. Herbert Hoover refused to join the Liberty League, recalling how much grief these Democrats had given him as president, and he commented that if they had not spent so much effort attacking him, "the country would not be writhing in this situation." Flush with financial contributions, the Liberty League wielded a bigger staff than the Republican National Committee, and it outspent it on anti–New Deal publicity. The public perceived the league as an affluent and upper-class organization—at one Liberty League dinner in Washington, a woman in a wine red evening dress, ermine muff, and sparkling diamonds approached the press table to assure the reporters, "Boys, I hate the New Deal as much as you do and I came all the way down from Philly to say so!" The league's vitriolic opposition only strengthened support for Roosevelt among the poor and the middle class. The president told his audiences that during his first administration, "the forces of selfishness" had met their match: "I should like to have it said of my second Administration that in it these forces met their master." The Liberty League later disbanded, in 1940, after it proved helpless to prevent Roosevelt's reelection.[50]

Herbert Hoover implicitly reminded Republicans of his availability for their presidential nomination in 1936. His former White House staff interpreted reports of audiences applauding Hoover at movie newsreels as a sign of the restoration of his public standing. But party leaders considered him the last man the Republicans should nominate, and the RNC declined to reprint his speeches. Hoover could not comprehend that his carping might assist Roosevelt's reelection by reminding the voters why they had chosen him the first time around. In the 1936 election, Hoover's former secretary, Walter Newton, ran again for his old House seat from Minnesota and received warnings from party pros not to mention his connections with Hoover in his campaign literature. Newton remained loyal to "the Chief," however, and went down to defeat in November.[51]

Republican leaders calculated that Roosevelt had won in 1932 because Hoover had split the Republican vote, and they counted on the return of the dissidents to the fold in 1936. "Literally millions of Republicans, mad with Mr. Hoover about prohibition, sore about the Depression and bad times, voted the Democratic ticket," wrote the conservative columnist Frank Kent. As a result, Hoover was unattractive to his party, in spite of his relentless efforts to articulate Republican policies. Disappointing poll results finally convinced the former president to announce that he would not be a candidate for the nomination. Addressing the convention, Hoover accused the New Deal of "the poisoning of Americanism," calling on Republicans to lead the country back to genuine recovery and stability. "Stop the retreat," he implored. Kansas governor Alf Landon won the nomination, keeping Hoover at a distance for most of the campaign. Although Landon called Social Security "a cruel hoax," he was less critical of the New Deal than Hoover wanted him to be. The former president regarded Landon's campaign as a "me-too-but-cheaper" version of the New Deal.[52]

Many signs seemed to point to Roosevelt's defeat in 1936. Maine went Republican in September, and throughout the fall, the *Literary Digest* showed Landon heading for a landslide victory. The magazine had sent thousands of postcard ballots to people selected from telephone directories and car registrations, without attempting to determine their economic status. The possession of cars and telephones during the Depression skewered the results in favor of the views of the better-off citizens. The *Digest* had employed the same polling methods in 1932, when it accurately predicted the outcome, indicating that in his first race, Roosevelt had drawn votes from all classes in roughly the same proportion. By 1936, his support among the wealthy fell off, and his popularity surged among those whom the *Literary Digest* editors called the "lower strata." Roosevelt's victory crushed the credibility of the *Digest*'s polls, driving the magazine out of business. Democrats had hired their own pollsters, who used more-scientific sampling and kept Roosevelt well informed of the shifts in public opinion. Although the Republicans did not nominate Hoover, Roosevelt ran against his former rival anyway. He also counted on his opponents to fall back on the "good old Republican tradition" of decrying government spending—not a popular tactic when federal funds were being used to feed, clothe, house, and employ millions of people. Attacking deficit spending pleased the Republicans' big contributors but did the party little good on election day.[53]

Defying Republican predictions, voters in 1936 swept Roosevelt into a second term and ratified the New Deal. The Roosevelt-Garner ticket took 60.8 percent of the vote and 523 electoral votes. Only Maine and Vermont gave majorities to Landon, causing Jim Farley to jest, "As Maine goes, so goes Vermont." More people turned out to vote—56.9 percent of the eligible voters, compared to 52.5 percent in 1932—and they boosted the Democrats' control of Congress to a historical high: in the 75th Congress, Democrats would hold 76 Senate seats to the Republicans' 16, and in the House, their margin was 334 to 88. A few Progressives and Farmer-Laborites added to the mix, mostly voting with the Democrats. The most dramatic voting shift took place among African Americans. In 1932, three out of every four black voters had cast their ballots for Hoover; in 1936, three out of every four went with Roosevelt. The New Deal had done little to advance racial integration, and southern Democrats had managed to exclude many African Americans from federal benefits (household domestics and farm laborers were left out of Social Security, for instance), but some federal relief programs reached into black communities. Furthermore, Roosevelt appointed some prominent African Americans to government positions, notably Mary McLeod Bethune, Roosevelt's special adviser on minority affairs; Robert C. Weaver, special assistant with the Housing Authority; and William H. Hastie, the first African American federal judge. They formed an unofficial "black cabinet" of top-ranked appointees within the administration who promoted civil rights.

Philadelphia provided a striking study of the New Deal's political dynamics. The City of Brotherly Love had been a Republican stronghold that gave 78 percent of its vote to Coolidge in 1924. Four years later, Al Smith enticed many new voters to the polls, especially Catholics, but still took only 40 percent of the city's vote. Without Smith on the ticket, the Democratic vote in Philadelphia slipped again during the 1930 congressional elections. In 1932, Franklin Roosevelt received 43 percent of the Philadelphia vote, better than Smith but the smallest percentage of the vote Roosevelt won in any major city. With a third of the city's workforce unemployed that year, the voter turnout in the poorest neighborhoods had been low. But after that, in 1936, Democrats won the local elections in Philadelphia, and Roosevelt carried the city with a smashing 60 percent of the vote.[54]

For the radical third parties, the 1936 elections proved just as disappointing as for the Republicans. The assassination of Senator Huey Long, who had toyed with running for president, sent the remnants of his following into the Union Party, whose colorless candidate, North Dakota representative William Lemke, ran an inconsequential campaign. The Socialist Party split apart, with most of its affiliated trade unions endorsing Roosevelt's reelection. The president had enacted many of their immediate issues, from unemployment insurance to old-age pensions, laying the groundwork for the welfare state, although he opposed their long-term goals for nationalization of finance and industry. Despite the desertion of his labor comrades, Socialist Party leader Norman Thomas was not interested in the Communist Party's suggestion that instead of fielding presidential candidates in 1936, both parties should get behind a labor party that would be sympathetic to Roosevelt. Thomas scoffed when commentators credited Roosevelt with carrying out the Socialist platform, "unless he carried it out on a stretcher." The New Deal was not socialism, Thomas insisted, just a form of state capitalism that kept the same old economic system in place, but he remained a voice crying in the political wilderness. The Socialists' vote fell off by three-quarters from four years earlier. Roosevelt had been elected in 1932 because "he was *not* Mr. Hoover," Thomas concluded. "In later campaigns he was elected because he *was* Mr. Roosevelt."[55]

Paradoxically, the Communist vote dropped despite the party's growth in membership during the Depression. Communist leaders now disdained elections as a diversion from the struggle of the masses. Regarding Republicans and Democrats as identical and liberals as anathema, the Communists at first viewed Roosevelt as trying to "sneak past a social catastrophe" to bolster capitalism. Then, in 1935, the Comintern (the Communist International) dictated a switch in policy. The U.S. party abandoned its call for a "Soviet America" and forged a Popular Front with liberals, finding common ground on such issues as labor organizing and civil rights—while at the same time, an underground wing of the party infiltrated various government agencies. "Overnight we adjusted our evaluation of Roosevelt and the New Deal," recalled George Charney, who joined the Communist Party in 1933, adding that the more positive attitude "reflected what many of us believed but could not articulate." In 1936, the Communists debated endorsing Roosevelt but decided that would do him more harm than good. Instead, the party dropped William Z. Foster as their candidate in favor of Earl Browder, who conducted a less aggressive campaign that received only 80,171 votes. Meanwhile, mounting fear and outrage over fascism in Germany and Italy swelled membership in the U.S. party, until the Soviet Union abruptly reversed itself and signed a nonaggression agreement with Nazi Germany in

1939. The shock of the Hitler-Stalin pact disillusioned thousands of American Communists and fellow travelers and wrecked the Popular Front. Those such as George Charney who stuck with the party once again "turned on FDR, the New Deal, and even Mrs. Roosevelt."[56]

Roosevelt owed his reelection to a prevailing sense that prosperity was at long last returning. General Robert E. Wood, head of Sears, Roebuck and later a bitter foe of the New Deal, admitted that he had voted for FDR in 1932 because he "couldn't help liking him." Wood observed that the economy had begun to pick up in 1934 and was going strong by 1936. But after the election, a severe recession wiped out most of the earlier gains. Eliot Janeway, a journalist and avid New Dealer, called the recession a "resumption of the Hoover Depression under New Deal auspices." Assuming that the Depression was over, Roosevelt and Treasury Secretary Henry Morgenthau had reverted to economic orthodoxy, reducing federal spending to balance the budget. These cuts occurred at the same time that the first Social Security payroll deductions were reducing consumers' discretionary income. The Federal Reserve Board made matters worse by tightening credit to dampen inflation. This combination of deflationary practices caused the economic relapse. The British economist John Maynard Keynes, having just published his *General Theory of Unemployment, Interest, and Money*, urged Roosevelt to pursue large-scale deficit spending to stimulate business investment. The president abandoned budget balancing and asked Congress for more funding of unemployment relief. But his efforts were not enough to keep Republicans from making significant gains in Congress in 1938, for the first time in a decade, although they were still far from regaining the majority. The New Deal's priming of the pump did not bring the Depression to a close. Federal spending had almost doubled by the end of Roosevelt's second term, and federal relief sustained the unemployed. By 1940, industrial output had returned to 1929 levels—with real wages 44 percent higher than before—but the labor force had grown by 6.5 million over the decade, an increase equivalent to 80 percent of those still out of work. It took the massive defense spending during World War II to eliminate substantial unemployment.[57]

Politically as well as economically, Roosevelt suffered significant reversals in his second term. In 1937, Congress balked at his plan to expand the size of the Supreme Court. The nine justices had struck down key New Deal agencies, leaving the fate of Social Security and other programs uncertain. Roosevelt had no opportunity to affect the ideological composition of the court through new appointments during his first term. Flush with political capital from his landslide reelection, he announced a plan to expand the size of the Supreme Court by adding a new justice for each one over seventy (there were six at the time), supposedly to reduce their burden of work. His opponents denounced this as an attempt to pack the Supreme Court. The tiny Republican minority in the Senate shrewdly stayed silent and let the Democrats fight among themselves, splitting the majority party in two. (It took considerable effort for Senate Republicans to persuade Herbert Hoover to stay out of this debate.) A bitterly divided Senate then killed Roosevelt's court plan. As the elderly justices retired, FDR ultimately won the judicial war, getting the rare opportunity to name all but one member of the Supreme Court—but at the cost of losing control of the legislative branch. In their opposition to court packing, conservative Democrats and Republicans forged an alliance that stymied further liberal legislative initiatives. Some progressives also grew wary of Roosevelt's concentration of power in the executive branch. People who had once urged the president to assume the powers of a dictator to meet the economic crisis now began accusing him of behaving like one. Roosevelt further failed, in 1938, in an attempt to purge the Democratic Party of its more reactionary members, primarily from the South. Insisting that all Democratic candidates should stand for the party's common principles, he discovered that his personal popularity did not transfer to the liberal primary challengers he endorsed. Most of the targeted conservatives won renomination and reelection. At the same time, his administration's effort to enforce antitrust laws more vigorously deepened the business community's resistance to its programs. All combined, these setbacks suggested that the New Deal's last card had been dealt.[58]

MUSTERING FOR WAR

Franklin Roosevelt had rarely referred to foreign policy while campaigning in 1932 or in 1936, but after his second-term triumph, international issues increasingly preoccupied him, from the rise of Japanese militarism in Asia to the rearming of Nazi Germany, Fascist Italy's invasion of Ethiopia, and the Spanish civil war. Although public sentiment in the United States favored isolation, Roosevelt felt that unchecked aggression would eventually pose a danger to American security. He began inching back toward the internationalism he had renounced during his first presidential campaign. Effective foreign policy required building a national consensus, and during his second term, he used the dramatically unfolding events abroad to educate a divided nation, balancing Americans' desire to stay out of another European war against their sympathy for the European democracies.[59]

Herbert Hoover saw the New Deal as a greater threat to American democracy than either the Nazis or the Japanese militarists. In 1938, he traveled to Europe and met with German chancellor Adolf Hitler, whom he judged "partly insane" but better informed than he had expected. Returning to the United States, Hoover went on national radio to warn Americans that in case war broke out in Europe, they must not become involved. "If the world is to keep peace," he advised, "then we must keep peace with dictatorships as well as with democratic governments." He blamed President Roosevelt for exacerbating the situation in Europe by encouraging the democracies to think that the United States would support them. When Germany invaded Poland, pulling Britain and France into the conflict, Hoover called it a senseless war and reiterated that the United States should remain neutral.

Roosevelt fundamentally believed that the United States could not allow Germany to defeat Britain and France. He reached out to Republican internationalists to build a united front on military policy. Hoover's secretary of state, Henry Stimson, joined Roosevelt's cabinet as secretary of war, and Landon's running mate, Frank Knox, became secretary of the navy. Roosevelt also dispatched intermediaries to sound out Hoover about taking charge of relief efforts in Europe. If the former president had indicated he would accept the job, Roosevelt would have met with him to talk it over. But Hoover declined, both because of the indirect way the post was offered and because he still harbored presidential hopes. Eleanor Roosevelt regretted that Hoover "felt a little hurt that Franklin had not talked to him himself. I think he has a right to feel that way because I think Franklin should have talked to him, but many of the men around Franklin felt it was wiser to sound Mr. Hoover out first." (Unlike their husbands, who had not seen each other since 1933, Eleanor Roosevelt and Lou Hoover had met on friendly terms over the years at Girl Scout conventions.) When reporters questioned why Hoover had not been enlisted to help with war relief, Roosevelt's press secretary explained that the administration had made overtures but "nothing came of the effort, it appears that Mr. Hoover did not accept the offer." A White House butler overheard an exasperated Roosevelt telling yet another visitor who had urged him to find a job for Herbert Hoover, "Well, I'm not a Jesus Christ. I'm not going to raise him from the dead."[60]

As 1940 approached, Roosevelt remained coy about seeking a third term. To lessen opposition to breaking the two-term tradition, he wanted the party to draft him. Keeping his intentions to himself, he encouraged a number of other Democrats to enter the crowded field. The one who concerned him the most was Vice President Garner, who led in the public opinion polls. John Nance Garner had been an effective presiding officer in the Senate, and he retained influence in the House. The New Deal had disenchanted him as it moved to the left, and he objected to its spending, taxation, and relief policies. "He seems to be pretty much against everything," Roosevelt commented, "and he hasn't got a single concrete idea to offer on any of these programs." The seventy-one-year-old Garner lost weight, stopped drinking, and bought expensive suits before he formally announced his candidacy for president on December 16, 1939. By allowing his own name to appear in party primaries, Roosevelt set up a direct contest between the president and vice president. On April 9, 1940, the day that Germany invaded Denmark and Norway, Roosevelt defeated Garner by an eight-to-one margin in the Illinois primary, dashing his presidential hopes.[61]

Garner always regretted giving up the House Speakership for the vice presidency, which he regarded as "the spare tire on the automobile of government." He left office without regret and retired to Uvalde, Texas. Interviewed in 1957, he commented wistfully that if he had not run for vice president, he "might still be Speaker today." To replace him on the Democratic ticket, Roosevelt selected his secretary of agriculture, Henry Wallace, originally a progressive Republican, and imposed him on the Democratic convention, once again held at the Chicago Stadium. By then totally loyal to Roosevelt, the city's Democratic machine orchestrated a "spontaneous" demonstration for him, led by the booming voice of Tom Garry, Chicago's superintendent of sewers. Operating unseen from a booth in the basement, Garry chanted for forty-five minutes over the stadium's loudspeakers: "We want Roosevelt!" "The party wants Roosevelt!" "The world needs Roosevelt!" "Roosevelt! Roosevelt! Roosevelt." On the stadium organ, Al Melgard accompanied him with "Happy Days Are Here Again." The energized delegates paraded through the hall and the following day nominated the president for a third term.[62]

On the Republican side, Herbert Hoover estimated that Roosevelt had staked his third-term chances on an Allied victory, which German military advances were rapidly making unlikely. Rumors spread about a Hoover-Lindbergh isolation ticket, but Hoover did not consider himself an isolationist. He wanted to spare his country from another European war and envisioned campaigning as someone who could deal with Germany diplomatically rather than militarily. Like Roosevelt, Hoover encouraged as many potential candidates as possible to stay in the race for the presidential nomination, trusting that he would stand tall over the pack and emerge as a consensus candidate. His staff conducted some dubious polls in which Hoover detected "a very extraordinary turn in the tide" in his favor, believing that a lack of foreign policy expertise would diminish the chances of other Republican prospects. The independent Gallup Polls shattered his illusions by revealing that only 2 percent of Republicans favored the former president's nomination.[63]

Hoover's last hope was to rouse and challenge the delegates at the 1940 convention. To this end, he delivered the fieriest speech of his career, but his habitual unease with large audiences undermined his efforts. Because he did not speak directly into the microphone, most of the crowd could not hear his fighting speech about saving the United States from "totalitarian liberals." Delegates shouted for him to speak louder, and the convention manager walked onto the stage to put the microphone directly in his hand. Afterward, Hoover and Larry Richey felt sure that his opponents had sabotaged him, but his performance was just another self-inflicted wound. Hoover was not the front-runner in any event, and the delegates stampeded to a dark-horse candidate, power company executive Wendell Willkie—who as a Democrat had worked for Newton Baker's nomination in 1932.[64]

Willkie conducted an energetic campaign, but the grim news from Europe and gratitude for the sitting president's past leadership made voters turn back to Roosevelt for security. The president won his third term with 54.8 percent of the vote. With the nation still divided between isolationists and internationalists, Roosevelt pledged not to send American troops to fight overseas unless the nation was attacked. At the same time, he was constructing an alliance with British prime minister Winston Churchill to bolster England against the German assault. His efforts alienated the implacably isolationist Republicans in Congress, both conservatives and progressives, but helped reunite Roosevelt with some of the southern Democrats who remained Wilsonian internationalists. He proceeded cautiously, seeking to amend or repeal neutrality legislation that limited the ability of the United States to resist aggressor nations, once commenting that it was a terrible thing "to look over your shoulder when you're trying to lead, and find no one there." Roosevelt's initiatives, from Lend-Lease measures to destroyers-for-bases programs, aided Great Britain and the Allies and stretched American neutrality to a point just short of war. In a fireside address on December 1940, he described the "undeniable threat" to the nation and sought to convince his listeners that it was in their strategic interests to increase defense production and become "the great arsenal of democracy."[65]

Not buying Roosevelt's arguments, Hoover went back on the radio after Germany invaded the Soviet Union in June 1941 and predicted that a fratricidal war between Hitler and Stalin would weaken both dictators. He recommended that the United States hold on to its aid for the postwar reconstruction of Europe, after the dictators had eliminated each other. Hoover charged Roosevelt with violating the spirit of the Neutrality Act by allowing American merchant ships to supply the Allies. But polls showed that the public had turned a deaf ear to the former president. According to one poll, 70 percent of Americans believed it was more important to defeat Hitler than to avoid war. In any case, on December 7, 1941, the Japanese rendered Hoover's arguments moot. After Pearl Harbor, he volunteered to serve the government in any useful capacity, but he heard nothing back. Roosevelt "frigidly declined any association with me," Hoover later recalled, reasoning that his speeches against the president's foreign policy "were probably hard for him to bear."[66]

Once the nation entered the war, Roosevelt signaled that the New Deal was over. He abandoned his antitrust efforts and mustered the business community for war production. At a press conference, he described the New Deal as having come into existence to treat "an awfully sick patient" suffering from a grave internal disorder. The doctor had prescribed remedies, and "a long, long process" of recuperation followed, but then the patient suffered a bad accident. "Old Doctor New Deal" knew about internal medicine but not about surgery, so he brought in an orthopedic surgeon, "Dr. Win-the-War," to put the patient back on his feet. Now that defense work and conscription had wiped out unemployment, Congress disbanded the WPA, the CCC, and other job-creating agencies. Still, Roosevelt suggested that reform would return once the war had been won. In 1944, he proposed an economic bill of rights that guaranteed Americans useful jobs, decent homes, good educations, adequate health care, and "freedom from want." His wartime administration sponsored the National Housing Agency to find housing for war workers, the Fair Employment Practices Committee to end racial discrimination in the defense industries, and the GI Bill of Rights to enable returning veterans to continue their educations and obtain low-cost home mortgages (and avoid a repeat of the World War I bonus fiasco). He insisted that he remained a little to the left of center. When a reporter asked if was not typical for someone his age to grow more conservative, he retorted, "You must be older than I am!"[67]

The alliance of government and business during World War II promoted the concept of a continually expanding national economy in which producers, labor, and consumers would all share in the economic growth. Business leaders discovered in the liberal Roosevelt an unexpected "master of production," who oversaw a massive military production effort, leading a nearly ruined economy back into full industrial capacity. The political Left regarded this development suspiciously, noting that capitalists "saw a great light" during the war and abandoned their old economic pieties about public thrift in favor of greater federal spending. Having long feared a powerful national government, industrialists now embraced the federal government as a lucrative customer. Widely praised for their part in producing war matériel, business leaders emerged from the war with their stature and their ties to the government enhanced.[68]

The British parliamentary system delayed general elections until after the war, but the American electoral process went ahead like clockwork in 1944. Roosevelt stood as the Democratic presidential candidate for a fourth time. Once again holding their convention at the Chicago Stadium, Democrats took the precaution of dropping Vice President Henry Wallace, whose eccentricities had antagonized too many congressional leaders. With seeming indifference, Roosevelt accepted the party's choice of Missouri senator Harry Truman as his running mate. "Go 4th to Win War" read their campaign buttons. Before the election, Roosevelt's doctors had diagnosed him with serious, life-threatening hypertension, yet they never informed him of the actual nature of his illness, and he never asked. It seemed essential to everyone around him that the commander in chief remain in office for the duration of the war. Just as his aides had disguised his polio, they cloaked his heart disease in 1944. Still, Roosevelt managed to outlive nearly all of his original rivals. Melvin Traylor died in 1934, Albert Ritchie in 1936, Newton Baker in 1937, William G.

McAdoo in 1941, and Al Smith in 1944; only John Nance Garner and Herbert Hoover would survive him. By his last race, Roosevelt had also separated from many of those who had made his election possible in 1932. The long list of New Deal defectors included William Randolph Hearst, John Nance Garner, Jim Farley, Raymond Moley, and others who broke with the president after he stopped taking their advice. Other talented advisers—including Thomas G. Corcoran, Harry Hopkins, and James F. Byrnes—took their places. Regardless of the changing cast, Roosevelt kept winning elections.

The majority of voters in 1944 regarded FDR as the leader who had guided them out of the Depression and was now leading them to victory in the war. His forty-two-year-old Republican challenger, the liberal New York governor Thomas E. Dewey, seemed too young and untested for wartime leadership. At seventy, Herbert Hoover no longer envisioned a political comeback, and he wearily told the 1944 convention that the people had not believed him each time he warned them about the impairment of their freedom; he claimed that the only flaw in those warnings was that they were too cautious. Yet when Dewey privately contended that Hoover "would have signed practically all the legislation that F.D.R. signed," the former president reflected for a minute and agreed, stating, "I think I would have."[69]

Roosevelt used the war as an excuse for not campaigning extensively in 1944. When his absence from the stump fanned rumors about his health, he demonstrated his vitality by riding in an open car through the boroughs of New York for four hours during a bitterly cold rainstorm. He also deftly regained his standing in his nationally broadcast "Fala speech" to the Teamsters Union. He accused the Republicans of attacking not only himself and his family but also his little Scotch terrier, Fala, who had "not been the same dog since." He could accept criticism about himself, he said, "but I think I have a right to object to libelous statements about my dog." More seriously, he pointed out that his administration had generated the greatest war machine the world had ever seen and was busily laying the foundation for peace. In the last speech of his last campaign, he defined victory as not simply defeating the Axis but also vanquishing poverty, disease, ignorance, and intolerance. "At the end of this war," he pledged, "this country will have the greatest material power of any nation in the world." Roosevelt won his last contest with 54 percent of the vote, and the Democrats retained majorities in Congress, although with reduced ranks.

Following an abbreviated inauguration on January 20, 1945, at the White House, Roosevelt traveled seven thousand miles to Yalta to negotiate with Stalin and Churchill over common methods of winning the war and establishing the peace. On his return, he appeared before a joint session of Congress to report on his trip, and he apologized for speaking while seated because "it makes it a lot easier for me not having to carry about ten pounds of steel around the bottom of my legs"—a rare public reference to his disability. Planning a trip to San Francisco to address the conference that would adopt the United Nations Charter, he went first to Warm Springs to rest. In a syndicated newspaper column on April 7, his longtime critic Walter Lippmann paid tribute to Roosevelt as a remarkable strategist in the military and diplomatic aspects of a global war. Despite his past disagreements with the president, Lippmann judged that FDR's estimate of the nation's vital interests had been accurate and farsighted. "He has served these interests with audacity and patience, shrewdly and with calculation," wrote the columnist, "and he has led this country out of the greatest peril in which it has ever been to the highest point of security, influence, and respect which it has ever attained." Five days later, on April 12, 1945, Roosevelt died at Warm Springs after suffering a cerebral hemorrhage. He was sixty-three. His death caused a genuine outpouring of grief around the world. Herbert Hoover joined the many thousands who sent condolences to his widow. Eleanor Roosevelt, having never liked Warm Springs, was not with her husband on his last trip, but she went there immediately after receiving the news. When she arrived at midnight, she was chagrined to learn that Lucy Mercer had been visiting when he died.[70]

For a dozen demanding years, Franklin D. Roosevelt gave the nation hope and confidence. As chief executive and chief legislator, he won a commitment from the federal government to promote the national welfare by creating a safety net of minimum wages and maximum hours, unemployment insurance, old-age pensions, and assurances for labor's right to bargain collectively. New Deal reforms made American capitalism work more fairly and reliably than before, affording greater protection for workers, investors, and consumers. Roosevelt's administration shifted power from the states to the federal government, and it placed the national economy under federal regulation. Although his opponents frequently accused him of being a dictator, he led a democratic government through an age of totalitarianism and left it intact. He understood that the presidency required more than administrative expertise; it could serve, with the right leadership, as a source of moral leadership to inspire positive change. His personal determination and courage lifted the nation out of its pessimism and economic shambles.[71]

His legacy also advanced the science that conquered polio. As president, Roosevelt was a symbol for other polio victims, and he helped to raise considerable revenues for polio-related research. Throughout his presidency, his birthdays became national fund-raising occasions for the March of Dimes—occasions when theaters across the country collected contributions and children sent in dimes. In 1945, in keeping with this crusade, the Treasury Department authorized the late president's face to be minted on the dime. Ten years after Roosevelt died, the government declared Jonas Salk's vaccine safe and effective for immunizing against polio.[72]

Roosevelt's opponents—and some of his supporters—regarded him at times as devious and vindictive, and he committed his share of blunders, among them his clumsy attempt to pack the Supreme Court, his insensitivity to the plight of European Jewish refugees, his authorization of the wartime internment of Japanese Americans, and his misjudgment of Stalin's trustworthiness at Yalta. His critics accused him of using federal relief funds in effect to buy his reelections and of relying on corrupt city machines to get out the vote. They credited his victories to inept opponents and to the special circumstances of the Depression and the war. They underestimated his keen political instincts and the appeal of his positive leadership on the voters. Roosevelt had a knack for assessing the political landscape realistically, enabling him to build an effective political organization that kept him in the White House and his party in the majority in Congress. He spoke eloquently and directly to citizens, educating by explaining his goals without ranting or lecturing. A Republican precinct captain observed with admiration that whereas most politicians stopped at the voter's doorstep, Roosevelt became one of the family.[73]

THE VERDICT OF HISTORY

A month into his presidency, Harry Truman invited Herbert Hoover back to the White House to give his views on the food shortages in postwar Europe. The former president reentered the West Wing on May 28, 1945, for the first time since he left it in 1933. He stayed for an hour, did most of the talking, and provided copious statistics and cogent recommendations that impressed the new president. Hoover privately questioned Truman's motives for inviting him but concluded that he was simply trying to establish "a feeling of good will in the country." He doubted that anything more would come of the meeting, yet the relationship between the two men lasted for the rest of their lives. Truman put Hoover back to work on a series of prominent assignments, from dealing with food crises abroad to reorganizing the executive branch of government.[74]

Many applauded the tapping of Hoover's talents. A minister from New York wrote that he had not cared for Hoover's policies in the past but that since the former president was no longer fired with ambition, he could "speak with sense and sobriety." Still, Truman's mail ran two-to-one against his decision to invite Hoover to visit the White House. A salesman asked, "Why dig him out of the mothballs into which the people put him in 1932?" A California woman complained that "workers never got any consideration from Mr. Hoover and though he forgot them and their just demands, he is much mistaken if he thinks they have forgotten him. He is remembered with acute distaste whenever working people gather." A farmer could not believe that Truman would consult with "that contemptible character, Herbert Hoover. He has been a butt of jokes since his administration of the presidency." An angry Democrat protested that having Hoover look into the food shortages in Europe was a waste of taxpayers' money, "since everyone with an inch of memory keenly remembers how Herbie couldn't even feed his own people—while he was President." A Philadelphia judge reminded Truman that Hoover's name had "a connotation that can never be erased from the memories of democratic minded Americans—Hoovervilles, apples on the street corners, soup lines—no we want none of Mr. Hoover in any capacity."[75]

Truman tapped this lingering resentment effectively in the election of 1948. Speaking in North Carolina, he reminded southerners of the Hoover cart pulled by a mule. "First you had the Hoovercrats, and then you had the Hoover carts," he warned. "One always follows the other. Bear that in mind now, carefully." The Republicans were just trying to "sell you the same old brand of Hoover carts," he said. In Boston, Truman appealed to Irish Catholics by recalling the anti-Catholic prejudice that Al Smith had suffered in 1928, when he was defeated by "that well-known engineer—Herbert Hoover. He was one engineer who really did a job of running things backwards." Truman added: "I say to you people of Boston that if Al Smith—and not Herbert Hoover—had been chosen President in 1928, we and the world would have been spared untold misery and suffering." Under Roosevelt's leadership, Truman insisted, Democrats had "licked the Hoover Depression" and rebuilt a strong United States. Hoover could not believe that after so many friendly exchanges, the president would slam him so mercilessly. "Oh, that was nothing but politics," Truman assured him. "I didn't mean it personally and you shouldn't have paid any attention to it."[76]

The New Deal political coalition held together to give Truman an improbable victory in 1948. It took twenty years after Hoover's defeat for the Republicans to recapture the presidency, running the popular general Dwight D. Eisenhower as their candidate. New Deal programs and the GI Bill had elevated much of the urban working class into a suburban middle class, but some voters interviewed during the 1952 campaign had not forgotten how their salaries had been cut and their jobs jeopardized under Hoover. The "Depression generation" retained those views long into the postwar prosperity, with Democrats stoking their memories at every election. During the 1950s, Eisenhower restored the Republicans' image by demonstrating that economic good times could exist while they occupied the White House. But Ike was a moderate who traded the support of congressional Democrats for his foreign policies in return for not trying to dismantle the New Deal's domestic reforms. The historian Richard Hofstadter commented to a friend that "the New Deal may have been a failure in the thirties but it sure is a success in the fifties!" As a young radical in the 1930s, Hofstadter thought that Roosevelt had not gone far enough with his economic reforms, but the New Deal had left the postwar United States more prosperous and secure, and Roosevelt's successors made his liberalism look much stronger in retrospect.[77]

The specter of the New Deal haunted Herbert Hoover for the three decades between his presidency and his death in 1964, at the age of ninety. Hoover was an ardent fisherman, noted one of his admirers, and that hobby endowed him "with patience and confidence in the ultimate catch"—that history would prove him right. Over time, his public image mellowed into that of a wise elder statesman. At private gatherings, he could surprise people with his humor and abundance of information. After one dinner party in the 1950s, a guest turned to her host and exclaimed, "That just can't be Herbert Hoover!" The Washington correspondent William S. White met the elderly former president and judged him "a warm personality encased in a rigid outer shell from which he was psychologically unable and emotionally unwilling to break out."[78]

Driven by a desire for historical vindication, Hoover published his memoirs in 1952. Still unwilling to retract any of the campaign accusations or admit any failings, he undermined his case with his narrow view of the Depression's causes and effects. He wrote, quite seriously, that "many persons left their jobs for the more profitable one of selling apples." Nor, for all his dread of audiences, did Hoover ever stop his public speaking. He addressed every Republican convention through 1960, though he opposed the choice of Landon, Willkie, Dewey, and Eisenhower as the party's nominees. He found a kindred spirit in another Quaker candidate, Richard Nixon. In 1946, Hoover and Lawrence Richey raised funds for Nixon's first congressional race, and Hoover offered paternal advice throughout Nixon's early political career. (Richey remained Hoover's loyal right-hand man until his death on a flight to Washington in 1957, after spending Christmas with his chief.) Illness kept Hoover away from the Republican convention in 1964, but the presidential nominee, Senator Barry Goldwater, paid a special tribune to him in his acceptance speech. The most conservative Republican candidate since Coolidge, Goldwater decried the widening government intervention in society since the New Deal. A few weeks after Hoover died, Goldwater went down to a worse electoral defeat than the former president had experienced in 1932.[79]

As the Great Depression faded from public memory, the Democratic Party retired "Happy Days Are Here Again" for more modern tunes. Into the 1960s, the Democrats maintained a strong lead in voter registration over the Republicans because the urban, ethnic population that Roosevelt attracted stayed with the party and grew at a rate the Republican constituencies did not match. But as the core of New Deal Democrats aged, the New Deal coalition began to fray. In 1963, John F. Kennedy's assassination made Lyndon B. Johnson president. Johnson had entered Congress in 1937 as a disciple of Roosevelt's, and as president, he established his Great Society programs, which would complete and attempt to outdo the New Deal. Johnson achieved long-sought advances in civil rights, Medicare, education, and environmental reform but also caused friction through a massive antipoverty program that encouraged maximum participation by the poor and wound up pitting them against local governments that administered the program. In the 1960s and 1970s, federal guarantees began to be called entitlements—a label originally identified with veterans' benefits—for health care, pensions, and welfare. They consumed an increasingly prominent share of the national budget, which made them targets for those seeking to reduce the size and cost of government. Johnson's decision to send combat troops to South Vietnam created a fiscal tension between "guns and butter," making it impossible for his administration to service its diverse constituencies. Vietnam also raised questions about Roosevelt's internationalist legacy; Hoover-style noninterventionism suddenly seemed more appealing to antiwar activists.

Some social welfare advocates attributed failures in the Great Society's antipoverty program to its inability to break from the New Deal's ideological limitations in redistributing wealth. They lamented that Roosevelt had not instituted a more extensive, European-style social welfare state to disburse the nation's resources more equitably among the poor. Growing consciousness of the inequalities in society prompted Democrats to adopt an egalitarian, rights-oriented agenda that gave greater voice to women and racial minorities (issues more closely identified with Eleanor rather than Franklin Roosevelt). This shift encompassed Democratic support for school busing, affirmative action, open housing, welfare payments, abortion, and women's liberation, further fragmenting the New Deal coalition. Disaffected cultural conservatives within the coalition, particularly among Catholics and evangelical Protestants, abandoned it to join the emerging grassroots conservative movement, fearful that liberal policies were threatening their traditional values. Southern conservatives drifted away from the Democrats after the passage of civil rights and voting rights legislation. A cadre of formerly liberal intellectuals grew disillusioned with the inability of social policy, as formulated by the heirs of the New Deal, to change society and demanded more hard-line military and foreign policies; they gravitated into the Republican ranks as neoconservatives.[80]

Democrats split in 1968 over social issues and the Vietnam War, with the segregationist George Wallace running as an independent against the liberal Democratic candidate Hubert Humphrey, thereby enabling Richard Nixon to win the White House with only 43.4 percent of the popular vote. The New Deal coalition held together in maintaining large Democratic majorities in both houses of Congress throughout Nixon's presidency. Those majorities masked the sharp divisions between southern conservatives and northern liberals that Nixon ably exploited. Pursuing a southern strategy not unlike Hoover's in 1928 and playing on the divisions between antiwar protesters and the "silent majority," Nixon won reelection by a huge majority over George McGovern in 1972. He appealed to blue-collar, urban, ethnic groups that had been voting Democratic since Roosevelt but had become agitated over feminism, Black Power, the counterculture, and "limousine liberalism"—an epithet suggesting that an out-of-touch elite was making social policy. These impulses were captured in the 1970s television situation comedy *All in the Family,* whose theme song included the line "Mister, we could use a man like Herbert Hoover again." The 1977 Broadway musical *Annie* caught Hoover's more enduring image in its chorus of the Depression-era homeless singing, "We'd like to thank you, Herbert Hoover. You made us what we are today."

The Watergate scandal resulted in Nixon's resignation on August 9, 1974, the day before the president was scheduled to speak at a ceremony honoring the centennial of Herbert Hoover's birth. Rather than restoring New Deal liberalism, Watergate further fueled the voters' cynicism and alienation from the government. Democrats won congressional victories that year, which enhanced their chances of regaining the presidency, but in 1976, when a pack of liberal senators with New Deal roots ran for the Democratic nomination, they all went down to defeat against the former governor of Georgia, James Earl "Jimmy" Carter, a genuine Washington outsider. Carter launched his general election campaign from Roosevelt's Little White House in Warm Springs, Georgia, and likened the incumbent president, Gerald Ford, to Herbert Hoover for promising that prosperity would soon return. When Carter won the presidency, the media attributed his victory to a revival of the old coalition that had elected Roosevelt, defining it as the South, the industrial Northeast, union labor, and minorities. Once in the White House, however, Carter distanced himself from the old New Dealers, many of whom had stayed in Washington as lobbyists. He saw them as representing the chummy insider politics he had run against. Rexford Tugwell offered advice to the new president, only to receive a perfunctory response from a Carter subordinate. On March 4, 1978, the surviving members of Roosevelt's administration held a last reunion in Washington, to mark the forty-fifth anniversary of his first inauguration. No one from the Carter administration bothered to attend.[81]

As an engineer, Jimmy Carter presented himself as a problem-solving president, but like the earlier engineer Herbert Hoover, he confronted problems that were too complex for straightforward solutions, and events often seemed to overwhelm him. Faced with "stagflation"—a stagnant economy combined with soaring inflation—Carter cut spending and raised taxes, while the Federal Reserve Board tightened credit to control the runaway inflation. The columnists Rowland Evans and Robert Novak pointed out that Carter's policies repudiated the New Deal and resembled "Hoover's economics that condemned the Republican Party to a half-century in the wilderness." Carter's presidency then suffered a lethal blow to its prestige in 1979 when Iranian militants seized the American embassy staff in Tehran, holding them hostage. Running for reelection in a climate of economic distress and impotence in foreign affairs, Carter suffered from a lower approval rating than any president since Hoover. He sought to rekindle his party's historical identity by returning to Warm Springs at the start of his second campaign.[82]

In 1980, the Republican presidential nomination went to Ronald Reagan, a former California governor, Hollywood actor, and New Deal Democrat turned conservative Republican. As a spokesman for General Electric during the 1950s, Reagan had made speeches on what he thought was wrong with the government, eventually talking himself out of his liberalism, convinced that government had grown too intrusive and taxes had climbed too high. After he left the Democratic Party in 1962, he urged conservatives to develop new issues and a new tone. Since the New Deal, they had allowed liberals to dominate the political debate. "Their ideas were new; they had momentum; they captivated the imagination of the American people," said Reagan. "The left held sway for a good time. There was a right, but it was, by the forties and fifties, diffuse and scattered, without a unifying voice." Reagan now provided that voice.[83]

Viewing Reagan as someone outside the political mainstream, Carter's advisers expected the nomination of the former California governor to scare moderate Republicans and liberal Democrats into rallying around the Carter candidacy. They were counting on polls that showed 50 percent of the country was still registered or leaning Democratic compared to 30 percent for the Republicans—echoing the erroneous assumptions that Hoover had once made about Roosevelt and the Democrats. Comparisons to 1932 surfaced during the campaign in editorials about "Jimmy Hoover" and "Franklin Delano Reagan." Carter became the first elected incumbent president since Herbert Hoover to be defeated at the polls, and like Hoover, he wound up taking only six states. Liberal Democrats argued that Reagan did not win so much as the unpopular Carter lost, but Reagan's coattails also carried the first Republican majority in the Senate in a quarter century. In the House, a trimmed-down Democratic majority increased the clout of conservative Democrats, who allied with Republicans to enact Reagan's programs.[84]

Just as progressive Republicans had joined the New Deal coalition, working-class "Reagan Democrats" turned Republican. In his acceptance speech at the Republican convention in Detroit, Reagan described casting his first vote in 1932 for Franklin Roosevelt, and he quoted FDR's warnings against federal deficits and promises to balance the budget. Trying to show that the Democratic Party had changed more than he had, Reagan was indulging in some personal revisionist history. During the Depression, his family had depended on the spending side of the New Deal. A Democrat in solidly Republican Dixon, Illinois, Reagan's father, desperately in need of work, had volunteered to campaign for Roosevelt. The Democrats rewarded him with jobs providing food to the destitute and running the local WPA office, where he put the unemployed to work cleaning parks and building bridges. Long after Roosevelt turned from balanced budgets to deficit spending, Ronald Reagan voted for him again and again. Like Roosevelt, Reagan would talk about balanced budgets without achieving one.[85]

Reagan's platform in 1980 read like Hoover's, but his jaunty personal style resembled Roosevelt's, demonstrating, in the words of one conservative commentator, that Republicans could form a party of hope and opportunity, no longer seeking leadership from "dour men like Herbert Hoover." Modeling himself after Roosevelt, Reagan became an activist president and an able communicator with an open-ended desire to change the way things had been done. Rather than appeal to voters' fears, he promised them a fresh start and better times. By then, the New Deal generation was collecting Social Security, and their children, the baby boomers, no longer responded viscerally to Depression-era arguments. Republican strategists counted on the Reagan coalition reshaping American politics well into the future, as his landslide reelection over the liberal Democrat Walter Mondale signaled in 1984. "If Republicans have finally escaped the stigma of Herbert Hoover and the Great Depression," wrote the political correspondent David Broder, "then it is possible that a political epoch has ended."[86]

Ronald Reagan took care not to set himself against the New Deal. Despite his earlier rhetoric, as president he preserved Social Security, did not sell off the TVA, and shaved neither the size nor the cost of the federal government. To stimulate the economy, he shifted emphasis from domestic spending to tax cuts, insisting that the poverty-stricken, the disabled, the elderly, and others truly in need could rest assured that the social safety net of programs they depended upon were exempt from any reductions in the federal budget. Reagan and his successors talked about ending the era of big government, but they recognized that the voters would not tolerate passive government in the face of either natural or man-made disasters. Conservatives aimed to abolish such "New Deal dinosaurs" as the TVA and the Federal Communications Commission, but by the end of the twentieth century, Roosevelt's handprint remained clearly visible in the pages of the *United States Government Manual* in the dozens of agencies and programs still functioning that had begun between 1933 and 1945.

As the Republicans made peace with Roosevelt, Democrats exhausted the negative value of Hoover's name. During the presidential campaign of 2004, the Democratic candidate, John F. Kerry, repeatedly assailed George W. Bush as the first president since Hoover to have the sum total of American jobs decline during his administration. When Bush responded that the nation had "turned the corner" on jobs, Kerry reminded listeners that the last president to campaign on such a slogan had been Hoover. That message left the voters largely indifferent, however, perhaps because polls showed that more than half the electorate could not distinguish between Herbert Hoover and J. Edgar Hoover, the late FBI director. One survey revealed that fewer than 7 percent of those who responded could connect President Hoover to either the stock market crash or the Great Depression.[87]

William Allen White once called Herbert Hoover the country's "great innocent bystander," and he expressed the hope that history would credit Hoover for being "an earnest, honest, intelligent man, full of courage and patriotism, undaunted to the last." Presidents cannot afford to be bystanders, however, and Hoover's many fine qualities did not make for a successful presidency. His ideological rigidity, his trouble in coping with contrary opinions, his alienation of large segments of his party, and his aloofness from the press and the public all contributed to a failure in leadership. Although Hoover has attracted his share of sympathetic biographers, in nearly every presidential ratings poll, historians have placed Franklin Roosevelt near the top and Herbert Hoover somewhere in the bottom half. At the close of the twentieth century, a group of distinguished historians, polled by *Time* magazine, identified Roosevelt as the century's greatest president for having "changed the landscape of American life" and Hoover as the worst for being dogmatic and ineffective in responding to the Great Depression, although they conceded that he had been a "victim of bad luck." Monuments in Washington reflect these assessments. Hoover's name is affixed to the stodgy Department of Commerce Building, whereas a short distance away, visitors wander through the parklike Franklin Delano Roosevelt Memorial, amid waterfalls, depictions of the Depression and World War II, and statues of Franklin and Eleanor Roosevelt and their little dog, Fala.[88]

Economists have seconded the historians. Through monetary analysis, economists endorsed Roosevelt's response to a seriously deflated economy. The economic consensus blamed the stock market crash and the severity of the Depression on the Federal Reserve Board for keeping interest rates too low in the 1920s and then raising them too abruptly after 1928. Economists also faulted Hoover's orthodox approach of balancing the budget, imposing higher taxes, and preserving the gold standard for worsening the economic slide. Fighting the Great Depression called for unorthodox thinking. Many had feared that inflation would prolong the downturn, but the crisis called for reflation to reverse a deflation so severe that it nearly halved the value of the nation's goods and services. The Depression indeed had been worldwide, as Herbert Hoover insisted, but nations emerged from the economic crisis individually according to their internal policies, depending on when they left the gold standard and let their currencies float and when they instituted deficit spending to stimulate wages and prices and restore employment and consumer spending. With the influx of wartime spending, the economy fully revived, and the United States entered a postwar era of sustained prosperity. Roosevelt put the nation back on its feet.[89]

No twentieth-century election more profoundly affected the United States than Franklin Roosevelt's victory over Herbert Hoover in 1932. The ferocity of the Great Depression forced the American people to reevaluate their expectations of government and their party loyalties. Voters elected the New Deal without knowing precisely what it meant or where Roosevelt would lead, gambling on his promise of a flexible, compassionate, liberal approach to resolve the economic crisis and construct a more secure society. As president, he confounded his political opponents by adopting a varied and creative program of relief, recovery, and reform that appealed broadly to the electorate. A momentous political realignment took place, with the majority of voters repeatedly ratifying Roosevelt's leadership and uniting in a coalition that long survived him, ensuring that his programs would endure and expand. Although Hoover's warnings against big government continue to resonate, Roosevelt's vision of a responsive government has prevailed.

FRANKLIN D. ROOSEVELT RADIO ADDRESS ON UNEMPLOYMENT AND SOCIAL WELFARE, OCTOBER 13, 1932

[Governor Roosevelt spoke at 10 P.M. EST from the Governor's Mansion in Albany. The Columbia Broadcasting System carried the address.]

I am speaking to you from my desk in the Executive Mansion in Albany of a subject which is not in the narrower sense of the word political, but which, because it is connected with Government, vitally affects the life of almost every man, woman and child in the United States.

I cannot, of course, answer the hundreds of questions which come to me in every mail, but a letter signed by ten of the leading social welfare workers permits me to use their questions as a text for the expression of certain great basic principles which are vital to us in this time of stress.

The first question asks my position in relation to the duty of the Federal and State and local Governments to provide funds and aid for the relief of those who are out of work.

The problem therein outlined is one which is very real in every section of the country, as I have good reason to know. This was accentuated by what I saw and heard on my recent trip to the Pacific Coast.

Let me answer it by laying down what I believe to be certain cardinal principles.

In the first place, even in an ideal community where no one is out of work, there would always be the needs of welfare work conducted through the churches, through private charity and by local government—the need for clinics and hospitals and vocational training, the need for the care of aged, for care of mental cases and for care of the crippled.

Such communities where there is no unemployment are almost utopian, for even in times of prosperity there are always some unemployed—people who want to work but can find no work.

The first principle I would lay down is that the primary duty rests on the community, through local government and private agencies, to take care of the relief of unemployment. But we then come to a situation where there are so many people out of work that local funds are insufficient.

It seems clear to me that the organized society known as the State comes into the picture at this point. In other words, the obligation of Government is extended to the next higher unit.

I practice what I preach. In 1930 the State of New York greatly increased its employment service and kept in close touch with the ability of localities to take care of their own unemployed. But by the summer of 1931 it became apparent to me that actual State funds and a State-supervised system were imperative.

I called a special session of the Legislature and they appropriated a fund of $20,000,000 for unemployment relief, this fund to be reimbursed to the State through the doubling of our income taxes. Thus the State of New York became the first among all the States to accept the definite obligation of supplementing local funds where these local funds were insufficient.

The administration of this great work has become a model for the rest of the country. Without setting up any complex machinery or large overhead, the State of New York is working successfully through local agencies, and in spite of the fact that over a million people are out of work and in need of aid in this one State alone, we have so far met at least the bare necessities of the case.

This past spring the Legislature appropriated another $5,000,000 and on November 8 the voters will pass on a $30,000,000 bond issue to tide us over this winter and at least up to next summer.

Finally, let me come to the last step in the statement of the principle. I am very certain that the obligation extends beyond the States and to the Federal Government itself if and when it becomes apparent that States and communities are unable to take care of the necessary relief work.

It may interest you to have me read a short quotation from my message to the Legislature in 1931:

"What is the State? It is the duly constituted representative of an organized society of human beings, created by them for their mutual protection and well being. One of the duties of the State is that of caring for those of its citizens who find themselves the victims of such adverse circumstances as make them unable to obtain even the necessities of mere existence without the aid of others.

"In broad terms, I assert that modern society, acting through its Government, owes the definite obligation to prevent the starvation or the dire want of any of its fellow men and women who try to maintain themselves but cannot. To these unfortunate citizens aid must be extended by the Government—not as a matter of charity, but as a matter of social duty."

That principle which I laid down in 1931, I reaffirm. I not only reaffirm it, I go a step further and say that where the State itself is unable successfully to fulfill this obligation which lies upon it, it then becomes the positive duty of the Federal Government to step in to help.

In the words of our Democratic national platform, the Federal Government has a "continuous responsibility for human welfare, especially for the protection of children." That duty and responsibility the Federal Government should carry out promptly, fearlessly and generously.

It took the present Republican Administration in Washington almost three years to recognize this principle. I have recounted to you in other speeches, and it is a matter of general information, that for at least two years after the crash, the only efforts made by the national Administration to cope with the distress of unemployment, were to deny its existence.

When finally this year, after attempts at concealment and minimizing had failed, it was at last forced to recognize the fact of suffering among millions of unemployed, appropriations of Federal funds for assistance to States were finally made.

I think it is fair to point out that a complete program of unemployment relief was on my recommendation actually under way in the State of New York over a year ago, and that in Washington relief funds in any large volume were not provided until this Summer and at that they were pushed through at the demand of Congress rather than through the leadership of the President of the United States.

At the same time, I have constantly reiterated my conviction that the expenditures of cities, States and the Federal Government must be reduced in the interest of the Nation as a whole. I believe that there are many ways in which such reduction of expenditure can take place, but I am utterly unwilling that economy should be practiced at the expense of starving people.

We must economize in other ways, but it shall never be said that the American people have refused to provide the necessities of life for those who, through no fault of their own, are unable to feed, clothe and house themselves. The first obligation of Government is the protection of the welfare and well-being, indeed the very existence of its citizens.

So much for that.

The next question asks my attitude toward appropriations for public works as an aid to unemployment. I am perfectly clear as to the principles involved in this case also.

From the long-range point of view it would be advisable for Governments of all kinds to set up in times of prosperity what might be called a nest egg to be used for public works in times of depression. That is a policy which we should initiate when we get back to good times.

But there is the immediate possibility of helping the emergency through appropriations for public works. One question, however, must be answered first, because of the simple fact that these public works cost money.

We all know that Government treasuries, whether local or State or Federal, are hard put to it to keep their budgets balanced, and in the case of the Federal Treasury thoroughly unsound financial policies have made its situation not exactly desperate, but at least threatening to future stability, if the policies of the present Administration are continued.

All public works, including the Federal, must be considered from the point of view of the ability of the Government treasury to pay for them. There are two ways of paying for public works.

One is by the sale of bonds. In principle such bonds should be issued only to pay for self-sustaining projects or for structures which will without question have a useful life over a long period of years.

The other method of payment is from current revenues, which in these days means in most cases added taxes. We all know that there is a very definite limit to the increase of taxes above the present level.

From this standpoint, therefore, I can go on and say that if funds can be properly provided by the Federal Government for increased appropriations for public works, we must examine the character of those public works. I have already spoken of that type which is self-sustaining. These should be greatly encouraged.

The other type is that of public works which are honestly essential to the community. Each case must rest on its own merits. It is impossible, for example, to say that all parks or all playgrounds are essential. One may be and another may not be.

If a school, for instance, has no playground, it is obvious that the furnishing of a playground is a necessity to the community. But if the school already has a playground and some people seek merely to enlarge it, there may be a definite question as to how necessary that enlargement is.

Let me cite another example. I am much interested in providing better housing accommodations for the poor in our great cities. If a slum area can be torn down and new modern buildings put up, I should call that almost a human necessity, but on the other hand, the mere erection of new buildings in some other part of the city while allowing the slums to remain raises at once a question of necessity. I am confident that the Federal Government working in cooperation with States and cities can do much to carry on increased public works and along lines which are sound from the economic and financial point of view.

Now I come to another question. I am asked whether I am in favor of a system of unemployment insurance reserves made compulsory by the States, supplemented by a system of federally coordinated State employment offices to facilitate the reemployment of jobless workers.

The first part of the question is directly answered by the Democratic platform, which advocates unemployment insurance under State laws.

This is no new policy for me. I have advocated unemployment insurance in my own State for some time, and indeed last year six Eastern Governors were my guests at a conference which resulted in the drawing up of what might be called an ideal plan of unemployment insurance.

This type of insurance is not a cure-all, but it provides at least a cushion to mitigate unemployment in times of depression. It is sound if, after starting it, we stick to the principle of sound insurance financing. It is only where Governments, as in some European countries, have failed to live up to these sound principles that unemployment insurance has been an economic failure.

As to the coordinated employment offices, I can only tell you that I was for the bills sponsored by Senator Wagner of my own State and passed by Congress. They created a nationally coordinated system of employment offices operated by the Individual States with the advisory cooperation of joint boards of employers and employees.

To my very great regret, this measure was vetoed by the President of the United States. I am certain that the Federal Government can, by furnishing leadership, stimulate the various States to set up and coordinate practical, useful systems.

These first three questions which I have discussed related to the relief of those who are unemployed, and it is perhaps logical that the next two questions should relate to children, because we know that unemployment works a great hardship on the young people of the coming generation.

I certainly favor the continuance of the fine work which has been done by the Children's Bureau in Washington, but at the same time we must not forget that the Federal Government through several other agencies is constantly working for the welfare of children.

Attempts have been made to cut the appropriations for child welfare work. It seems to me that this is the last place in which we should economize. I cannot agree with the member of President Hoover's Cabinet who suggests that this depression is not altogether a bad thing for our children.

You and I know the appalling fact that malnutrition is one of the saddest by-products of unemployment. The health of these children is being affected not only now but for all the rest of their lives.

Furthermore, a depression takes thousands of children away from schools and puts them to work to help the family income. They are underpaid and only too often work under conditions which, physically and morally, are often dangerous. It is well to remember, too, that the use of these untrained children in industry keeps many adults out of employment and has the effect of cutting down wages below a decent standard of living.

These are only a few of the many reasons why the Federal Government must continue to act as an agency to disseminate information about child welfare and to encourage State and local governments to raise their standards to the highest possible levels.

The last question relates to keeping children in school to the age of sixteen. I am in favor of that. Furthermore, I go along with the thought that we must increase vocational education for those children who otherwise would not receive adequate training. That kind of vocational training will raise the standards of worthwhile employment, not only now but also in normal times.

My own observation leads me to believe that in many parts of the country we have tended to an educational system devised too greatly for academic training and professional careers.

We know that already many of the professions are oversupplied, and it is a fair guess that during the coming generation we shall devote more attention to educating our boys and girls for vocational pursuits which are just as honorable, just as respectable and in many instances just as remunerative as are the professions themselves.

The Federal Government, without in any way taking away the right and the duty of the several States to manage their own educational affairs, can act as a clearing house of information and as an incentive to higher standards.

But the Federal Government has had no continuing policy for dealing with problems of public health and social welfare. In this as in other activities a multiplicity of unrelated agencies has been developed hit-or-miss to deal with aspects of the same problem. The result has been waste of men and money and a more costly and less efficient service than we should have.

The Administration has done nothing to reorganize this or other branches of the Federal Government, in spite of campaign promises at the last three Presidential elections. I propose to inaugurate a definite long-range plan for dealing with all phases of public health and welfare, which are a proper concern of the Federal Government.

May I add that in the State of New York during the past four years we have accomplished definite and practical results by coordinating and planning the work of the State?

I cite as a simple example the public health program, which is a part of my Administration. It has been referred to in other States as the most important contribution to practical public health work during this generation. And all of this we have taken out of politics.

The same principles can and should be applied to the health and welfare work of the Federal Government.

In closing, will you let me make an appeal to the entire country—an appeal with all my heart, with all my mind and with all my soul—to let nothing interfere with the duty and obligation of coming forward as individuals and as groups to the support of the unemployed and their dependants during the coming winter.

By proclamation I can make official appeal to the State of which I am Governor, but I think I have the right as a Presidential candidate, to make an unofficial appeal to my fellow Americans in every other State.

I wish that every man, woman and child above the age of reason in the whole country would make the coming Thanksgiving Day and coming Christmas Day occasions to contribute with money or food or clothing, or all three, to the direct relief of local needs.

Let us remember that in addition to whatever it may be possible for the Federal Government or State Government or municipalities to do in relieving the tremendous and increasing burden of relief work, misery and distress will still be great unless individuals, societies and churches practice actual charity—actual love of their neighbor—to an extent even greater than at any time in the past.

Let us who have jobs or money or shelter for ourselves and our own families share with the less fortunate. Thanksgiving Day and Christmas Day of 1932 will take on an added significance—the significance of a higher American ideal of social justice.

Source: Samuel I. Rosenman, ed., *The Public Papers and Addresses of Franklin D. Roosevelt,* vol. 1, *The Genesis of the New Deal, 1928–1932* (New York: Random House, 1938), 786–95.

HERBERT HOOVER RADIO ADDRESS FROM ELKO, NEVADA, NOVEMBER 7, 1932

[The president spoke at 7:40 PST from the lounge car of his train while stopped at Elko, Nevada. The National Broadcasting Company and the Columbia Broadcasting System radio networks carried the address.]

My fellow citizens:

We have been through an arduous campaign. It has been almost unique as a campaign of education in the great domestic and international problems which have arisen out of events of the last 15 years.

I have endeavored to place these problems before the people as I see them from the facts and experience that have come to me in these past years. I wished the people to realize more intimately the difficulties with which their Government has been confronted, the disasters which have been averted, and the forces which have been mobilized for their support and their protection.

I hope from these discussions that the people will realize the great crisis that we have successfully passed and the unprecedented measures taken which have been designed solely that we might protect and restore the system of life and of government endeared to us for over 150 years—a government that has given to us protection from distress and allayed the forces which would otherwise have wrecked our homes and our firesides. But more than that, I hope I have given an understanding of these measures that have been designed for counterattack upon this crisis. These measures are now demonstrating their strength and effectiveness not only at home but abroad, evidences of which are multiplying throughout the country in the return of more than half a million men to work monthly, and that we have again resumed the road to prosperity.

I might add that the figure which I have given during the last few days of the return of 1 million men to work since the adjournment of the Congress have been added to during the day today by the estimates of the American Federation of Labor which increased the estimates, which I have given to you, by nearly 300,000 men.

I wish to emphasize the greatest function of the American citizen, the one which each of us should perform tomorrow. The ballot is that most sacred individual act which preserves the great system of self-government which we have inherited and which should carry forward at any cost. It is a direct opportunity for every man and woman to express their views in terms of equality with every other citizen as to the policies and kind of a government that they wish carried out in the next 4 years. And I have a deep feeling that the choice that you make now is more than the choice for another 4 years. There is great divergence in the philosophy of government between the parties which may affect events over a generation; a mistaken choice may hazard the welfare of our children and our children's children. I have been fighting that the wrong course may not be adopted, not by appeal to destructive emotion, but by truth and logic. I have tried to dissolve the mirage of promises by the reality of facts.

I am a believer in party government. It is only through party organization that our people can give coherent expression to their views upon public affairs. There is no other way except by revolution, but we in America have ordained that the ballot shall be used for peaceful determination and not violence.

We are a nation of progressives. We wish to see our Nation march forward. We differ strongly as to the method to progress. I differ widely with the principles and views advocated by our opponents, but it is not my purpose to review them at this moment. I feel deeply that the Republican Party has been the party of progress in our history from the days of Abraham Lincoln. It has built the progress of the Nation upon the foundations of national principles and national ideals.

We are a nation of homes from which the accomplishment of individuals is nurtured by the maximum freedom in an ordered liberty. The ultimate goal of our progress is to build for security and happiness in these homes where the inspiration of our religious faiths will implant in our children those principles of social order and idealism, and where our Government will contribute in safeguarding their future opportunity for them.

The action of our Nation has been modified and benefited by the enfranchisement of women. They equally with the men bear the shocks from economic disaster. With them lies largely the guardianship of the fundamental ideals, because concentrated in their lives and their responsibilities is a solicitude for the preservation of the home and the inspiration for the future. And in these labors our Government can contribute to strengthen their accomplishment and their influence.

Our women give with lavish hands, not only to childhood, but, as well, to the creation of those conserving customs upon which are builded all the blessings of our ordered Government. They thus give to government a large measure of the true strength of its foundations. It is but just that they receive back, in return, all that the Government can give them to assure them of security and the enlargement of the equal opportunity to their children and to themselves, to widen the field for the use of their own powers of mind and spirit.

It is they who are mobilizing new public regard to our obligations to home and children of the future; it is they who are mobilizing the public opinion on the maintenance of peace in the world.

The men of our country carry the frontline of battle through their initiative, their enterprise, their hopes, their courage.

The immediate question before our country is in whose direction shall be the measures by which we shall emerge from our present difficulties. In the longer view our problems are the questions that the world should have peace; that prosperity of the Nation shall be diffused to all, and that we shall build more strongly the ideal of equal opportunity amongst all our people; that we shall secure that obedience to law which is essential to assurance of life in our institutions; that honesty and righteousness in business shall confirm the confidence of our people in our institutions and laws; that our Government shall contribute to leadership in these matters.

It is my deep conviction for the welfare of the United States the Republican Party should continue to administer the Government. Those men and women who have supported the party over these many years should not be led astray by false gods arrayed in the rainbow colors of promises. They have but to review the performance and the sense of responsibility, the constructive action, the maintenance of national ideals by the Republican Party, in every national crisis including the present, always in opposition to the destructive forces of sectional and group action of our opponents.

Election Day is more than a day set aside for casting of our several ballots. There is a solemnity in the feeling of that day, the sense of being in the presence of a great invisible power when the united people of a great nation give their final judgment on great issues. We cannot feel that any human power alone can give us such emotions; rather we must trust that we are sensing the movements of the Ruler of the universe in whose beneficence and in whose favor we have been blessed throughout our history.

As a final word, I wish to convey my deep gratitude to the many hundreds of thousands of people who have come to stations and to meetings to welcome and encourage me during the past month and to the many millions more who have responded to me over the radio. I wish to express my gratitude to the young men and the young women who have organized their special movement to my support, for in them lies a special energy and idealism which drives and inspires the country; to the veterans' service leagues whose tested patriotism has supported me in this campaign; to the devoted women who, realizing the results at stake, have worked untiringly for the return of this administration; and to the organizations of men throughout the country who have been unceasing through this campaign in their presentation to the American people of the principles and ideas for which I have stood.

Four years ago I stated that I conceived the Presidency as more than administrative office: it is a power for leadership in bringing coordination of the forces of business and cultural life in every city, town, and countryside. The Presidency is more than executive responsibility. It is the symbol of America's high purpose. The President must represent the Nation's ideals, and he must also represent them to the nations of the world. After 4 years of experience I still regard this as a supreme obligation.

Source: *Public Papers of the Presidents of the United States: Herbert Hoover, Containing the Public Messages, Speeches, and Statements of the President, January 1, 1931 to March 4, 1933* (Washington, D.C.: Government Printing Office, 1977), 795–99.

1932 GENERAL ELECTION RESULTS

	Roosevelt (Democrat)	Popular Vote Hoover (Republican)	Thomas (Socialist)	Electoral Vote	
Alabama	207,910 (84.8)	34,675 (14.1)	2,030 (.8)	11	
Arizona	79,264 (67)	36,104 (30.5)	2,616 (2.2)	3	
Arkansas	186,829 (86.3)	27,465 (12.7)	1,166 (.5)	9	
California	1,324,157 (58.4)	847,902 (37.4)	63,299 (2.8)	22	
Colorado	250,877 (54.8)	189,617 (41.4)	13,591 (3)	6	
Connecticut	281,632 (47.4)	288,420 (48.5)	20,480 (3.4)		8
Delaware	54,319 (48.1)	57,073 (50.6)	1,376 (1.2)		3
Florida	206,307 (74.5)	69,170 (25)	775 (.3)	7	
Georgia	234,118 (91.6)	19,863 (7.8)	461 (.2)	12	
Idaho	109,479 (58.7)	71,312 (38.2)	526 (.3)	4	
Illinois	1,882,304 (55.2)	1,432,756 (42)	67,258 (2)	29	
Indiana	862,054 (54.7)	677,184 (42.9)	21,388 (1.4)	14	
Iowa	598,019 (57.7)	414,433 (40)	20,467 (2)	11	
Kansas	424,204 (53.6)	349,498 (44.1)	18,276 (2.3)	9	
Kentucky	580,574 (59.1)	394,716 (40.2)	3,853 (.4)	11	
Louisiana	249,418 (92.8)	18,853 (7)	—	10	
Maine	128,907 (43.2)	166,631 (55.8)	2,489 (.8)		5
Maryland	314,314 (61.5)	184,184 (36)	10,489 (2.1)	8	
Massachusetts	800,148 (50.6)	736,959 (46.6)	34,305 (2.2)	17	
Michigan	871,700 (52.4)	739,894 (44.4)	39,205 (2.4)	19	
Minnesota	600,806 (59.9)	363,959 (36.3)	25,476 (2.5)	11	
Mississippi	140,168 (96)	5,180 (3.5)	686 (.5)	9	
Missouri	1,025,406 (63.7)	564,713 (35.1)	16,374 (1)	15	
Montana	127,286 (58.8)	78,078 (36.1)	7,891 (3.6)	4	
Nebraska	359,082 (63)	201,177 (35.3)	9,876 (1.7)	7	
Nevada	28,756 (69.4)	12,674 (30.6)	—	3	
New Hampshire	100,680 (49)	103,629 (50.4)	947 (.5)		4
New Jersey	806,630 (49.5)	775,684 (47.6)	42,998 (2.6)	16	
New Mexico	95,089 (62.7)	54,217 (35.8)	1,776 (1.2)	3	
New York	2,534,959 (54.1)	1,937,963 (41.3)	177,397 (3.8)	47	
North Carolina	497,566 (69.9)	208,344 (29.3)	5,588 (.8)	13	
North Dakota	178,350 (69.6)	71,772 (28)	3,521 (1.4)	4	
Ohio	1,301,695 (49.9)	1,227,319 (47)	64,094 (2.5)	26	
Oklahoma	516,468 (73.3)	188,165 (26.7)	—	11	
Oregon	213,871 (58)	136,019 (36.9)	15,450 (4.2)	5	
Pennsylvania	1,295,948 (45.3)	1,453,540 (50.8)	91,119 (3.2)		36
Rhode Island	146,604 (55.1)	115,266 (43.3)	3,138 (1.2)	4	

		Popular Vote		
	Roosevelt (Democrat)	Hoover (Republican)	Thomas (Socialist)	Electoral Vote
South Carolina	102,347 (98)	1,978 (1.9)	82 (.1)	8
South Dakota	183,515 (63.6)	99,212 (34.4)	1,551 (.5)	4
Tennessee	259,473 (66.5)	126,752 (32.5)	1,796 (.5)	11
Texas	771,109 (88.2)	98,218 (11.2)	4,414 (.5)	23
Utah	116,750 (56.5)	84,795 (41)	4,087 (2)	4
Vermont	56,266 (41.1)	78,984 (57.7)	1,533 (1.1)	3
Virginia	203,979 (68.5)	89,637 (30.1)	2,382 (.8)	11
Washington	353,260 (57.5)	208,645 (33.9)	17,080 (2.8)	8
West Virginia	405,124 (54.5)	330,731 (44.5)	5,133 (.7)	8
Wisconsin	707,410 (63.5)	347,741 (31.2)	53,379 (4.8)	12
Wyoming	54,370 (56.1)	39,583 (40.8)	2,829 (2.9)	3
Total	22,829,501 (57.4)	15,760,684 (39.6)	884,649 (2.2)	472 59

Figures in parentheses are percentages.

Source: John L. Moore, ed., *Congressional Quarterly's Guide to U.S. Elections* (Washington, D.C.: Congressional Quarterly, 1994).

CIVILIAN EMPLOYMENT STATISTICS, 1929–1945 (IN THOUSANDS)

Year	Total	Employed	Agriculture	Industry and Commerce	Unemployed	Percent Unemployed
1929	49,180	47,630	10,450	37,180	1,550	3.2
1930	49,820	45,480	10,340	35,140	4,340	8.7
1931	50,420	42,400	10,290	32,110	8,020	15.9
1932	51,000	38,940	10,170	28,770	12,060	23.6
1933	51,590	38,760	10,090	28,670	12,830	24.9
1934	52,230	40,890	9,900	30,990	11,340	21.7
1935	52,870	42,260	10,110	32,150	10,610	20.1
1936	53,440	44,410	10,000	34,410	9,030	16.9
1937	54,000	46,300	9,820	36,480	7,700	14.3
1938	54,610	44,220	9,690	34,530	10,390	19.0
1939	55,230	45,750	9,610	36,140	9,480	17.2
1940	55,640	47,520	9,540	37,980	8,120	14.6
1941	55,910	50,350	9,100	41,250	5,560	9.9
1942	56,410	53,750	9,250	44,500	2,660	4.7
1943	55,540	54,470	9,080	45,390	1,070	1.9
1944	54,630	53,960	8,950	45,010	670	1.2
1945	53,860	52,820	8,580	44,240	1,040	1.9

Source: HS-29, Employment Status of the Civilian Population, 1929 to 2003, U.S. Census Bureau, *Statistical Abstract of the United States, 2003,* available at http://www.census.gov/statab/hist/HS-29.pdf.

NOTES

ABBREVIATIONS

Columbia Oral History Research Office, New York, N.Y.
    Arthur Krock oral history (Krock oral history)
    Eugene Meyer oral history (Meyer oral history)
Herbert C. Hoover Presidential Library, West Branch, Iowa (Hoover Library)
    Theodore Joslin Papers (Joslin Papers)
    Walter Newton Papers (Newton Papers)
    Lawrence Richey Papers (Richey Papers)
    George Ackerman Jr. oral history (Ackerman oral history)
    Edward Anthony oral history (Anthony oral history)
    Joel T. Boone oral history (Boone oral history)
    George C. Drescher oral history (Drescher oral history)
    Alonzo Fields oral history (Fields oral history)
    Byron Price oral history (Price oral history)
Library of Congress, Washington, D.C.
    Newton D. Baker Papers (Baker Papers)
    Edward Clark Papers (Clark Papers)
    Felix Frankfurter Papers (Frankfurter Papers)
    Everett Sanders Papers (Sanders Papers)
Franklin D. Roosevelt Presidential Library, Hyde Park, N.Y. (Roosevelt Library)
    Adolph Berle Papers (Berle Papers)
    Louis Howe Papers (Howe Papers)
Harry S. Truman Presidential Library, Independence, Mo. (Truman Library)

CHAPTER 1 THE POLITICS OF PROSPERITY

1 Daniel J. Boorstin, ed., *An American Primer* (Chicago: University of Chicago Press, 1966), 802–21.

2 Arthur M. Schlesinger Jr., Fred L. Israel, and David J. Frent, eds., *Running for President: The Candidates and Their Images,* vol. 1, *1789–1896* (New York: Simon & Schuster, 1994), 425–41.

3 Robert H. Wiebe, *The Search for Order, 1877–1920* (New York: Hill & Wang, 1967), 299–302.

4 Herbert Hoover, *The Ordeal of Woodrow Wilson* (New York: McGraw-Hill, 1958), 297; President's Research Committee on Social Trends, *Recent Social Trends in the United States* (New York: McGraw-Hill, 1933), 2:1356–57.

5 Douglas B. Craig, *After Wilson: The Struggle for the Democratic Party, 1920–1934* (Chapel Hill: University of North Carolina Press, 1992), 19–20, 25–26.

6 *New York Times,* December 11, 1931.

7 President's Research Committee, *Recent Social Trends in the United States,* 1:230–38.

8 *New York Times,* April 19, 1925; Robert F. Martin, *Hero of the Heartland: Billy Sunday and the Transformation of American Society, 1862–1935* (Bloomington: Indiana University Press, 2002), 88, 111, 122–35.

9 David A. Horowitz, *America's Political Class under Fire: The Twentieth Century's Great Cultural War* (New York: Routledge, 2003), 13–36.

10 Charles W. Eagles, *Democracy Delayed: Congressional Reapportionment and Urban-Rural Conflict in the 1920s* (Athens: University of Georgia Press, 1990), 38, 58.

11 *New York Times,* October 2, 1920; *Los Angeles Times,* November 21, 1920.

12 David M. Chalmers, *Hooded Americanism: The History of the Ku Klux Klan* (New York: Franklin Watts, 1981), 33, 47, 202, 206, 281.

13 Calvin Coolidge, *The Autobiography of Calvin Coolidge* (New York: Cosmopolitan, 1929), 107; Charles Willis Thompson, *Presidents I Have Known and Two Near Presidents* (Indianapolis, Ind.: Bobbs-Merrill, 1929), 354–55; Donald A. Ritchie, *Press Gallery: Congress and the Washington Correspondents* (Cambridge, Mass.: Harvard University Press, 1991), 210.

14 Lawrence W. Levine, *Defender of the Faith: William Jennings Bryan—The Last Decade, 1915–1925* (New York: Oxford University Press, 1965), 116–24, 248, 254, 327, 340–41; Michael Kazin, *A Godly Hero: The Life of William Jennings Bryan* (New York: Alfred A. Knopf, 2006), 299.

15 See K. Austin Kerr, *Organized for Prohibition: A New History of the Anti-saloon League* (New Haven, Conn.: Yale University Press, 1985).

16 Gaines M. Foster, *Moral Reconstruction: Christian Lobbyists and the Federal Legislation of Morality, 1865–1920* (Chapel Hill: University of North Carolina Press, 2002), 224; President's Research Committee, *Recent Social Trends in the United States,* 2:1136, 1366.

17 Herbert Hoover, *Memoirs,* vol. 1, *Years of Adventure, 1874–1920* (New York: Macmillan, 1951), 5, 7; Steve Neal, *McNary of Oregon: A Political Biography* (Portland: Oregon Historical Society Press, 1985), 3–4; Theodore G. Joslin, *Hoover off the Record* (Garden City, N.Y.: Doubleday, 1935), 6.

18 Marvin Eisenstadt, André Haynal, Pierre Rentchnick, and Pierre De Senarclens, *Parental Loss and Achievement* (Madison, Conn.: International Universities Press, 1989), xi, 25–27, 40, 73–74.

19 Hoover, *Memoirs,* 1:98; Hoover, *The Ordeal of Woodrow Wilson,* v; Fred L. Israel, ed., *Taught to Lead: The Education of the Presidents of the United States* (Philadelphia: Mason Crest, 2004), 324–35.

20 David Burner, *Herbert Hoover: A Public Life* (New York: Alfred A. Knopf, 1979), 25–62; Nancy Beck Young, *Lou Henry Hoover: Activist First Lady* (Lawrence: University Press of Kansas, 2004), 10–11.

21 Irwin Hood Hoover, *Forty-two Years in the White House* (Boston: Houghton Mifflin, 1934), 185–86; Carol Green Wilson, *Herbert Hoover: A Challenge for Today* (New York: Evans, 1968), 184.

22 Will Irwin, "The Autocrat of the Dinner Table," *Saturday Evening Post,* June 23, 1917, 56; Young, *Lou Henry Hoover,* 25.

23 *Congressional Record,* 65th Cong., 1st sess., 1917, vol. 55, pt. 5, 5157, and pt. 8, app. 372; Richard Lowitt, *George W. Norris: The Persistence of a Progressive, 1913–1933* (Urbana: University of Illinois Press, 1971), 80.

24 Meg Jacobs, William J. Novak, and Julian E. Zelizer, eds., *The Democratic Experiment: New Directions in American Political History* (Princeton, N.J.: Princeton University Press, 2003), 229–30; Nathan Miller, *FDR: An Intimate History* (Garden City, N.Y.: Doubleday, 1983), 152.

25 Robert D. Cuff, "Herbert Hoover, the Ideology of Voluntarism, and War Organization during the Great War," *Journal of American History* 64 (September 1977): 358–72; Arthur M. Schlesinger Jr., *The Cycles of History* (Boston: Houghton Mifflin, 1986), 381.

26 Will Irwin, *Herbert Hoover: A Reminiscent Biography* (New York: Grosset & Dunlap, 1928), 255.

27 *New York Times,* November 20, 1932; Melvin I. Urofsky and David M. Levy, eds., *Letters of Louis D. Brandeis* (Albany: State University of New York Press, 1975), 3:3, 444, 448; Louis B. Wehle, *Hidden Threads of History: Wilson through Roosevelt* (New York: Macmillan, 1953), 83.

28 Herbert Hoover, *Memoirs,* vol. 2, *The Cabinet and the Presidency, 1920–1933* (New York: Macmillan, 1952), 35; John Morton Blum, ed., *Public Philosopher: Selected Letters of Walter Lippmann* (New York: Ticknor & Fields, 1985), 134.

29 *New York Times,* January 15, February 9, March 10, 1920; Hoover, *The Ordeal of Woodrow Wilson,* 17, 297.

30 [Clinton Gilbert], *The Mirrors of Washington* (New York: G. P. Putnam's Sons, 1921), 113–15; Melvin I. Urofsky and David M. Levy, eds., *Letters of Louis D. Brandeis* (Albany: State University of New York Press, 1978), 5:10.

31 Herbert Hoover, *American Individualism* (Garden City, N.Y.: Doubleday, 1922); Joan Hoff Wilson, *Herbert Hoover: Forgotten Progressive* (Boston: Little, Brown, 1975), 68–69, 79; Martin L. Fausold, *The Presidency of Herbert C. Hoover* (Lawrence: University Press of Kansas, 1985), 15–18; William Starr Myers and Walter H. Newton, *The Hoover Administration: A Documented Narrative* (New York: Charles Scribner's Sons, 1936), 25.

32 Andrew Sinclair, *Prohibition, the Era of Excess* (Boston: Little, Brown, 1962), 293–94.

33 Pete Daniel, *Deep'n as It Come: The 1927 Mississippi River Flood* (New York: Oxford University Press, 1977), 87–91.

34 David Greenberg, *Calvin Coolidge* (New York: Henry Holt, 2006), 132–35.

35 George C. Drescher oral history, 6, Hoover Library; Hoover, *Memoirs,* 2:55–56.

36 Alice Roosevelt Longworth, *Crowded Hours* (New York: Charles Scribner's Sons, 1933), 327; Marion Elizabeth Rodgers, ed., *The Impossible Mencken: A Selection of His Best Newspaper Stories* (New York: Doubleday, 1991), 306.

37 See Donald J. Lisio, *Hoover, Blacks and Lily-Whites: A Study of Southern Strategies* (Chapel Hill: University of North Carolina Press, 1985).

38 Edward Anthony oral history, 39, Hoover Library; Mark O. Hatfield, Donald A. Ritchie, Jo Anne McCormick Quantannens, Richard A. Baker, and William T. Hull, *Vice Presidents of the United States, 1793–1993* (Washington, D.C.: Government Printing Office, 1997), 373–81.

39 See David Von Drehle, *Triangle: The Fire That Changed America* (New York: Atlantic Monthly Press, 2003).

40 *New York Times,* October 23, 1932, May 22, 1985.

41 Matthew Josephson and Hannah Josephson, *Al Smith: Hero of the Cities* (Boston: Houghton Mifflin, 1969), 378–87; Robert A. Slayton, *Empire Statesman: The Rise and Redemption of Al Smith* (New York: Free Press, 2001), 206–11, 274–75.

42 Craig, *After Wilson,* 112–30, 158–61, 165.

43 Elliot Roosevelt, ed., *F.D.R.: His Personal Letters* (New York: Duell, Sloan & Pearce, 1947), 109–10; Blum, ed., *Public Philosopher,* 216.

44 Anthony oral history, 68–69; David E. Kyvig, *Repealing National Prohibition* (Kent, Ohio: Kent State University Press, 2000), 100–102.

45 Claude Bowers, *My Life: The Memoirs of Claude Bowers* (New York: Simon & Schuster, 1962), 177; Cecil Edward Weller Jr., *Joe T. Robinson: Always a Loyal Democrat* (Fayetteville: University of Arkansas Press, 1998), 115; *Washington Post,* March 3, 1929.

46 Lewis L. Gould, *Grand Old Party: A History of the Republicans* (New York: Random House, 2003), 252.

47 Dorothy M. Brown, *Mabel Walker Willebrandt: A Study of Power, Loyalty, and Law* (Knoxville: University of Tennessee Press, 1984), 160–65.

48 Byron Price oral history, 1, Hoover Library; Thomas L. Stokes, *Chip off My Shoulder* (Princeton, N.J.: Princeton University Press, 1940), 244–45; *Washington Post,* March 3, 1929; Jacobs, Novak, and Zelizer, *The Democratic Experiment,* 231; Hoover, *American Individualism,* 24–25.

49 Anthony oral history, 24; Oliver Grambling, *AP: The Story of News* (New York: Farrar and Rinehart, 1940), 349–51.

50 Slayton, *Empire Statesman,* 272; advertisement in *New York Times,* October 28, 1928.

51 Boorstin, *An American Primer,* 802–20; *New York Times,* October 24, 1928.

52 *Baltimore Sun,* November 5, 1928; Clarence E. Wunderlin Jr., Frank L. Byrne, Bette J. Sawicki, and Anita M. Weber, eds., *The Papers of Robert A. Taft,* vol. 1, *1889–1939* (Kent, Ohio: Kent State University Press, 1997), 354–55.

53 Allan J. Lichtman, *Prejudice and the Old Politics: The Presidential Election of 1928* (Chapel Hill: University of North Carolina Press, 1979), 77, 138; Kerr, *Organized for Prohibition,* 254–66.

54 Timothy Walch and Dwight M. Miller, *Herbert Hoover and Franklin D. Roosevelt: A Documentary History* (Westport, Conn.: Greenwood, 1998), 26–27.

CHAPTER 2 PREFIX FOR POVERTY

 1 Charles Michelson, *The Ghost Talks* (New York: G. P. Putnam's Sons, 1944), 4, 15–17, 133–34.

2 Frank R. Kent, *The Great Game of Politics* (Garden City, N.Y.: Doubleday, Doran, 1930), 148–55.

3 Cornelius P. Cotter and Bernard C. Hennessey, *Politics without Power: The National Party Committees* (New York: Atherton Press, 1964), 7–8, 68, 138–39; Frank R. Kent, "Charley Michelson," *Scribner's*, September 1930, 291.

4 David Burner, *The Politics of Provincialism: The Democratic Party in Transition, 1918–1932* (New York: Alfred A. Knopf, 1968), 142–57; Douglas B. Craig, *After Wilson: The Struggle for the Democratic Party, 1920–1934* (Chapel Hill: University of North Carolina Press, 1992), 86–87; Marion Elizabeth Rodgers, ed., *The Impossible Mencken: A Selection of His Best Newspaper Stories* (New York: Doubleday, 1991), 292.

5 Louise Overacker, "Campaign Funds in a Depression Year," *American Political Science Review* 27 (October 1933): 769–83; Cotter and Hennessey, *Politics without Power*, 72–73.

6 Donald A. Ritchie, *Press Gallery: Congress and the Washington Correspondents* (Cambridge, Mass.: Harvard University Press, 1991), 203–4; Michelson, *The Ghost Talks*, 4, 15–17, 133–34; *Washington Post*, May 10, 1973; *New York Times*, January 9, 1948; Raymond Moley, *27 Masters of Politics, in a Personal Perspective* (New York: Funk & Wagnalls, 1949), 147–49.

7 Kent, "Charley Michelson," 291.

8 James E. Watson, *As I Knew Them: Memoirs of James E. Watson* (Indianapolis, Ind.: Bobbs-Merrill, 1936), 261–63; Edward Clark to Calvin Coolidge, August 19, 1929, Edward Clark Papers, Library of Congress; Joel T. Boone oral history, 124, Hoover Library; *Washington Post*, June 5, 1929.

9 *Washington Post*, September 8, 1929; Raymond Clapper, *Racketeering in Washington* (Boston: L. C. Page, 1933), 53; John L. Nethers, "'Driest of the Drys': Simeon D. Fess," *Ohio History* 79 (Summer-Autumn 1970): 178–92.

10 *New York Times*, July 12, August 6, December 23, 1930, October 14, 1947.

11 Clark to Coolidge, August 17, 1931, Clark Papers.

12 *New York Times*, August 13, December 20–25, 1930, January 17, 1931; Clark to Coolidge, November 29, 1930, January 10, 1931, Clark Papers.

13 *Wall Street Journal*, March 7, 1930.

14 Mark O. Hatfield, ed., *Herbert Hoover Reassessed: Essays Commemorating the Fiftieth Anniversary of the Inauguration of Our Thirty-first President*, S. Doc. 96-63 (Washington, D.C.: Government Printing Office, 1981), 33; Walter Johnson, ed., *Selected Letters of William Allen White, 1899–1943* (1947; repr., New York: Greenwood, 1968), letter to David Hinshaw, December 3, 1929.

15 Joslin diary, February 29, 1932, Theodore Joslin Papers, Hoover Library; Clark to Coolidge, October 31, 1929, Clark Papers; Irwin Hood (Ike) Hoover, *Forty-two Years in the White House* (Boston: Houghton Mifflin, 1934), 184, 187–88; Donald R. Richberg, *My Hero: The Indiscreet Memoirs of an Eventful but Unheroic Life* (New York: G. P. Putnam's Sons, 1954), 149–50.

16 Eugene Meyer oral history, 693, and Agnes Meyer diary entry, A42, Columbia Oral History Research Office; Clark to Coolidge, November 14, 1932,

Clark Papers; *New York Times*, August 9, 1964; H. G. Wells, *Experiment in Autobiography* (New York: Macmillan, 1934), 679.

17 Dorothy Detzer, *Appointment on the Hill* (New York: Henry Holt, 1948), 92–97.

18 *New York Herald Tribune*, May 5, 1929; Meyer oral history, 694; A Washington Correspondent, "The Secretariat," *American Mercury* 18 (December 1929): 385–95.

19 *New York Times*, February 26, 1933; Roberta Barrows oral history, 15, 18–19, Truman Library; Ruth Steadman White Durno oral history, 6, 11, George Akerson Jr. oral history, 5–6, Hoover Library; Charles E. Walcott and Karen M. Hult, *Governing the White House: From Hoover through LBJ* (Lawrence: University Press of Kansas, 1995), 31–32, 53–55, 62, 76–77, 148–49, 224–25.

20 Hiram Johnson, *The Diary Letters of Hiram Johnson*, vol. 4 (New York: Garland, 1983), February 3, 1928; James Burnham, *Congress and the American Tradition* (Chicago: Henry Regnery, 1965), 130; Claudius O. Johnson, *Borah of Idaho* (Seattle: University of Washington Press, 1936), 429–30.

21 Clark to Coolidge, May 24, 1929, Clark Papers; Lawrence H. Chamberlain, *The President, Congress and Legislation* (New York: Columbia University Press, 1946), 124–32.

22 Paul H. Douglas, *In the Fullness of Time: The Memoirs of Paul H. Douglas* (New York: Harcourt Brace Jovanovich, 1971), 71; Walter Newton to Herbert Hoover, February 27, 1940, Walter Newton Papers, Hoover Library.

23 Michelson, *The Ghost Talks*, 29–30.

24 Hood, *Forty-two Years in the White House*, 231; *New York Times*, February 26, 1933.

25 Watson, *As I Knew Them*, 259–60, 265; Donald J. Lisio, *Hoover, Blacks and Lily-Whites: A Study of Southern Strategies* (Chapel Hill: University of North Carolina Press, 1985), 124, 229–32.

26 David E. Hamilton, "Herbert Hoover and the Great Drought of 1930," *Journal of American History* 68 (March 1982): 875; Watson, *As I Knew Them*, 256–59; Arthur W. Macmahon, "First Session of the Seventy-first Congress," *American Political Science Review* 24 (February 1930): 39–42; Clark to Coolidge, October 31, 1929, Clark Papers.

27 David F. Burg, *The Great Depression: An Eyewitness History* (New York: Facts on File, 1996), 96; Maury Klein, *Rainbow's End: The Crash of 1929* (New York: Oxford, 2001), xiii–xiv, 190–206.

28 Allan H. Meltzer, *A History of the Federal Reserve* (Chicago: University of Chicago Press, 2003), 1:137–270; Barry Eichengreen, "Still Fettered after All These Years," *NBER Working Paper no. 9276*, National Bureau of Economic Research, Cambridge, Mass., 2002; Christina D. Romer, "The Nation in Depression," *Journal of Economic Perspectives* 7 (Spring 1993): 19–39.

29 Herbert Hoover, *Memoirs*, vol. 3, *The Great Depression, 1929–1941* (New York: Macmillan, 1952), 29–32; David Cannadine, *Mellon: An American Life* (New York: Alfred A. Knopf, 2006), 55, 391–95.

30 Byron E. Shafer and Anthony J. Badger, eds., *Contesting Democracy: Substance and Structure in American Political History, 1775–2000* (Lawrence: University Press of Kansas, 2001), 172.

31 Walter Lippmann, *Interpretations, 1931–1932* (New York: Macmillan, 1932), 67–68; Clark to Coolidge, November 14, 1932, Clark Papers; John A. Garraty, *The Great Depression* (New York: Harcourt Brace Jovanovich, 1986), 35.

32 *New York Times*, November 6, 1930; David Burner, *Herbert Hoover: A Public Life* (New York: Alfred A. Knopf, 1979), 243–53; Ben S. Bernanke, "Money, Gold, and the Great Depression," lecture presented at Washington and Lee University, Lexington, Va., March 2, 2004.

33 *New York Times*, February 7, 1932; Garraty, *The Great Depression*, 4–5, 15.

34 Joslin diary, August 10, 1931; *New York Times*, October 30, 1929; *Congressional Record*, 71st Cong., special sess., 1929, vol. 17, pt. 1, 117; *Congressional Record*, 71st Cong., 2nd sess., 1930, vol. 72, pt. 11, 12635, 12642.

35 Hamilton, "Herbert Hoover and the Great Drought," 850–75.

36 Nan Elizabeth Woodruff, *As Rare As Rain: Federal Relief in the Great Southern Drought of 1930–31* (Urbana: University of Illinois Press, 1985), 10–14, 40, 44–45, 62, 86, 94, 103, 178.

37 Franklin D. Roosevelt to Felix Frankfurter, April 18, 1930, Felix Frankfurter Papers, Library of Congress; Clark to Coolidge, July 1, August 2, 1930, Clark Papers; Arthur M. Schlesinger Jr., *The Crisis of the Old Order, 1918–1933* (Boston: Houghton Mifflin, 1957), 213.

38 Kenneth L. Kusmer, *Down and Out, on the Road: The Homeless in the Great Depression* (New York: Oxford University Press, 2002), 193–203; *New York Times*, August 19, 1948.

39 Byron Price to Theodore Joslin, May 5, 1931, Joslin Papers; Louis W. Liebovich, *Bylines in Despair: Herbert Hoover, the Great Depression, and the U.S. News Media* (Westport, Conn.: Praeger, 1994), 111, 137, 146.

40 Will Irwin, *Propaganda and the News, or What Makes You Think So?* (New York: Whittlesey House, 1936), 295; Ishbel Ross, *Ladies of the Press: The Story of Women in Journalism by an Insider* (New York: Harper & Brothers, 1936), 314.

41 *Washington Post*, July 10, 1931; James E. Pollard, *The Presidents and the Press* (New York: Macmillan, 1947), 746–47.

42 Frank R. Kent, *Without Gloves* (New York: William Morrow, 1934), 28; Kent, "Charley Michelson," 292–94; *Washington Post*, May 10, 1973; Clark to Coolidge, August 19, 1929, Clark Papers; Watson, *As I Knew Them*, 262.

43 Kent, "Charley Michelson," 290–96; Irwin, *Propaganda and the News*, 292; Michelson, *The Ghost Talks*, 28–30; *New York Times*, September 30, 1930.

44 Kent, "Charley Michelson," 295; *Washington Post*, February 9, 11, June 12, September 6, 1930; *Congressional Record*, 72nd Cong., 1st sess., 1932, vol. 75, pt. 14, 15623.

45 [Drew Pearson and Robert S. Allen], *Washington Merry-Go-Round* (New York: Horace Liveright, 1931), 55; Pollard, *The Presidents and the Press*, 742; Clark to

Coolidge, November 11, 14, 1932, Clark Papers; Jeffery M. Dorwart, *Conflict of Duty: The U.S. Navy's Intelligence Dilemma, 1919–1945* (Annapolis, Md.: Naval Institute Press, 1983), 3–4.

46 Leo C. Rosten, *The Washington Correspondents* (New York: Harcourt, Brace, 1937), 40–46.

47 Andrew Sinclair, *Prohibition: The Era of Excess* (Boston: Little, Brown, 1962), 366.

48 *Washington Post,* October 26, 29, 1930.

49 Clark to Coolidge, March 28, 1931, Clark Papers; Liebovich, *Bylines in Despair,* 146.

50 *New York Herald Tribune,* January 1, 1932.

51 Marquis James, *Mr. Garner of Texas* (Indianapolis, Ind.: Bobbs-Merrill, 1939), 113; Michael Barone, *Our Country: The Shaping of America from Roosevelt to Reagan* (New York: Free Press, 1990), 45–49; Andrew E. Busch, *Horses in Midstream: U.S. Midterm Elections and Their Consequences, 1894–1998* (Pittsburgh, Pa.: University of Pittsburgh Press, 1999), 71–82.

52 *New York Times,* November 6, 1930; Clark to Coolidge, November 6, 29, 1930, Clark Papers.

53 Martin L. Fausold, *The Presidency of Herbert C. Hoover* (Lawrence: University Press of Kansas, 1985), 101–3.

54 Hoover, *Memoirs,* 101; Clark to Coolidge, August 17, 1931, Clark Papers.

55 Craig, *After Wilson,* 200–203; Clark to Coolidge, November 29, 1930, Clark Papers.

56 Claude Bowers, *My Life: The Memoirs of Claude Bowers* (New York: Simon & Schuster, 1962), 258; Andrew Bergman, *We're in the Money: Depression America and Its Films* (New York: New York University Press, 1971), 3–17.

57 Olive Ewing Clapper, *Washington Tapestry* (New York: Whittlesey House, 1946), 3–5; Richard M. Ketchum, *Will Rogers and His Times* (New York: McGraw-Hill, 1973), 285–88.

58 *New York Times,* February 25, 1932.

59 Byron Price oral history, 11, Hoover Library; Turner Catledge, *My Life and the Times* (New York: Harper & Row, 1971), 62.

60 James Stuart Olson, *Herbert Hoover and the Reconstruction Finance Corporation, 1931–1933* (Ames: Iowa State University Press, 1977), 33–39; Lawrence H. Chamberlain, *The President, Congress and Legislation* (New York: Columbia University Press, 1946), 289–96.

61 Richard Langham Riedel, *Halls of the Mighty: My 47 Years at the Senate* (Washington, D.C.: Robert B. Luce, 1969), 172–73; E. Pendelton Herring, "First Session of the Seventy-second Congress," *American Political Science Review* 26 (October 1932): 846–74.

62 Arthur W. Macmahon, "Third Session of the Seventy-first Congress," *American Political Science Review* 25 (November 1931): 945–46; James L. Sundquist, *Dynamics of the Party System: Alignment and Realignment of Political Parties in the United States* (Washington, D.C.: Brookings Institution, 1983), 202.

63 J. Joseph Hutmacher, *Senator Robert F. Wagner and the Rise of Urban Liberalism* (New York: Atheneum, 1968), 70–92, 100–101; David Robertson, *Sly and Able: A Political Biography of James F. Byrnes* (New York: W. W. Norton, 1994), 132–33.

64 Burton Hendrick, "Shall We Have Responsible Government?" *World's Work*, January 28, 1916, 275; Neil MacNeil, *Forge of Democracy: The House of Representatives* (New York: David MacKay, 1963), 91; Bascom N. Timmons, *Garner of Texas: A Personal History* (New York: Harper & Brothers, 1948), 137–39, 147–49; *Chicago Tribune*, March 31, 1932.

65 Olson, *Herbert Hoover and the Reconstruction Finance Corporation*, 62–75; Stephen Skowronek, *The Politics Presidents Make: Leadership from John Adams to Bill Clinton* (Cambridge, Mass.: Harvard University Press, 1997), 260–85.

66 Timothy Walch and Dwight M. Miller, *Herbert Hoover and Franklin D. Roosevelt: A Documentary History* (Westport, Conn.: Greenwood, 1998), 26–27, 32; Harold Brayman, *The President Speaks Off-the-Record* (Princeton, N.J.: Dow Jones Books, 1976), 197–98.

67 Joseph Alsop, *FDR, 1882–1945: A Centenary Remembrance* (New York: Viking Press, 1982), 20, 33–34.

68 Ibid., 9–12, 20, 32–34, 41; Geoffrey C. Ward, ed., *Closest Companion: The Unknown Story of the Intimate Friendship between Franklin Roosevelt and Margaret Suckley* (Boston: Houghton Mifflin, 1995), 172.

69 Alsop, *FDR*, 73.

70 Ibid., 34–36; Nathan Miller, *FDR: An Intimate History* (Garden City, N.Y.: Doubleday, 1983), 6–34.

71 Miller, *FDR*, 63–66.

72 Robert H. Jackson, *That Man: An Insider's Portrait of Franklin D. Roosevelt*, ed. John Q. Barrett (New York: Oxford University Press, 2003), 3; Alsop, *FDR*, 61–62; Miller, *FDR*, 86–88.

73 Alsop, *FDR*, 73.

74 Kenneth S. Davis, *FDR: The Beckoning of Destiny, 1882–1928—A History* (New York: Putnam, 1972), 607–8; *Chicago Tribune*, May 30, 1919; *New York Times*, May 30, 1919; Alsop, *FDR*, 58, 93.

75 David Oshinsky, *Polio: An American Story* (New York: Oxford University Press, 2005), 24–42, 282.

76 Richard Thayer Goldberg, *The Making of Franklin D. Roosevelt: Triumph over Disability* (Cambridge, Mass.: Abt Books, 1981), 130–32; Ward, *Closest Companion*, 172, 420.

77 Frances Perkins, *The Roosevelt I Knew* (New York: Viking Press, 1946), 29; Hugh Gregory Gallagher, *FDR's Splendid Deception* (New York: Dodd, Mead, 1985), 60–62.

78 James A. Farley, *Jim Farley's Story: The Roosevelt Years* (New York: Whittlesey House, 1948), 60; Alsop, *FDR*, 70.

79 Gallagher, *FDR's Splendid Deception*, 72; Walch and Miller, *Herbert Hoover and Franklin D. Roosevelt*, 30.

80 "Howe," *New Yorker,* April 25, 1932, 13; *New York Times,* December 30, 1928; Samuel I. Rosenman, *Working with Roosevelt* (New York: Harper & Brothers, 1952), 16.

81 Kenneth S. Davis, *FDR: The New York Years, 1928–1933* (New York: Random House, 1985), 135, 155–57.

82 Alsop, *FDR,* 103–5.

83 Davis, *FDR,* 85–101.

84 Rosenman, *Working with Roosevelt,* 40–43.

85 Farley, *Jim Farley's Story,* 6–7, 9.

86 David E. Kyvig, *Repealing National Prohibition* (Kent, Ohio: Kent State University Press, 2000), xvii, 84, 144–45.

87 Ibid., 147–52; Alsop, *FDR,* 103–5.

CHAPTER 3 A COUPLE OF CONVENTIONS IN CHICAGO

1 Marion Elizabeth Rodgers, *Mencken: The American Iconoclast* (New York: Oxford, 2005), 380–81.

2 *Washington Post,* January 1, 1932; Frank R. Kent, "Charley Michelson," *Scribner's,* September 1930, 290.

3 When I began graduate studies at the University of Maryland in 1967, the History Department chairman, David Shannon, asked whether I was related to Albert C. Ritchie, for whom the campus coliseum had been named. I said no, and Professor Shannon replied that it was no matter, since Ritchie had been "the worst governor the state ever had." Steve Neal, *Happy Days Are Here Again: The 1932 Democratic Convention, the Emergence of FDR— And How America Was Changed Forever* (New York: William Morrow, 2004), 22.

4 Sean J. Savage, *Roosevelt: The Party Leader, 1932–1945* (Lexington: University Press of Kentucky, 1991), 1–3, 17–18.

5 Kenneth S. Davis, *FDR: The New York Years, 1928–1933* (New York: Random House, 1985), 204; Frank Freidel, *Franklin D. Roosevelt: The Triumph* (Boston: Little, Brown, 1956), 9–10.

6 Louis Howe to Col. E. M. House, August 17, 1931, Steve Early to Howe, October 13, 1931, Louis Howe Papers, Roosevelt Library.

7 "The Squire of Hyde Park," *Time,* February 1, 1932, 12–14; James Farley to Franklin Roosevelt, July 11, 1932, Howe Papers; Thomas L. Stokes, *Chip off My Shoulder* (Princeton, N.J.: Princeton University Press, 1940), 322.

8 Roy V. Peel and Thomas C. Donnelly, *The 1932 Campaign: An Analysis* (1935; repr., New York: DaCapo Press, 1973), 68–69; Arthur F. Mullen, *Western Democrat* (New York: Wilfred Funk, 1940), 262; Robert H. Jackson, *That Man: An Insider's Portrait of Franklin D. Roosevelt* (New York: Oxford University Press, 2003), 6; Farley to Roosevelt, July 17, 1931, Howe Papers.

9 Elliot A. Rosen, *Hoover, Roosevelt, and the Brains Trust: From Depression to New Deal* (New York: Columbia University Press, 1977), 23–24.

10 Davis, *FDR,* 207–8; Neal, *Happy Days Are Here Again,* 238–39.

11 Robert A. Slayton, *Empire Statesman: The Rise and Redemption of Al Smith* (New York: Free Press, 2001), 341–47; Edward J. Flynn, *You're the Boss* (New York: Viking Press, 1947), 86.

12 Elliott Roosevelt, ed., *F.D.R.: His Personal Letters, 1928–1945* (New York: Duell, Sloan & Pearce, 1950), 229–32.

13 David Robertson, *Sly and Able: A Political Biography of James F. Byrnes* (New York: W. W. Norton, 1994), 121; Roger H. Davidson, Susan Webb Hammond, and Raymond W. Smock, eds., *Masters of the House: Congressional Leadership over Two Centuries* (New York: Westview Press, 1998), 146–48.

14 *New York Times*, March 13, 1932; Rodney P. Carlisle, *Hearst and the New Deal: The Progressive as Reactionary* (New York: Garland, 1979), 55–56.

15 Carlisle, *Hearst and the New Deal*, 57.

16 "Democracy's Week," *Time*, January 18, 1932, 11; *Washington Post*, February 8, 1932.

17 Kathleen E. Kendall, *Communication in the Presidential Primaries: Candidates and the Media, 1912–2000* (Westport, Conn.: Praeger, 2000), 58–62; Samuel I. Rosenman, *Working with Roosevelt* (New York: Harper & Brothers, 1952), 11, 22–23, 32.

18 Rosenman, *Working with Roosevelt*, 65; Rosen, *Hoover, Roosevelt, and the Brains Trust*, 4–5, 141; Beatrice Bishop Berle and Travis Beal Jacobs, eds., *Navigating the Rapids, 1918–1971: From the Papers of Adolph A. Berle* (New York: Harcourt Brace Jovanovich, 1973), 31; Daniel Scroop, *Mr. Democrat: Jim Farley, the New Deal, and the Making of Modern American Politics* (Ann Arbor: University of Michigan Press, 2006), 74–75.

19 *New York Times*, May 23, 1932; Rosen, *Hoover, Roosevelt, and the Brains Trust*, 111, 131–32.

20 *Washington Post*, April 8, 14, 15, 1932; Slayton, *Empire Statesman*, 368–70; Rosen, *Hoover, Roosevelt, and the Brains Trust*, 134–38.

21 Rexford G. Tugwell, *The Brains Trust* (New York: Viking Press, 1968), 105, 161.

22 Rosenman, *Working with Roosevelt*, 82–83.

23 James Roosevelt and Sidney Shalatt, *Affectionately, F.D.R: A Son's Story of a Lonely Man* (New York: Harcourt, Brace, 1959), 224; James Michael Curley, *I'd Do It Again: A Record of All My Uproarious Years* (Englewood Cliffs, N.J.: Prentice-Hall, 1957), 231–34.

24 "Again 'Chock,'" *Time*, May 16, 1932, 18.

25 Douglas B. Craig, *After Wilson: The Struggle for the Democratic Party, 1920–1934* (Chapel Hill: University of North Carolina Press, 1992), 238; Jordan A. Schwarz, *The Speculator: Bernard M. Baruch in Washington, 1917–1965* (Chapel Hill: University of North Carolina Press, 1981), 267; James A. Farley, *Jim Farley's Story: The Roosevelt Years* (New York: Whittlesey House, 1948), 19.

26 Alex Gottfried, *Boss Cermak of Chicago: A Study of Political Leadership* (Seattle: University of Washington Press, 1962), 205, 242–51, 257–58, 298–308; Ray Eldon Hiebert, *Courtier for the Crowd: The Story of Ivy Lee and the Development of Public Relations* (Ames: Iowa State University Press, 1966), 218–21.

27 Peel and Donnelly, *The 1932 Campaign*, 41–42; *New York Times*, July 1, 1932.

28 Rosen, *Hoover, Roosevelt, and the Brains Trust*, 236–37; "June and Duty," *Time*, May 23, 1932, 10–11.

29 Baker to Hayes, July 29, 1930, April 27, 1931, Baker to Elliott Biskand, September 27, 1930, Baker to Walter Lippmann, August 16, 1931, Hayes to Baker, March 13, 17, 18, 1932, Newton D. Baker Papers, Library of Congress; Adolph Berle memorandum, November 7, 1932, Adolph Berle Papers, Roosevelt Library; Claude Bowers, *My Life: The Memoirs of Claude Bowers* (New York: Simon & Schuster, 1962), 225–26, 236.

30 Baker to Hayes, January 18, 1932, Hayes to Baker, September 19, 1931, January 29, 27, 1932, Lippmann to Baker, November 24, 1931, Baker Papers.

31 *New York Herald Tribune*, January 8, 1932; Roosevelt, *F.D.R.*, 254.

32 Peyton C. March to Baker, April 5, 1932, Hayes to Baker, April 18, 1932, Baker to Hayes, April 14, 1932, April 29, 1932, Baker Papers.

33 Joslin diary, April 26, 1932, Theodore Joslin Papers, Hoover Library; Louis W. Liebovich, *Bylines in Despair: Herbert Hoover, the Great Depression, and the U.S. News Media* (Westport, Conn.: Praeger, 1994), 186–87.

34 Eleanor Roosevelt told the biographer Frank Freidel that she and her husband were "absolutely convinced" that Hoover had purposefully stayed away "to try to prove that Roosevelt would collapse and was not capable of being president." Freidel considered this "absolutely preposterous," believing that it would have been out of character for Hoover to do such a thing. See Frank Freidel, "Hoover and FDR: Reminiscent Reflections," in Leo Nash, ed., *Understanding Herbert Hoover* (Stanford, Calif.: Hoover Institution Press, 1987), 138–39; Alonzo Fields oral history, 6–9, 11, Hoover Library; Eleanor Roosevelt, *This I Remember* (New York: Harper & Brothers, 1949), 61.

35 Joel T. Boone oral history, 241–42, Hoover Library.

36 Hugh Gregory Gallagher, *FDR's Splendid Deception* (New York: Dodd, Mead, 1985), xiv, 16–17; Davis W. Houck, *Rhetoric and Currency: Hoover, Roosevelt, and the Great Depression* (College Station: Texas A&M Press, 2001), 54; Joslin diary, April 30, 1932.

37 "Candidature," *Time*, January 25, 1932, 9; Peel and Donnelly, *The 1932 Campaign*, 51.

38 Joslin diary, November 30, 1931, May 3, 1932; Richard F. Shepard, *The Paper's Papers: A Reporter's Journey through the Archives of the "New York Times"* (New York: Random House, 1996), 212–14; Kendall, *Communication in the Presidential Primaries*, 62, 143–45.

39 Peel and Donnelly, *The 1932 Campaign*, 54–55; Joslin diary, May 6, 1932; "A Serious Hour," *Time*, May 16, 1932, 15.

40 Joslin diary, May 1, 1932; Ronald L. Feinman, *Twilight of Progressivism: The Western Republican Senators and the New Deal* (Baltimore, Md.: Johns Hopkins University Press, 1981), 33–47.

41 Peel and Donnelly, *The 1932 Campaign*, 24–25; *Washington Star*, January 26, 1939; *New York Times*, September 8, 1932, January 27, 1939.

42 *Chicago Tribune*, July 3, 1932.

43 Joslin diary, June 7, 1932; Richard Oulahan, *The Man Who . . . The Story of the 1932 Democratic National Convention* (New York: Dial Press, 1971), 38.

44 David E. Kyvig, *Repealing National Prohibition* (Kent, Ohio: Kent State University Press, 2000), 147–52; Joe Martin, *My First Years in Politics* (New York: McGraw-Hill, 1960), 67–68; Oliver Pilat, *Pegler: Angry Man of the Press* (Boston: Beacon Press, 1963), 112.

45 Studs Terkel, *Hard Times: An Oral History of the Great Depression* (1970; repr., New York: New Press, 2000), 290; *New York Times*, June 14, 1932; H. L. Mencken, *Making a President: A Footnote to the Saga of Democracy* (New York: Alfred A. Knopf, 1932), 57–63, 74; Kyvig, *Repealing National Prohibition*, 155.

46 *Philadelphia Inquirer*, June 17, 1932; *New York Times*, June 17, 1932; *Washington Post*, January 27, 1939; Mencken, *Making a President*, 45–48, 66–72.

47 Oulahan, *The Man Who*, 64; Bowers, *My Life*, 243.

48 Bess Furman, *Washington By-line: The Personal History of a Newspaperwoman* (New York: Alfred A. Knopf, 1949), 109; Joslin diary, June 15, 1932; *Chicago Tribune*, June 14, 1932; *Kansas City Star*, October 10, 1964; Clark to Coolidge, April 11, June 11, 1932, Edward Clark Papers, Library of Congress.

49 Joslin diary, June 12, 1932; Calvin Coolidge to Everett Sanders, June 17, 1932, Sanders to Coolidge, June 20, 1932, Everett Sanders Papers, Library of Congress; Arthur Krock, "And Now 'The Man Who—'" *New York Times Magazine*, June 7, 1936, 1–2, 19.

50 Arthur Krock, *Memoirs: Sixty Years on the Firing Line* (New York: Funk & Wagnalls, 1968), 138; *New York Times*, July 3, 1932; Liebovich, *Bylines in Despair*, 192–93.

51 *New York Times*, July 3, 1932; J. Leonard Bates, *Senator Thomas J. Walsh: Law and Public Affairs, from TR to FDR* (Urbana: University of Illinois Press, 1999), 308–11.

52 William Ivy Hair, *The Kingfish and His Realm: The Life and Times of Huey P. Long* (Baton Rouge: Louisiana State University Press, 1991), 244–45; Joslin diary, June 24, 1932.

53 Kyvig, *Repealing National Prohibition*, 156–59.

54 Rosen, *Hoover, Roosevelt, and the Brains Trust*, 244–45.

55 Shana Alexander, *Happy Days: My Mother, My Father, My Sister and Me* (New York: Doubleday, 1995), 114–16.

56 Alfred B. Rollins Jr., *Roosevelt and Howe* (1962; repr., New Brunswick, N.J.: Transaction Publications, 2002), 4–5; Flynn, *You're the Boss*, 99.

57 Neal, *Happy Days Are Here Again*, 258–59; Rosen, *Hoover, Roosevelt, and the Brains Trust*, 252–53; D. B. Hardeman and Donald C. Bacon, *Rayburn: A Biography* (Austin: Texas Monthly Press, 1987), 138–39.

58 Rosen, *Hoover, Roosevelt, and the Brains Trust*, 246–49; *New York Times*, June 11, July 1, 1932.

59 Transcript of Franklin D. Roosevelt's phone conversation with Felix Frankfurter, July 5, 1932, Felix Frankfurter Papers, Library of Congress; Mencken, *Making a President*, 113, 121–22, 134, 147; Peel and Donnelly, *The 1932 Campaign*, 101; *Washington Post*, July 1, 1932.

60 Farley, *Jim Farley's Story*, 21; *Washington Evening Star*, June 26, 1932.

61 *New York Times*, June 28, July 3, 1932; Mencken, *Making a President*, viii, 152–58; Peel and Donnelly, *The 1932 Campaign*, 101; Neal, *Happy Days Are Here Again*, 266; Mullen, *Western Democrat*, 272.

62 *Chicago Tribune*, July 2, 1932.

63 Ralph Hayes to Newton Baker, July 15, 1932, Baker Papers.

64 Arthur Krock oral history, 8, Columbia Oral History Research Office; *New York Times*, July 2, 1932; Joslin diary, June 28, 30, July 1, 1932.

65 David Nasaw, *The Chief: The Life of William Randolph Hearst* (Boston: Houghton Mifflin, 2000), 456; Oulahan, *The Man Who*, 116–17; Carlisle, *Hearst and the New Deal*, 63.

66 Hardeman and Bacon, *Rayburn*, 140–41; Oulahan, *The Man Who*, 121–23; *New York Times*, July 2, 3, 15, 1932.

67 Rosen, *Hoover, Roosevelt, and the Brains Trust*, 256–63.

68 Ibid., 258; Baker to Charles E. Diehl, July 6, 1932, Baker to Nathan Straus Jr., July 7, 1932, Hayes to Baker, July 8, 1932, Baker Papers.

69 *New York Times*, July 2, 1932.

70 Marion Elizabeth Rogers, ed., *The Impossible Mencken: A Selection of His Best Newspaper Stories* (New York: Doubleday, 1991), 322, 328; *New York Times*, July 3, 1932; Charles Michelson, *The Ghost Talks* (New York: G. P. Putnam's Sons, 1944), 139–40; Bowers, *My Life*, 246.

71 "The Roosevelt Week," *Time*, July 11, 1932, 10; Rosen, *Hoover, Roosevelt, and the Brains Trust*, 269, 272; *New York Times*, July 3, 1932.

72 Furman, *Washington By-line*, 120.

73 Gary Dean Best, *Peddling Panaceas: Popular Economists in the New Deal Era* (New Brunswick, N.J.: Transaction, 2005), 117–67.

74 Rogers, *The Impossible Mencken*, 328–29; Mencken, *Making a President*, 161–69, 173–74, 184; "Roosevelt Wins!" *Nation*, July 13, 1932, 22; Osward Garrison Villard, "The Democratic Trough at Chicago," *Nation*, July 13, 1932, 26–27; Bowers, *My Life*, 245.

75 *New York Times*, July 1, 1932; *Wall Street Journal*, July 14, 1932.

76 John Dos Passos, *Travel Books and Other Writings, 1916–1941* (New York: Library of America, 2003), 408.

77 David A. Shannon, *The Socialist Party of America: A History* (New York: Macmillan, 1955), 182–226.

78 *New York Times*, May 23, November 1, 1932.

79 *New York Times*, May 1–2, 1932.

80 Albert Fried, *Communism in America: A History in Documents* (New York: Columbia University Press, 1997), 166–76.

81 Harvey Klehr, John Earl Haynes, and Fridrikh Igorevich Firsov, *The Secret World of American Communism* (New Haven, Conn.: Yale University Press, 1995), 7; Terkel, *Hard Times*, 297–301; *Chicago Tribune*, May 29, 30, June 1, 29, 1932.

82 *Philadelphia Inquirer*, June 19, 1932; *New York Times*, June 18, July 16, August 15, 1932.

83 *New York Times*, January 8, 17, April 3, July 2, 8, 29, 1932, March 20, 1951.

CHAPTER 4 A CAMPAIGN OF HOPE AND FEAR

1 Joel T. Boone oral history, Hoover Library, 241–42; Arthur M. Schlesinger Jr., Fred L. Israel, and William P. Hansen, eds., *The Coming to Power: Critical Presidential Elections in American History* (New York: Chelsea House, 1972), 346–47.

2 Roger Burlingame, *Don't Let Them Scare You: The Life and Times of Elmer Davis* (Philadelphia: J. B. Lippincott, 1961), 113–15; John L. Heaton, *Tough Luck—Hoover Again!* (New York: Vanguard Press, 1932), 11–13; Walter Lippmann to Newton Baker, July 18, 1932, Newton Baker Papers, Library of Congress.

3 Joslin diary, July 20, 1932, Theodore Joslin Papers, Hoover Library; *New York Times*, July 13, November 6, 1932; Raymond Moley, *27 Masters of Politics, in a Personal Perspective* (New York: Funk & Wagnalls, 1949), 37–38.

4 Joslin diary, June 2, 10, 1932; see also Paul Dickson and Thomas B. Allen, *The Bonus Army: An American Epic* (New York: Walker, 2004).

5 *New York Times*, July 31, 1932; James E. Watson, *As I Knew Them* (Indianapolis, Ind.: Bobbs-Merrill, 1936), 277.

6 Donald J. Lisio, *The President and Protest: Hoover, Conspiracy, and the Bonus Riot* (Columbia: University of Missouri Press, 1974), 190–225.

7 Joslin diary, July 28, 1932; Herbert Hoover, *Memoirs*, vol. 3, *The Great Depression, 1929–1941* (New York: Macmillan, 1952), 225–27; Thomas L. Stokes, *Chip off My Shoulder* (Princeton, N.J.: Princeton University Press, 1940), 301–4.

8 Rexford G. Tugwell, *The Brains Trust* (New York: Viking Press, 1968), 259, 357–58.

9 *New York Times*, August 21, September 5, 1932; *Nation*, August 31, 1932, 181.

10 *New York Times*, September 4, 1932.

11 Bill Marsh and Bub Marsh, *Why You Should Vote for President Hoover* (New Mitford, Conn.: Privately published, 1932), 7; Arthur M. Schlesinger Jr., Fred L. Israel, and David J. Frent, eds., *Running for President: The Candidates and Their Images* (New York: Simon & Schuster, 1994), 2:163–79.

12 Joslin diary, September 15, 1932.

13 *New York Times*, August 12, 19, 1932; Joslin diary, August 17, 1932.

14 Joslin diary, August 8, 1932; Tugwell, *The Brains Trust*, 295–96, 410–11, 498.

15 Louis Howe article, distributed by the North American Newspaper Alliance, December 10, 1932, Louis Howe Papers, Roosevelt Library; transcript of Franklin D. Roosevelt's phone conversation with Felix Frankfurter, July 5, 1932, Felix Frankfurter Papers, Library of Congress; *New York Times*, July 24, 1932; Tugwell, *The Brains Trust*, 94.

16 Donald R. Richberg, *My Hero: The Indiscreet Memoirs of an Eventful but Unheroic Life* (New York: G. P. Putnam's Sons, 1954), 155; Beatrice Bishop Berle and Travis Beal Jacobs, eds., *Navigating the Rapids, 1918–1971: From the Papers of Adolph A. Berle* (New York: Harcourt Brace Jovanovich, 1973), 71.

17 Tugwell, *The Brains Trust*, 314–15; Claude Bowers, *My Life: The Memoirs of Claude Bowers* (New York: Simon & Schuster, 1962), 254–55.

18 "Shareholders in America" coupons in the Howe Papers; Louise Overacker, "Campaign Funds in a Depression Year," *American Political Science Review* 27 (October 1933): 769–83; *Washington Post*, June 25, 1932; *Chicago Tribune*, November 18, 1932; Edward Anthony oral history, 81, Hoover Library.

19 Roosevelt memorandum for Jim [Farley], July 27, 1931, Howe Papers; Joslin diary, July 31, 1932.

20 Tugwell, *The Brains Trust*, 500–503; *New York Times*, September 28, 1932.

21 Hugh Gregory Gallagher, *FDR's Splendid Deception* (New York: Dodd, Mead, 1985), 85.

22 Charles Michelson, *The Ghost Talks* (New York: G. P. Putnam's Sons, 1944), 11–12; Tugwell, *The Brains Trust*, 503–5; James A. Farley, *Jim Farley's Story: The Roosevelt Years* (New York: Whittlesey House, 1948), 28; Bowers, *My Life*, 251.

23 Richard Thayer Goldberg, *The Making of Franklin D. Roosevelt: Triumph over Disability* (Cambridge, Mass.: Abt Books, 1981), 171; "The Squire of Hyde Park," *Time*, February 1, 1932, 12–14.

24 Gallagher, *FDR's Splendid Deception*, 93–95; see also George Wolfskill and John A. Hudson, *All but the People: Franklin D. Roosevelt and His Critics, 1933–1939* (New York: Macmillan, 1969).

25 Kathleen E. Kendall, *Communication in the Presidential Primaries: Candidates and the Media, 1912–2000* (Westport, Conn.: Praeger, 2000), 601; *Los Angeles Times*, September 20, 1932.

26 *Washington Post*, October 3, 1932; Boone oral history, 215–19.

27 Gil Troy, *See How They Ran: The Changing Role of the Presidential Candidate* (Cambridge, Mass.: Harvard University Press, 1996), 161–64; *New York Times*, September 10, 11, 1932.

28 Arthur F. Mullen, *Western Democrat* (New York: Wilfred Funk, 1940), 290.

29 Joslin diary, September 13, 1932; *Washington Post*, September 14, 1932.

30 *Chicago Tribune*, November 3, 1932.

31 *New York Times*, September 15, 18, 1932; James H. Madison, ed., *Heartland: Comparative Histories of the Midwestern States* (Bloomington: Indiana University Press, 1988), 290.

32 *New York Times*, September 15, 17, 1932.

33 Harold F. Gosnell, *Champion Campaigner, Franklin D. Roosevelt* (New York: Macmillan, 1952), 123–34; Thomas K. McCraw, *TVA and the Power Fight, 1933–1939* (Philadelphia: J. B. Lippincott, 1971), 1–34.

34 *New York Times*, September 23, 1932; Robert H. Jackson, *That Man: An Insider's Portrait of Franklin D. Roosevelt* (New York: Oxford University Press, 2003), 17–18.

35 Michael Barone, *Our Country: The Shaping of America from Roosevelt to Reagan* (New York: Free Press, 1990), 54–55; Davis W. Houck, *Rhetoric and Currency: Hoover, Roosevelt, and the Great Depression* (College Station: Texas A&M Press, 2001), 140, 149–51, 153.

36 "Bob Shuler's Red-Hot Race for the Senate," *Literary Digest* 114 (October 29, 1932): 20; "Side Fights," *Time*, October 31, 1932, 14.

37 *Los Angeles Times*, September 25, 1932.

38 Adolph Berle to John Crane, October 31, 1932, Berle memorandum, November 7, 1932, Adolph Berle Papers, Roosevelt Library.

39 Roosevelt and Shalatt, *Affectionately, F.D.R.*, 231.

40 *Congressional Record*, 72nd Cong., 1st sess., 1932, vol. 75, pt. 13, 14629; Edward Clark to Calvin Coolidge, September 29, 1931, October 31, 1932, Coolidge to Clark, October 21, December 31, 1932, Edward Clark Papers, Library of Congress; *New York Times*, October 23, 1932.

41 Hoover, *Memoirs*, 3:176; Joslin diary, October 8, 1932.

42 David E. Hamilton, *From New Day to New Deal: American Farm Policy from Hoover to Roosevelt, 1928–1933* (Chapel Hill: University of North Carolina Press, 1991), 209–15; *Chicago Tribune*, October 11, 1932.

43 Berle memoranda, August 5, October 17, 1932, Berle to Roosevelt, August 10, 1932, Berle to Nicholas Murray Butler, September 29, 1932, Berle Papers.

44 Tugwell, *The Brains Trust*, 507–8; Carol Green Wilson, *Herbert Hoover: A Challenge for Today* (New York: Evans, 1968), 228; *New York Times*, September 17, October 23, 1932.

45 Irwin Hood (Ike) Hoover, *Forty-two Years in the White House* (Boston: Houghton Mifflin, 1934), 217–18, 248; Joslin diary, October 16, 17, 19, 1932.

46 Joslin diary, October 6, 1932; Hoover, *Memoirs*, 3:233–34; *New York Times*, November 3, 1932, March 13, 1933.

47 Frances Perkins, *The Roosevelt I Knew* (New York: Viking Press, 1946), 113; Raymond Moley, *After Seven Years: A Political Analysis of the New Deal* (1939; repr., Lincoln: University of Nebraska Press, 1971), 9–11, 58; Tugwell, *The Brains Trust*, 410–11.

48 Samuel I. Rosenman, *Working with Roosevelt* (New York: Harper & Brothers, 1952), 86–87; Moley, *After Seven Years*, 45–55, 63; James MacGregor Burns, *Roosevelt: The Lion and the Fox* (New York; Harcourt, Brace, 1956), 143.

49 *New York Times*, August 23, 1932; Houck, *Rhetoric and Currency*, 94, 108; Watson, *As I Knew Them*, 279.

50 *Boston Transcript*, November 2, 1932.

51 *New York Times*, August 23, 1932.

52 Nancy Beck Young, *Lou Henry Hoover: Activist First Lady* (Lawrence: University Press of Kansas, 2004), 154, 160; Bess Furman, *Washington By-line: The Personal History of a Newspaperwoman* (New York: Alfred A. Knopf, 1949), 8–9, 133.

53 Blanche Wiesen Cook, *Eleanor Roosevelt, 1884–1933* (New York: Viking Press, 1992), 412–76; *New York Times*, July 18, October 24, 1932.

54 Tugwell, *The Brains Trust*, 307, 310; Otis L. Graham Jr., *Toward a Planned Society: From Roosevelt to Nixon* (New York: Oxford University Press, 1976), 18–20.

55 Houck, *Rhetoric and Currency*, 155–62; John Kennedy Ohl, *Hugh S. Johnson and the New Deal* (DeKalb: Northern Illinois University Press, 1985), 88–90.

56 "The Campaign in the 'Fear' Stage," *Literary Digest* 114 (November 5, 1932): 1–2; *New York Times,* October 30, 1932.

57 Tugwell, *The Brains Trust,* 506; *New York Times,* October 20, 1932.

58 Rosenman, *Working with Roosevelt,* 86–87; Tugwell, *The Brains Trust,* 465.

59 John Gerring, *Party Ideologies in America, 1828–1996* (New York: Cambridge University Press, 1998), 126–30, 140, 147, 188, 205–30.

60 W. J. Cash, *The Mind of the South* (New York: Alfred A. Knopf, 1941), 371; Kari Frederickson, *The Dixiecrat Revolt and the End of the Solid South, 1932–1968* (Chapel Hill: University of North Carolina Press, 2001), 15; Tugwell, *The Brains Trust,* 514–15.

61 *New York Times,* October 5, 1932, June 28, 1936; Farley, *Jim Farley's Story,* 29–30.

62 *New York Times,* October 29, 1932; Alan Brinkley, *Voices of Protest: Huey Long, Father Coughlin, and the Great Depression* (New York: Alfred A. Knopf, 1982), 104, 108, 130.

63 Furman, *Washington By-line,* 132; Edmund W. Starling, *Starling of the White House* (New York: Simon & Schuster, 1946), 289, 298–300; Stokes, *Chip off My Shoulder,* 305.

64 Theodore G. Joslin, *Hoover off the Record* (Garden City, N.Y.: Doubleday, Doran, 1934), 321–23; *New York Times,* October 23, November 6, 1932.

65 David Robertson, *Sly and Able: A Political Biography of James F. Byrnes* (New York: W. W. Norton, 1994), 141–43; Moley, *27 Masters of Politics,* 39–40; Michelson, *The Ghost Talks,* 46.

66 Joslin diary, February 15; Troy, *See How They Ran,* 165; Richard Langham Riedel, *Halls of the Mighty: My 47 Years at the Senate* (Washington, D.C.: Robert B. Luce, 1969), 141.

67 *Chicago Tribune,* October 29, 1932; *New York Times,* October 29, 1932.

68 Wilson, *Herbert Hoover,* 229–30.

69 Moley, *After Seven Years,* 63–64; *New York Times,* November 4, 1932.

70 *New York Times,* November 1, 1932.

71 Becky M. Nicolaides, "Radio Electioneering in the American Presidential Campaigns of 1932 and 1936," *Historical Journal of Film, Radio and Television* 6 (1988): 116; H. L. Pettey to Howe, November 30, 1932, Howe Papers; *New York Times,* November 6, 1932.

72 Leo C. Rosten, *The Washington Correspondents* (New York: Harcourt, Brace, 1937), 46; Louis W. Liebovich, *Bylines in Despair: Herbert Hoover, the Great Depression, and the U.S. News Media* (Westport, Conn.: Praeger, 1994), 189.

73 Ronald Steel, *Walter Lippmann and the American Century* (Boston: Little, Brown, 1980), 295–96.

74 Barone, *Our Country,* 55; Tugwell, *The Brains Trust,* 488, 495; Matthew Josephson, *Infidel in the Temple: A Memoir of the Nineteen-thirties* (New York: Alfred A. Knopf, 1967), 59–60, 103–4; George Charney, *A Long Journey* (Chicago: Quadrangle, 1968), 23–49.

75 James R. Barrett, *William Z. Foster and the Tragedy of American Radicalism* (Urbana: University of Illinois Press, 1999), 178–88; Roy V. Peel and

Thomas C. Donnelly, *The 1932 Campaign: An Analysis* (New York: Farrar & Rinehart, 1935), 194; *Time*, July 11, 1932, 12; *New York Times*, October 28, November 6, 1932.

76 *New York Times*, October 28, November 7, 1932.

77 Bernard K. Johnpoll, *Pacifist's Progress: Norman Thomas and the Decline of American Socialism* (Chicago: Quadrangle, 1970), 93–98; *New York Times*, September 4, October 22, November 4, 1932.

78 "Governor Roosevelt's Campaign," *Nation*, November 2, 1932, 414; Walter Lippmann to Newton Baker, July 18, 1932, Baker Papers; Peel and Donnelly, *The 1932 Campaign*, 129.

79 *Chicago Tribune*, November 8, 1932; Tugwell, *The Brains Trust*, 286–87; Jerry Voorhis, *Confessions of a Congressman* (Garden City, N.Y.: Doubleday, 1948), 16; Rita James Simon, ed., *As We Saw the Thirties: Essays on Social and Political Movements of a Decade* (Urbana: University of Illinois Press, 1967), 119.

80 Fred W. Johnson to James A. Farley, October 21, 1932, Howe Papers.

81 *Los Angeles Times*, September 26, 1932; George Gallup, *A Guide to Public Opinion Polls* (Princeton, N.J.: Princeton University Press, 1944), 20–31.

82 "'Digest' Poll Scrutinized by an Expert," *Literary Digest* 114 (October 8, 1932): 37–39.

83 See the following articles in *Literary Digest*, vol. 114: "First Poll Figures Give Hoover a Slight Lead" (September 24, 1932): 7–8; "Roosevelt Slips Ahead in a See-saw Race" (October 1, 1932): 8–9; "The Stampede across the Old Party Lines" and "Looks a Bit Like a Roosevelt Week in the Poll" (October 8, 1932): 1–2, 8–9; "Roosevelt Leads, but It's Anybody's Race Yet" (October 15, 1932): 10–11.

84 "Roosevelt Bags 41 States out of 48," *Literary Digest* 114 (November 5, 1932): 8–9, 44–47.

85 "Nailing a Lie!" *Literary Digest* 114 (November 5, 1932): 1; *Washington Post*, October 29, 1932; *New York Times*, October 15, November 5, 1932.

86 *Los Angeles Times*, October 27, 1932; Allan H. Meltzer, *A History of the Federal Reserve, 1913–1951* (Chicago: University of Chicago Press, 2003), 358–74.

87 Joslin diary, October 10, November 1, 5, 1932; Boone oral history, 223; Starling, *Starling of the White House*, 289, 298–300.

88 Joslin diary, November 8, 1932; Boone oral history, 231; Farley, *Jim Farley's Story*, 31; Edward J. Flynn, *You're the Boss* (1947; repr., Westport, Conn.: Greenwood Press, 1975), 122.

89 "Press Gives Net Election Returns," *Broadcasting* 4 (November 15, 1932): 8.

90 *New York Times*, November 6, 1932; Everett Sanders to Calvin Coolidge, November 28, 1932, Everett Sanders Papers, Library of Congress; Theodore Joslin to Henry J. Allen, November 14, 1932, Joslin Papers; Hoover, *Memoirs*, 3:vi.

91 Everett Carll Ladd Jr., with Charles D. Hadley, *Transformations of the American Party System: Political Conditions from the New Deal to the 1970s* (New York: W. W. Norton, 1978), 54–60.

92 Kai Bird and Martin J. Sherwin, *American Prometheus: The Triumph and Tragedy of J. Robert Oppenheimer* (New York: Alfred A. Knopf, 2005), 104.

93 Angus Campbell, Philip E. Converse, Warren E. Miller, and Donald E. Stokes, *The American Voter* (1960; repr., Chicago: University of Chicago Press, 1980), 89, 154–57; Jerome M. Clubb, William H. Flanigan, and Nancy H. Zingale, *Partisan Realignment: Voters, Parties, and Government in American History* (Boulder, Colo.: Westview Press, 1990), 254–60; James L. Sundquist, *Dynamics of the Party System: Alignment and Realignment of Political Parties in the United States* (Washington, D.C.: Brookings Institution, 1983), 198–239; Peel and Donnelly, *The 1932 Campaign*, 213–25.

94 Donald J. Lisio, *Hoover, Blacks and Lily-Whites: A Study of Southern Strategies* (Chapel Hill: University of North Carolina Press, 1985), 252–53, 260–66, 269, 273; Ladd, *Transformations of the American Party System*, 67, 93–104; *Chicago Defender*, November 19, 1932.

95 Byrd joined the freshman class late after winning a special election in November 1933. Patrick J. Maney, *The Roosevelt Presence: A Biography of Franklin D. Roosevelt* (New York: Twayne, 1992), 51–55.

96 John M. Allswang, *The New Deal and American Politics: A Study in Political Change* (New York: Wiley, 1978), 12–14; David E. Kyvig, *Repealing National Prohibition* (Kent, Ohio: Kent State University Press, 2000), 166–68.

97 "Texas Tangled in 'Ma's' Apron Strings," *Literary Digest* 114 (September 24, 1932): 34.

98 *Kansas City Star*, October 25, 1964.

CHAPTER 5 THE NEW DEAL EXPERIMENT

1 Joel T. Boone oral history, 231–34, Hoover Library.

2 Andrew J. Dunar and Dennis McBride, *Building Hoover Dam: An Oral History of the Great Depression* (New York: Twayne, 1993), 106–7; Lawrence Richey to Herbert Hoover, May 3, 1947, Lawrence Richey Papers, Hoover Library.

3 Raymond Moley, *After Seven Years* (New York: Harper & Brothers, 1939), 68; Elliot A. Rosen, *Hoover, Roosevelt, and the Brains Trust: From Depression to New Deal* (New York: Columbia University Press, 1977), 345–46.

4 Timothy Walch and Dwight M. Miller, *Herbert Hoover and Franklin D. Roosevelt: A Documentary History* (Westport, Conn.: Greenwood, 1998), 67–68.

5 *Chicago Tribune*, November 23, 1932; Joslin diary, November 12, 16, 17, 1932, Theodore Joslin Papers, Hoover Library; Frank Freidel, *Franklin D. Roosevelt: Launching the New Deal* (Boston: Little, Brown, 1973), 26–27.

6 Moley, *After Seven Years*, 71–77; Joslin diary, November 16, 22, 23, 1932; Freidel, *Franklin D. Roosevelt: Launching the New Deal*, 31–35.

7 Harold Brayman, *The President Speaks Off-the-Record* (Princeton, N.J.: Dow Jones, 1976), 229–32.

8 Adolph Berle to Raymond Moley, November 10, 1932, Adolph Berle Papers, Roosevelt Library; Edward J. Flynn, *You're the Boss* (1947; repr., Westport, Conn.: Greenwood, 1975), 126; Rexford G. Tugwell, *Roosevelt's Revolution: The First Year—A Personal Perspective* (New York: Macmillan, 1977), 21.

9   Joslin diary, December 20, 1932; Moley, *After Seven Years,* 84–89.

10 Calvin Coolidge to Edward Clark, December 31, 1932, Edward Clark Papers, Library of Congress; William Allen White, *A Puritan in Babylon: The Story of Calvin Coolidge* (New York: Macmillan, 1938), 434–38.

11 Joslin diary, December 21, 1932, January 4, 20, 23, February 1, 1933.

12 Joslin diary, November 29, 1932; Herbert Hoover, *Memoirs,* vol. 3, *The Great Depression, 1929–1941* (New York: Macmillan, 1952), 203–4; E. Pendleton Herring, "Second Session of the Seventy-second Congress, December 5, 1932 to March 4, 1933," *American Political Science Review* 27 (June 1933): 406.

13 Raymond Moley, *The First New Deal* (New York: Harcourt, Brace & World, 1966), 30–32; Herring, "Second Session of the Seventy-second Congress," 404–22; Arthur Krock oral history, 12–13, Columbia Oral History Research Office.

14 Susan Estabrook Kennedy, *The Banking Crisis of 1933* (Lexington: University Press of Kentucky, 1973), 69–73.

15 Gaines M. Foster, *Moral Reconstruction: Christian Lobbyists and the Federal Legislation of Morality, 1865–1920* (Chapel Hill: University of North Carolina Press, 2002), 224; Joslin diary, February 17, 1933.

16 *New York Times,* October 16, 1930; Joslin diary, March 30, 1932.

17 Adolph Berle to Franklin Roosevelt, July 20, 1932, Berle Papers.

18 Donald A. Ritchie, "The Pecora Stock Market Exposé," in Arthur M. Schlesinger Jr. and Roger Bruns, eds., *Congress Investigates: A Documented History, 1792–1974* (New York: R. R. Bowker, 1975), 2555–78.

19 Tugwell, *Roosevelt's Revolution,* 18–19.

20 Kennedy, *The Banking Crisis of 1933,* 4, 19–20.

21 Joslin diary, February 25, 1933; Kennedy, *The Banking Crisis of 1933,* 69–73, 135–43.

22 Bernard Sternsher, *Rexford Tugwell and the New Deal* (New Brunswick, N.J.: Rutgers University Press, 1964), 73–76; *New York Times,* April 11, 1934.

23 Moley, *After Seven Years,* 144–56; James Stuart Olson, *Herbert Hoover and the Reconstruction Finance Corporation, 1931–1933* (Ames: Iowa State University Press, 1977), 106–15; Eugene Meyer oral history, 674, Columbia Oral History Research Office.

24 James Roosevelt and Sidney Shalatt, *Affectionately, F.D.R: A Son's Story of a Lonely Man* (New York: Harcourt, Brace, 1959), 252; Flynn, *You're the Boss,* 125.

25 Grace Tully, *F.D.R., My Boss* (New York: Charles Scribner's Sons, 1949), 60–62; Moley, *The First New Deal,* 58, 151–52, 209–12.

26 *New York Times,* February 9, 1931; Moley, *The First New Deal,* 96–119.

27 Tom E. Terrill and Jerrold Hirsch, eds., *Such As Us: Southern Voices of the Thirties* (Chapel Hill: University of North Carolina Press, 1967), 167.

28 Joslin diary, March 2, 1933; Gary Dean Best, *Herbert Hoover: The Post Presidential Years, 1933–1964,* 2 vols. (Stanford, Calif.: Hoover Institution Press, 1983), 1:2–3; Nicholas Roosevelt oral history, 10–12, Hoover Library.

29 *New York Times,* March 25, 1933; Elmus Wicker, *The Banking Panics of the Great Depression* (New York: Cambridge University Press, 1996), 19–23, 57, 66, 77, 95, 146; Lawrence W. Levine and Cornelia R. Levine, *The People and the President: America's Conversation with FDR* (Boston: Beacon Press, 2002), 48.

30 Barry J. Eichengreen, *Golden Fetters: The Gold Standard and the Great Depression, 1919–1939* (New York: Oxford University Press, 1992); Eichengreen, "Still Fettered after All These Years," *NBER Working Paper no. 9276,* National Bureau of Economic Research, Cambridge, Mass., 2002.

31 William E. Leuchtenburg, *Franklin D. Roosevelt and the New Deal, 1932–1940* (New York: Harper & Row, 1963), 41–62; Patrick J. Maney, *The Roosevelt Presence: A Biography of Franklin Delano Roosevelt* (New York: Twayne, 1992), 53.

32 Tugwell, *The Roosevelt Revolution,* 98–99, 101.

33 David E. Hamilton, *From New Day to New Deal: American Farm Policy from Hoover to Roosevelt, 1928–1933* (Chapel Hill: University of North Carolina Press, 1991), 233–34, 240–51.

34 Donald A. Ritchie, *James M. Landis: Dean of the Regulators* (Cambridge, Mass.: Harvard University Press, 1980), 43–78.

35 Studs Terkel, *Hard Times: An Oral History of the Great Depression* (New York: Pantheon, 1970), 178; Donald A. Ritchie, *Reporting from Washington: The History of the Washington Press Corps* (New York: Oxford University Press, 2005), 7–27.

36 *New York Times,* January 27, 1933; Robert H. Jackson, *That Man: An Insider's Portrait of Franklin D. Roosevelt* (New York: Oxford University Press, 2003), 12, 15; Joseph Alsop, *FDR, 1882–1945: A Centenary Remembrance* (New York: Viking Press, 1982), 111–12, 143.

37 Ritchie, *James M. Landis,* 76.

38 Tully, *F.D.R., My Boss,* 66; H. G. Wells, *Experiment in Autobiography* (New York: Macmillan, 1934), 681; Thomas H. Eliot, *Recollections of the New Deal: When People Mattered* (Boston: Northeastern University Press, 1992), 23.

39 Doris Kearns Goodwin, *No Ordinary Time: Franklin and Eleanor Roosevelt—The Home Front in World War II* (New York: Simon & Schuster, 1994), 28; Eleanor Roosevelt, *This I Remember* (New York: Harper, 1949), 349.

40 Alsop, *FDR,* 10–12.

41 Matthew Josephson, *Infidel in the Temple: A Memoir of the Nineteen-thirties* (New York: Alfred A. Knopf, 1967), 234–47; Thomas L. Stokes, *Chip off My Shoulder* (Princeton, N.J.: Princeton University Press, 1940), 361.

42 *Washington Post,* May 6, 1934; Edward T. Clark to Calvin Coolidge, December 30, 1932, Clark Papers; Joslin diary, December 19, 1932.

43 Clyde P. Weed, *The Nemesis of Reform: The Republican Party during the New Deal* (New York: Columbia University Press, 1994), 30–39, 43–49.

44 Herbert Hoover, *The Challenge to Liberty* (New York: Charles Scribner's Sons, 1935), 108–13, 170–71, 203; *New York Times,* November 6, 1934; Best, *Herbert Hoover: The Post Presidential Years,* 1:29.

45 Charles A. Moser, *Watershed and Ratifying Elections: A Historical View of the 1934 and 1954 Midterm Elections* (Washington, D.C.: Free Congress Research & Education Foundation, 1982), 5–11; *Washington Post,* November 8, 1934.

46 Gareth Davies, "The Unsuspected Radicalism of the Social Security Act," in Robert A. Garson and Stuart S. Kidd, eds., *The Roosevelt Years: New Perspectives on American History, 1933–1945* (Edinburgh: Edinburgh University Press, 1999), 56–71.

47 *New York Times,* June 17, 1936; John Patrick Diggins, ed., *The Liberal Persuasion: Arthur M. Schlesinger, Jr. and the Challenge of the American Past* (Princeton, N.J.: Princeton University Press, 1997), 151–60; M. J. Heale, *Franklin D. Roosevelt: The New Deal and War* (New York: Routledge, 1999), 4–5.

48 Moley, *The First New Deal,* 376–79, 523–42.

49 William S. White, *Majesty and Mischief: A Mixed Tribute to F.D.R.* (New York: McGraw-Hill, 1961), 77–79; Marquis Childs, *They Hate Roosevelt!* (New York: Harper & Brothers, 1936), 26; George Wolfskill and John A. Hudson, *All but the People: Franklin D. Roosevelt and His Critics, 1933–39* (New York: Macmillan, 1969), 61–92, 215–16.

50 Best, *Herbert Hoover: The Post Presidential Years,* 1:28; *Washington Post,* January 26, 1936.

51 Walter Newton to Grace Newton, April 24, 1935, Newton to James H. McLafferty, June 18, 1936, Walter Newton Papers, Hoover Library; Nicholas Roosevelt oral history, 2, Hoover Library; Best, *Herbert Hoover: The Post Presidential Years,* 1:37–39, 54.

52 Frank R. Kent, *Without Grease* (New York: William Morrow, 1936), 169; Best, *Herbert Hoover: The Post Presidential Years,* 1:61–62, 66–67, 72–73.

53 *New York Times,* September 7, November 13, 1936; James L Sundquist, *Dynamics of the Party System: Alignment and Realignment of Political Parties in the United States* (Washington, D.C.: Brookings Institution, 1983), 218–19; Joe Martin, *My First Fifty Years in Politics* (New York: McGraw-Hill, 1960), 78.

54 John L. Shover, "The Emergence of a Two-Party System in Republican Philadelphia, 1924–1936," *Journal of American History* 60 (March 1974): 985–1002.

55 *New York Times,* February 3, 1936; Frances Perkins, *The Roosevelt I Knew* (New York: Viking Press, 1946), 34; Rita James Simon, *As We Saw the Thirties: Essays on Social and Political Movements of a Decade* (Urbana: University of Illinois Press, 1967), 46–75, 103–22.

56 Wells, *Experiment in Autobiography,* 672; George Charney, *A Long Journey* (Chicago: Quadrangle, 1968), 36–37, 59, 125; Simon, *As We Saw the Thirties,* 216–53.

57 Terkel, *Hard Times,* 442; Michael Janeway, *The Fall of the House of Roosevelt: Brokers of Ideas of Power from FDR to LBJ* (New York: Columbia University Press, 2004), 37; Allan H. Meltzer, *A History of the Federal Reserve* (Chicago: University of Chicago Press, 2003), 1:503–77.

58 Steve Neal, *McNary of Oregon: A Political Biography* (Portland: Oregon Historical Society Press, 1985), 165; David A. Horowitz, *Beyond Left and Right:*

Insurgency and the Establishment (Urbana: University of Illinois Press, 1997), 140–45, 158–61.

59 Robert Dallek, *Franklin D. Roosevelt and American Foreign Policy, 1932–1945* (New York: Oxford University Press, 1979), 530–31.

60 Best, *Herbert Hoover: The Post Presidential Years*, 1:102–42; David Burner, *Herbert Hoover: A Public Life* (New York: Alfred A. Knopf, 1979), 332; Walch and Miller, *Herbert Hoover and Franklin D. Roosevelt*, 169–79; Alonzo Fields oral history, 18, Hoover Library.

61 Robert A. Caro, *The Years of Lyndon Johnson: The Path to Power* (New York: Alfred A. Knopf, 1982), 557–605.

62 Mark O. Hatfield, Donald A. Ritchie, Jo Anne McCormick Quatannes, Richard A. Baker, and William T. Hull, *Vice Presidents of the United States, 1789–1993* (Washington, D.C.: Government Printing Office, 1997), 385–93; *New York Times*, July 18, 1940.

63 Herbert Hoover to Walter Newton, April 18, May 11, 1940, Newton Papers; Best, *Herbert Hoover: The Post Presidential Years*, 1:150–65.

64 Charles Peters, *Five Days in Philadelphia* (New York: Public Affairs, 2005), 78–93.

65 Leuchtenburg, *Franklin D. Roosevelt and the New Deal*, 226–27.

66 Frank Freidel, "Hoover and FDR: Reminiscent Reflections," in Leo Nash, ed., *Understanding Herbert Hoover* (Stanford, Calif.: Hoover Institute Press, 1987), 139.

67 Byron E. Shafer and Anthony J. Badger, eds., *Contesting Democracy: Substance and Structure in American Political History, 1775–2000* (Lawrence: University Press of Kansas, 2001), 189–93, 205–10.

68 Alan Brinkley, *The End of Reform: New Deal Liberalism in Recession and War* (New York: Alfred A. Knopf, 1995), 227–71; White, *Majesty and Mischief*, 179–85; Josephson, *Infidel in the Temple*, 509.

69 Burner, *Herbert Hoover*, 329.

70 *Washington Post*, April 7, 1945.

71 William E. Leuchtenburg, *The FDR Years: On Roosevelt and His Legacy* (New York: Columbia University Press, 1995), 1–34.

72 David Oshinsky, *Polio: An American Story* (New York: Oxford University Press, 2005), 24, 201.

73 Harold F. Gosnell, *Champion Campaigner, Franklin D. Roosevelt* (New York: Macmillan, 1952), 219–25.

74 Timothy Walch and Dwight M. Miller, eds., *Herbert Hoover and Harry S. Truman: A Documentary History* (Worland, Wyo.: High Plains Publishing, 1992), 35–36, 43, 53.

75 H. G. Powers to Truman, April 26, 1945, W. Hume Logan to Truman, April 25, 1945, Representative Jack Z. Anderson to Truman, May 22, 1945, Rev. John G. Pierce to Truman, August 14, 1945, Anna Martin to Truman, June 5, 1945, Mrs. Paul L. Wilson to Truman, June 5, 1945, Paul Crosbie to Truman, February 27, 1946, Mary Hoobler to Truman, May, 1945, Mrs. Alice A. Tollefson to Truman, July 21, 1946, Howard B. Norton to Truman, Septem-

ber 12, 1947, Justice Fitzpatrick Fletcher to Truman, June 7, 1945, Papers of Harry S. Truman, Official File, Truman Library.

76 Walch and Miller, *Herbert Hoover and Harry S. Truman*, 184–88; Walter Trohan, *Political Animals: Memoirs of a Sentimental Cynic* (Garden City, N.Y.: Doubleday, 1975), 206.

77 Angus Campbell, Philip E. Converse, Warren E. Miller, and Donald E. Stokes, *The American Voter* (1960; repr., Chicago: University of Chicago Press, 1980), 45–47, 401, 534; David S. Brown, *Richard Hofstadter: An Intellectual Biography* (Chicago: University of Chicago Press, 2006), 62.

78 Lester Merkel, *What You Don't Know Can Hurt You: A Study of Public Opinion and Public Emotion* (Washington, D.C.: Public Affairs Press, 1972), 60; Arthur Krock, *Memoirs: Sixty Years on the Firing Line* (New York: Funk & Wagnalls, 1968), 120; William S. White, *The Making of a Journalist* (Lexington: University Press of Kentucky, 1986), 43.

79 Hoover, *Memoirs*, 3:195; Homer F. Cunningham, *The Presidents' Last Years: George Washington to Lyndon B. Johnson* (Jefferson, N.C.: McFarland, 1989), 228–40.

80 Steve Fraser and Gary Gerstle, eds., *The Rise and Fall of the New Deal Order, 1930–1980* (Princeton, N.J.: Princeton University Press, 1989), 185–205, 243–66.

81 *Washington Post*, March 6, 1978, July 29, 1979.

82 *Washington Post*, March 10, 1980.

83 Andrew E. Busch, *Reagan's Victory: The Presidential Election of 1980 and the Rise of the Right* (Lawrence: University Press of Kansas, 2005), 29–36; Ronald Reagan, *Speaking My Mind: Selected Speeches* (New York: Simon & Schuster, 1989), 22–23, 213–14.

84 *New York Times*, July 20, 1980; *Los Angeles Times*, July 22, 1980; *Washington Post*, August 10, 1980.

85 Ronald Reagan, with Richard G. Hubler, *Where's the Rest of Me?* (New York: Duell, Sloan & Pearce, 1965), 42, 52–54.

86 David Frum, *Dead Right* (New York: Basic Books, 1994), 34; *Washington Post*, July 13, 1980.

87 *Minneapolis Star Tribune*, March 28, 2004; *New York Times*, October 24, 2004; *Washington Post*, October 28, 2004.

88 William Allen White, *The Autobiography of William Allen White* (New York: Macmillan, 1946), 635; *New York Times*, December 15, 1996; *Wall Street Journal*, June 10, 2004, September 12, 2005; "The Presidents: History's Judgment," *Time*, April 13, 1998, 106.

89 Ben S. Bernanke, *Essays on the Great Depression* (Princeton, N.J.: Princeton University Press, 2000); Bernanke, "Money, Gold, and the Great Depression," lecture presented at Washington and Lee University, Lexington, Va., March 2, 2004.

BIBLIOGRAPHIC ESSAY

The 1932 contest between Herbert Hoover and Franklin Roosevelt as well as their dueling presidencies has generated an abundance of literature. A good place to begin is with a selection of records from their presidential libraries compiled by Timothy Walch and Dwight M. Miller, *Herbert Hoover and Franklin D. Roosevelt: A Documentary History* (Westport, Conn.: Greenwood, 1998), and *Herbert Hoover and Harry S. Truman: A Documentary History* (Worland, Wyo.: High Plains Publishing, 1992). The collected public papers of the presidents are available in *Public Papers of the President of the United States, Herbert Hoover*, 6 vols. (Washington, D.C.: Government Printing Office, 1974–1977), and Samuel I. Rosenman, ed., *The Public Papers and Addresses of Franklin D. Roosevelt*, 13 vols. (New York: Russell & Russell, 1938–1950). Among the general studies of presidential politics, policies, and administrative styles that shed light on Hoover and Roosevelt are Stephen Skowronek, *The Politics Presidents Make: Leadership from John Adams to Bill Clinton* (Cambridge, Mass.: Harvard University Press, 1997); Gil Troy, *See How They Ran: The Changing Role of the Presidential Candidate* (Cambridge, Mass.: Harvard University Press, 1996); and Charles E. Walcott and Karen M. Hult, *Governing the White House: From Hoover through LBJ* (Lawrence: University Press of Kansas, 1995).

The economic and social backdrop for the election has been painted in a variety of hues by Ben S. Bernanke, *Essays on the Great Depression* (Princeton, N.J.: Princeton University Press, 2000); Barry Eichengreen, *Golden Fetters: The Gold Standard and the Great Depression, 1919–1939* (New York: Oxford University Press, 1992); Milton Friedman and Anna Schwartz, *The Great Contraction, 1929–33* (Princeton, N.J.: Princeton University Press, 1965); John Kenneth Galbraith, *The Great Crash* (Boston: Houghton Mifflin, 1955); John A. Garraty, *The Great Depression* (New York: Doubleday, 1986); Thomas E. Hall and J. David Ferguson, *The Great Depression: An International Disaster of Perverse Economic Policies* (Ann Arbor: University of Michigan Press, 1998); Charles P. Kindleberger, *The World in Depression, 1929–39* (Berkeley: University of California Press, 1973); Maury Klein, *Rainbow's End: The Crash of 1929* (New York: Oxford University Press, 2001); Robert S. McElvaine, *The Great Depression, 1929–1941* (New York: Times Books, 1984); Allan H. Meltzer, *A History of the Federal Reserve, 1913–1951* (Chicago: University of Chicago Press, 2003); Murray N. Rothbard, *America's Great Depression* (Princeton, N.J.: Van Nostrand, 1963); Peter Temin, *Lessons from the Great Depression* (Cambridge, Mass.: MIT Press, 1989); Tom H. Watkins, *The Hungry Years: A Narrative History of the Great Depression* (New York: Henry Holt, 1999); and Elmus Wicker, *The Banking Panics of the Great Depression* (New York: Cambridge University Press, 1996).

The concept of critical elections was originated by V. O. Key Jr., "A Theory of Critical Elections," *Journal of Politics* 17 (February 1955), and expanded upon by

Walter Dean Burnham in *Critical Elections and the Mainsprings of American Politics* (New York: Norton, 1970). Analyses of the political shifts around the election of 1932 can be found in John M. Allswang, *The New Deal and American Politics: A Study in Political Change* (New York: Wiley, 1978); Kristi Andersen, *The Creation of a Democratic Majority, 1928–1936* (Chicago: University of Chicago Press, 1979); Michael Barone, *Our Country: The Shaping of America from Roosevelt to Reagan* (New York: Free Press, 1990); David Burner, *The Politics of Provincialism: The Democratic Party in Transition, 1918–1932* (New York: Alfred A. Knopf, 1968); Angus Campbell, Philip E. Converse, Warren E. Miller, and Donald E. Stokes, *The American Voter* (New York: Wiley, 1960); Lizabeth Cohen, *Making a New Deal: Industrial Workers in Chicago, 1919–1939* (New York: Cambridge University Press, 1990); Jerome M. Clubb, William H. Flanigan, and Nancy H. Zingale, *Partisan Realignment: Voters, Parties, and Government in American History* (Boulder, Colo.: Westview Press, 1990); Douglas B. Craig, *After Wilson: The Struggle for the Democratic Party, 1920–1934* (Chapel Hill: University of North Carolina Press, 1992); Gerald H. Gamm, *The Making of New Deal Democrats: Voting Behavior and Realignment in Boston, 1920–1940* (Chicago: University of Chicago Press, 1989); John Gerring, *Party Ideologies in America, 1828–1996* (New York: Cambridge University Press, 1998); Otis L. Graham Jr., *Encore for Reform: The Old Progressives and the New Deal* (New York: Oxford University Press, 1967); John D. Hicks, *Republican Ascendancy, 1921–1933* (New York: Harper, 1960); Richard Hofstadter, *The Age of Reform: From Bryan to F.D.R.* (New York: Alfred A. Knopf, 1955); Davis W. Houck, *Rhetoric as Currency: Hoover, Roosevelt, and the Great Depression* (College Station: Texas A&M University Press, 2001); Peter B. Kovler, ed., *Democrats and the American Idea: A Bicentennial Appraisal* (Washington, D.C.: Center for National Policy Press, 1992); Everett Carll Ladd Jr., with Charles D. Hadley, *Transformations of the American Party System: Political Conditions from the New Deal to the 1970s* (New York: Norton, 1978); William E. Leuchtenburg, *The Perils of Prosperity, 1914–32* (Chicago: University of Chicago Press, 1958); David Plotke, *Building a Democratic Political Order: Reshaping American Liberalism in the 1930s and 1940s* (New York: Cambridge University Press, 1996); Elliot A. Rosen, *Hoover, Roosevelt, and the Brains Trust: From Depression to New Deal* (New York: Columbia University Press, 1977); Arthur M. Schlesinger Jr., ed., *History of U.S. Political Parties* (New York: Chelsea House, 1973); Byron E. Shafer and Anthony J. Badger, *Contesting Democracy: Substance and Structure in American Political History, 1775–2000* (Lawrence: University Press of Kansas, 2001); James L. Sundquist, *Dynamics of the Party System: Alignment and Realignment of Political Parties in the United States* (Washington, D.C.: Brookings Institution, 1983); and Clyde P. Weed, *The Nemesis of Reform: The Republican Party during the New Deal* (New York: Columbia University Press, 1994).

Frank Freidel, who first counted Hoover as a hero and later became an admirer of Roosevelt, offered observations on their friendship, "Hoover and Roosevelt: Reminiscent Reflections," in Leo Nash, ed., *Understanding Herbert Hoover* (Stanford, Calif.: Hoover Institution Press, 1987). Their philosophies and positions on the issues are compared in Edward O. Guerrant, *Herbert Hoover, Franklin Roose-*

velt: Comparisons and Contrasts (Cleveland, Ohio: H. Allen, 1960), and Gordon Lloyd, ed., *The Two Faces of Liberalism: How the Hoover-Roosevelt Debate Shapes the 21st Century* (Salem, Mass.: Scrivener Press, 2006). Their presidential contest is the subject of Frank Freidel, "Election of 1932," in Arthur M. Schlesinger Jr., Fred L. Israel, and William P. Hansen, eds., *The Coming to Power: Critical Presidential Elections in American History* (New York: Chelsea House, 1972), and also by Freidel in Arthur Schlesinger Jr., Fred L. Israel, and David J. Frent, eds., *Running for President: The Candidates and Their Images* (New York: Simon & Schuster, 1994); Harold F. Gosnell, *Champion Campaigner, Franklin D. Roosevelt* (New York: Macmillan, 1952); James H. Guilfoyle, *On the Trail of the Forgotten Man: A Journal of the Roosevelt Presidential Campaign* (Boston: Peabody Master Printers, 1933); H. L. Mencken, *Making a President: A Footnote to the Saga of Democracy* (New York: Alfred A. Knopf, 1932); Kathleen E. Kendall, *Communication in the Presidential Primaries: Candidates and the Media, 1912–2000* (Westport, Conn.: Praeger, 2000); Steve Neal, *Happy Days Are Here Again: The 1932 Democratic Convention, the Emergence of FDR—and How America Was Changed Forever* (New York: William Morrow, 2004); Roy V. Peel and Thomas C. Donnelly, *The 1932 Campaign: An Analysis* (New York: Farrar & Rinehart, 1935); and Richard Oulahan, *The Man Who . . . The Story of the 1932 Democratic National Convention* (New York: Dial Press, 1971).

Radical thought and politics in the Depression era are the subjects of James R. Barrett, *William Z. Foster and the Tragedy of American Radicalism* (Urbana: University of Illinois Press, 1999); David H. Bennett, *Demagogues in the Depression: American Radicals and the Union Party, 1932–1936* (New Brunswick, N.J.: Rutgers University Press, 1969); Albert Fried, ed., *Communism in America: A History in Documents* (New York: Columbia University Press, 1997); Bernard K. Johnpoll, *Pacifist's Progress: Norman Thomas and the Decline of American Socialism* (Chicago: Quadrangle, 1970); Matthew Josephson, *Infidel in the Temple: A Memoir of the Nineteen-thirties* (New York: Alfred A. Knopf, 1967); Harvey Klehr and John Earl Haynes, *The American Communist Movement: Storming Heaven Itself* (New York: Twayne, 1992); Harvey Klehr, *The Heyday of American Communism: The Depression Decade* (New York: Basic Books, 1984); R. Alan Lawson, *The Failure of Independent Liberalism, 1931–1940* (New York: Putnam, 1971); Richard Pells, *Radical Visions and American Dreams: Culture and Social Thought in the Depression Years* (New York: Harper & Row, 1973); and David A. Shannon, *The Socialist Party of America: A History* (New York: Macmillan, 1955). Assessments by some of the decade's leading leftists appear in Rita James Simon, ed., *As We Saw the Thirties: Essays on Social and Political Movements of a Decade* (Urbana: University of Illinois Press, 1967).

A leading Roosevelt scholar, William E. Leuchtenburg, has noted that historians no longer accept the image of a "do-nothing" Hoover and have come to credit his efforts, adding that perhaps because so many of them were liberal Democrats, they felt "a need to lean over backwards" in Hoover's behalf. Hoover's historiography starts with his three-volume self-defense, *Memoirs* (New York: Macmillan, 1951–1952), and his telling account of *The Ordeal of Woodrow Wilson*

(New York: McGraw-Hill, 1958). His historical reexamination began in Richard Hofstadter's *The American Political Tradition and the Men Who Made It* (New York: Alfred A. Knopf, 1948), and Carl Degler's "The Ordeal of Herbert Hoover," *Yale Review* 52 (Summer 1963). Analyses of his 1928 campaign are offered in Brian Balogh's "'Mirrors of Desires': Interest Groups, Elections, and the Targeted Style in Twentieth-Century America," in Meg Jacobs, William J. Novak, and Julian E. Zelizer, eds., *The Democratic Experiment: New Directions in American Political History* (Princeton, N.J.: Princeton University Press, 2003), and Allan J. Lichtman, *Prejudice and the Old Politics: The Presidential Election of 1928* (Chapel Hill: University of North Carolina Press, 1979). Hoover's biographers include Gary Dean Best, *The Politics of American Individualism: Herbert Hoover in Transition, 1918–1929* (Westport, Conn.: Greenwood, 1975); David Burner, *Herbert Hoover: A Public Life* (New York: Alfred A. Knopf, 1979); Craig Lloyd, *Aggressive Introvert: A Study of Herbert Hoover and Public Relations Management, 1912–1932* (Columbus: Ohio State University Press, 1972); George H. Nash, *The Life of Herbert Hoover* (New York: W. W. Norton, 1983–1996); Gene Smith, *The Shattered Dream: Herbert Hoover and the Great Depression* (New York: Morrow, 1970); Richard Norton Smith, *An Uncommon Man: The Triumph of Herbert Hoover* (New York: Simon & Schuster, 1984); and Joan Hoff Wilson, *Herbert Hoover: Forgotten Progressive* (New York: Simon & Schuster, 1975).

The Hoover administration is scrutinized in William J. Barber, *From New Era to New Deal: Herbert Hoover, the Economists, and American Economic Policy, 1921–1933* (New York: Cambridge University Press, 1985); Paul Dickson and Thomas B. Allen, *The Bonus Army: An American Epic* (New York: Walker, 2004); Martin L. Fausold and George T. Mazuzan, eds., *The Hoover Presidency: A Reappraisal* (Albany: State University of New York Press, 1984); Martin L. Fausold, *The Presidency of Herbert C. Hoover* (Lawrence: University Press of Kansas, 1985); Vincent Gaddis, *Herbert Hoover, Unemployment, and the Public Sphere: A Conceptual History, 1919–1933* (Lanham, Md.: University Press of America, 2005); David E. Hamilton, *From New Day to New Deal: American Farm Policy from Hoover to Roosevelt, 1928–1933* (Chapel Hill: University of North Carolina Press, 1991); Carl E. Krog and William R. Tanner, eds., *Herbert Hoover and the Republican Era: A Reconsideration* (Lanham, Md.: University Press of America, 1984); Donald J. Lisio, *Hoover, Blacks and Lily-Whites: A Study of Southern Strategies* (Chapel Hill: University of North Carolina Press, 1985), and *The President and Protest: Hoover, MacArthur, and the Bonus Riot* (Columbia: University of Missouri Press, 1974); James S. Olson, *Herbert Hoover and the Reconstruction Finance Corporation, 1931–1933* (Ames: Iowa State University Press, 1977); Albert U. Romasco, *The Poverty of Abundance: Hoover, the Nation and the Depression* (New York: Oxford University Press, 1965); Jordan A. Schwartz, *The Interregnum of Despair: Hoover, Congress and the Depression* (Urbana: University of Illinois Press, 1970); William Appleman Williams, *The Contours of American Democracy* (Cleveland, Ohio: World Publishing, 1961), and *The Tragedy of American Diplomacy* (New York: Dell, 1959); and Nan Elizabeth Woodruff, *As Rare as Rain: Federal Relief in the Great Southern Drought of 1930–31* (Urbana: University of Illinois Press, 1985).

While Hoover scholars puzzle over why the "forgotten progressive" turned conservative, Roosevelt's biographers grapple with how the "country squire" became a liberal activist. Roosevelt's biographers include Joseph Alsop, *FDR, 1882–1945: A Centenary Remembrance* (New York: Viking Press, 1982); Bernard Bellush, *Franklin D. Roosevelt as Governor of New York* (New York: Columbia University Press, 1955); Conrad Black, *Franklin Delano Roosevelt: Champion of Freedom* (New York: Public Affairs, 2003); James MacGregor Burns, *Roosevelt: The Lion and the Fox* (New York: Harcourt, Brace, 1956), and *Roosevelt: The Soldier of Freedom, 1940–1945* (New York: Harcourt Brace Jovanovich, 1970); Kenneth S. Davis, *FDR: The Beckoning of Destiny* (New York: Putnam, 1972), and *FDR: The New York Years* (New York: Random House, 1985); Frank Freidel, *Franklin D. Roosevelt* (Boston: Little, Brown, 1952–1973), and *Roosevelt: A Rendezvous with Destiny* (Boston: Little, Brown, 1990); Robert H. Jackson, *That Man: An Insider's Portrait of Franklin D. Roosevelt* (New York: Oxford University Press, 2003); Roy Jenkins, with Richard E. Neustadt, *Franklin Delano Roosevelt* (New York: Times Books, 2003); Patrick J. Maney, *The Roosevelt Presence* (New York: Twayne, 1992); Nathan Miller, *FDR: An Intimate History* (New York: New American Library, 1983); Sean J. Savage, *Roosevelt: The Party Leader, 1932–1945* (Lexington: University Press of Kentucky, 1991); Arthur M. Schlesinger Jr., *The Age of Roosevelt* (Boston: Houghton Mifflin, 1957–1960); Rexford G. Tugwell, *The Democratic Roosevelt: A Biography of Franklin D. Roosevelt* (Garden City, N.Y.: Doubleday, 1957); Geoffrey C. Ward, *A First-Class Temperament: The Emergence of Franklin Roosevelt* (New York: Harper & Row, 1989), and *Closest Companion: The Unknown Story of the Intimate Friendship between Franklin Roosevelt and Margaret Suckley* (Boston: Houghton Mifflin, 1995); and Allan M. Winkler, *Franklin D. Roosevelt and the Making of Modern America* (New York: Pearson/Longman, 2006). The impact of polio on Roosevelt is evaluated in Hugh Gregory Gallagher, *FDR's Splendid Deception* (New York: Dodd, Mead, 1985); Richard Thayer Goldberg, *The Making of Franklin D. Roosevelt: Triumph over Disability* (Cambridge, Mass.: Abt Books, 1981); and David Oshinsky, *Polio: An American Story* (New York: Oxford University Press, 2005).

For the New Deal in action, see Jonathan Alter, *The Defining Moment: FDR's Hundred Days and the Triumph of Hope* (New York: Simon & Schuster, 2006); Anthony J. Badger, *The New Deal: The Depression Years, 1933–1940* (Chicago: Ivan R. Dee, 2002); John Braeman, Robert H. Bremner, and David Brody, eds., *The New Deal* (Columbus: Ohio State University Press, 1975); Alan Brinkley, *The End of Reform: New Deal Liberalism in Recession and War* (New York: Alfred A. Knopf, 1995); Wilbur J. Cohen, ed., *The Roosevelt New Deal: A Program Assessment Fifty Years After* (Austin, Tex.: Lyndon B. Johnson School of Public Affairs, 1984); Ronald W. Edsforth, *The New Deal: America's Response to the Great Depression* (Malden, Mass.: Blackwell, 2000); Arthur A. Ekirch Jr., *Ideologies and Utopias: The Impact of the New Deal on American Thought* (Chicago: Quadrangle, 1969); Robert A. Garson and Stuart S. Kidd., eds., *The Roosevelt Years: New Perspectives on American History, 1933–1945* (Edinburgh: Edinburgh University Press, 1999); Colin Gordon, *New Deals: Business, Labor, and Politics in America,*

1920–1935 (New York: Cambridge University Press, 1994); Otis L. Graham Jr., *Toward a Planned Society: From Roosevelt to Nixon* (New York: Oxford University Press, 1976); Ellis W. Hawley, *The New Deal and the Problem of Monopoly* (Princeton, N.J.: Princeton University Press, 1966); Robert F. Himmelberg, *The Great Depression and the New Deal* (Westport, Conn.: Greenwood, 2001); David M. Kennedy, *Freedom from Fear: The United States, 1929–1945* (New York: Oxford University Press, 1999); William E. Leuchtenburg, *Franklin D. Roosevelt and the New Deal, 1932–1940* (New York: Harper & Row, 1963), and *The FDR Years: On Roosevelt and His Legacy* (New York: Columbia University Press, 1995); Thomas K. McCraw, *TVA and the Power Fight, 1933–1939* (Philadelphia: J. B. Lippincott, 1971); George T. McJimsey, *The Presidency of Franklin Delano Roosevelt* (Lawrence: University Press of Kansas, 2000); Patrick D. Reagan, *Designing a New America: The Origins of New Deal Planning, 1890–1943* (Amherst: University of Massachusetts Press, 1999); Elliot A. Rosen, *Roosevelt, the Great Depression, and the Economics of Recovery* (Charlottesville: University of Virginia Press, 2005); Albert U. Romasco, *The Politics of Recovery: Roosevelt's New Deal* (New York: Oxford University Press, 1983); Jordan A. Schwarz, *The New Dealers: Power Politics in the Age of Roosevelt* (New York: Alfred A. Knopf, 1993); James E. Sergent, *Roosevelt and the Hundred Days: Struggle for the Early New Deal* (New York: Garland, 1981); and George Wolfskill and John A. Hudson, *All but the People: Franklin D. Roosevelt and His Critics, 1933–39* (New York: Macmillan, 1969). Roosevelt's foreign policy and wartime leadership are covered in Robert Dallek, *Franklin D. Roosevelt and American Foreign Policy, 1932–1945* (New York: Oxford University Press, 1979); Alonzo L. Hamby, *For the Survival of Democracy: Franklin Roosevelt and the World Crisis of the 1930s* (New York: Free Press, 2004); and Richard Polenberg, *War and Society: The United States, 1941–1945* (Philadelphia: J. B. Lippincott, 1972).

The role of women and African Americans in the New Deal coalition is considered in George Martin, *Madam Secretary, Frances Perkins* (Boston: Houghton Mifflin, 1976); Lois Scharf, *To Work and to Wed: Female Employment, Feminism, and the Great Depression* (Westport, Conn.: Greenwood, 1980); Harvard Sitkoff, *A New Deal for Blacks: The Emergence of Civil Rights as a National Issue* (New York: Oxford University Press, 1978); Susan Ware, *Beyond Suffrage: Women and the New Deal* (Cambridge, Mass.: Harvard University Press, 1981); and Nancy J. Weiss, *Farewell to the Party of Lincoln: Black Politics in the Age of FDR* (Princeton, N.J.: Princeton University Press, 1983). The wives of the candidates are profiled in Maurine H. Beasley, *Eleanor Roosevelt and the Media: A Public Quest for Self-Fulfillment* (Urbana: University of Illinois Press, 1987); Doris Kearns Goodwin, *No Ordinary Time: Franklin and Eleanor Roosevelt—The Home Front in World War II* (New York: Simon & Schuster, 1994); Joseph P. Lash, *Eleanor and Franklin: The Story of Their Relationship* (New York: Norton, 1971); Eleanor Roosevelt, *This I Remember* (New York: Harper, 1949); Joan Hoff Wilson and Marjorie Lightman, eds., *Without Precedent: The Life and Career of Eleanor Roosevelt* (Bloomington: Indiana University Press, 1984); and Nancy Beck Young, *Lou Henry Hoover: Activist First Lady* (Lawrence: University Press of Kansas, 2004).

William Leuchtenburg evaluated Roosevelt's lasting impact on his presidential successors in *In the Shadow of FDR: From Harry Truman to George W. Bush* (New York: Cornell University Press, 2001). Aspects of the New Deal legacy are considered in William H. Chafe, ed., *The Achievement of American Liberalism: The New Deal and Its Legacies* (New York: Columbia University Press, 2003); Robert Eden, ed., *The New Deal and Its Legacy* (New York: Greenwood, 1989); Steve Fraser and Gary Gerstle, eds., *The Rise and Fall of the New Deal Order, 1930–1980* (Princeton, N.J.: Princeton University Press, 1989); Michael Janeway, *The Fall of the House of Roosevelt: Brokers of Ideas and Power from FDR to LBJ* (New York: Columbia University Press, 2004); Theodore J. Lowi, *The End of Liberalism: Ideology, Policy, and the Crisis of Public Authority* (New York: Norton, 1969); Sidney M. Milkis, *The President and the Party: The Transformation of the American Party System since the New Deal* (New York: Oxford University Press, 1993); and Cass R. Sunstein, *The Second Bill of Rights: FDR's Unfinished Bill of Rights and Why We Need It More than Ever* (New York: Basic Book, 2004).

Criticism of the New Deal from the Left can be found in Barton J. Bernstein, "The New Deal: The Conservative Achievements of Liberal Reform," in Bernstein, ed., *Towards a New Past: Dissenting Essays in American History* (New York: Pantheon, 1968); Paul K. Conkin, *The New Deal* (New York: Crowell, 1968); Ira Katznelson, *When Affirmative Action Was White: An Untold History of Racial Inequality in Twentieth-Century America* (New York: W. W. Norton, 2005); and Howard Zinn, *New Deal Thought* (Indianapolis, Ind.: Bobbs-Merrill, 1966), and *The Twentieth Century: A People's History* (New York: Harper & Row, 1984). Critics on the Right include Gary Dean Best, *Pride, Prejudice, and Politics: Roosevelt versus Recovery, 1933–1938* (New York: Praeger, 1991); John T. Flynn, *Country Squire in the White House* (New York: Doubleday, Doran, 1940); Paul Johnson, *Modern Times: The World from the Twenties to the Nineties* (New York: Harper & Row, 1983); and Jim Powell, *FDR's Folly: How Roosevelt and His New Deal Prolonged the Great Depression* (New York: Crown Forum, 2003).

Discussions of the congressional role in the political process can be found in Richard Franklin Bensel, *Sectionalism and American Political Development, 1880–1980* (Madison: University of Wisconsin Press, 1984); Andrew W. Busch, *Horses in Midstream: U.S. Midterm Elections and Their Consequences, 1894–1998* (Pittsburgh, Pa.: University of Pittsburgh Press, 1999); Roger H. Davidson, Susan Webb Hammond, and Raymond W. Smock, eds., *Masters of the House: Congressional Leadership over Two Centuries* (Boulder, Colo.: Westview Press, 1998); O. C. Fisher, *Cactus Jack* (Waco, Tex.: Texian Press, 1978); William Ivy Hair, *The Kingfish and His Realm: The Life and Times of Huey P. Long* (Baton Rouge: Louisiana State University Press, 1991); D. B. Hardeman and Donald C. Bacon, *Rayburn: A Biography* (Austin: Texas Monthly Press, 1987); David A. Horowitz, *Beyond Left and Right: Insurgency and the Establishment* (Urbana: University of Illinois Press, 1997); J. Joseph Huthmacher, *Senator Robert F. Wagner and the Rise of Urban Liberalism* (New York: Atheneum, 1968); Richard Lowitt, *George W. Norris: The Persistence of a Progressive, 1913–1933* (Urbana: University of Illinois

Press, 1971); Patrick Maney, "The Forgotten New Deal Congress," in Julian Zelizer, ed., *The American Congress: The Building of Democracy* (Boston: Houghton Mifflin, 2004), and *"Young Bob" La Follette: A Biography of Robert M. La Follette, Jr., 1895–1953* (Columbia: University of Missouri Press, 1978); James T. Patterson, *Congressional Conservatism and the New Deal: The Growth of the Conservative Coalition in Congress, 1933–1939* (Lexington: University Press of Kentucky, 1967); Robert V. Remini, *The House: The History of the House of Representatives* (New York: HarperCollins, 2006); David Robertson, *Sly and Able: A Political Biography of James F. Byrnes* (New York: Norton, 1994); Arthur M. Schlesinger Jr. and Roger Bruns, eds., *Congress Investigates: A Documented History, 1792–1975* (New York: Chelsea House, 1975); and Thomas P. Wolf, William D. Pederson, and Byron W. Daynes, eds., *Franklin D. Roosevelt and Congress: The New Deal and Its Aftermath* (Armonk, N.Y.: M. E. Sharpe, 2001).

Communications, from oratory to the news media, are analyzed in Bernard K. Duffy and Halford A. Ryan, eds., *American Orators of the Twentieth Century* (New York: Greenwood, 1987); Russell D. Buhite and David W. Levy, eds., *FDR's Fireside Chats* (Norman: University of Oklahoma Press, 1992); Douglas B. Craig, *Fireside Politics: Radio and Political Culture in the United States, 1920–1940* (Baltimore, Md.: Johns Hopkins University Press, 2000); Theodore G. Joslin, *Hoover off the Record* (Garden City, N.Y.: Doubleday, Doran, 1934); Louis W. Liebovich, *Bylines in Despair: Herbert Hoover, the Great Depression, and the U.S. News Media* (Westport, Conn.: Praeger, 1994); James E. Pollard, *The Presidents and the Press* (New York: Macmillan, 1947); Donald A. Ritchie, *Reporting from Washington: The History of the Washington Press Corps* (New York: Oxford University Press, 2005); Richard V. Steele, *Propaganda in an Open Society: The Roosevelt Administration and the Media, 1933–1941* (Westport, Conn.: Greenwood, 1985); Graham J. White, *FDR and the Press* (Chicago: University of Chicago Press, 1979); and Betty Houchin Winfield, *FDR and the News Media* (Urbana: University of Illinois Press, 1990). Journalists' memoirs include Turner Catledge, *My Life and the Times* (New York: Harper & Row, 1971); Bess Furman, *Washington By-line: The Personal History of a Newspaperwoman* (New York: Alfred A. Knopf, 1949); Charles Hurd, *When the New Deal Was Young and Gay* (New York: Hawthorn Books, 1965); H. V. Kaltenborn, *Fifty Fabulous Years, 1900–1950: A Personal Review* (New York: Putnam, 1950); Arthur Krock, *Memoirs: Sixty Years on the Firing Line* (New York: Funk & Wagnalls, 1968); Thomas L. Stokes, *Chip off My Shoulder* (Princeton, N.J.: Princeton University Press, 1940); and William Allen White, *The Autobiography of William Allen White* (New York: Macmillan, 1946).

There is no shortage of memoirs by other participants in the election, among them Claude Bowers, *My Life: The Memoirs of Claude Bowers* (New York: Simon & Schuster, 1962); James Michael Curley, *I'd Do It Again: A Record of All My Uproarious Years* (Englewood Cliffs, N.J.: Prentice-Hall, 1957); Paul H. Douglas, *In the Fullness of Time: The Memoirs of Paul H. Douglas* (New York: Harcourt Brace Jovanovich, 1971); James A. Farley, *Behind the Ballots: A Personal History* (New York: Harcourt, Brace, 1938), and *Jim Farley's Story: The Roosevelt Years* (New York: Whittlesey House, 1948); Edward J. Flynn, *You're the Boss* (New York:

Viking Press, 1947); Raymond Moley, *After Seven Years: A Political Analysis of the New Deal* (New York: Harper & Brothers, 1939); Charles Michelson, *The Ghost Talks* (New York: G. P. Putnam's Sons, 1944); Arthur F. Mullen, *Western Democrat* (New York; W. Funk, 1940); Samuel I. Rosenman, *Working with Roosevelt* (New York: Harper, 1952); James Roosevelt and Sidney Shalatt, *Affectionately, F.D.R: A Son's Story of a Lonely Man* (New York: Harcourt, Brace, 1959); Henry L. Stimson and McGeorge Bundy, *On Active Service in Peace and War* (New York: Harper, 1948); Rexford G. Tugwell, *The Brains Trust* (New York: Viking Press, 1968); Grace Tully, *F.D.R., My Boss* (New York: Charles Scribner's Sons, 1949); and James E. Watson, *As I Knew Them: Memoirs of James E. Watson* (Indianapolis, Ind.: Bobbs-Merrill, 1936). Biographies of some key players include Rodney P. Carlisle, *Hearst and the New Deal: The Progressive as Reactionary* (New York: Garland, 1979); C. H. Cramer, *Newton D. Baker: A Biography* (Cleveland, Ohio: World Publishing, 1961); Alex Gottfried, *Boss Cermak of Chicago: A Study of Political Leadership* (Seattle: University of Washington Press, 1962); Samuel B. Hand, *Counsel and Advise: A Political Biography of Samuel I. Rosenman* (New York: Garland, 1979); David Nasaw, *The Chief: The Life of William Randolph Hearst* (Boston: Houghton Mifflin, 2000); John Kennedy Ohl, *Hugh S. Johnson and the New Deal* (DeKalb: Northern Illinois University Press, 1985); Alfred B. Rollins Jr., *Roosevelt and Howe* (New York: Alfred A. Knopf, 1962); Jordan A. Schwarz, *The Speculator: Bernard M. Baruch in Washington, 1917–1965* (Chapel Hill: University of North Carolina Press, 1981); Daniel Scroop, *Mr. Democrat: Jim Farley, the New Deal, and the Making of Modern American Politics* (Ann Arbor: University of Michigan Press, 2006); Robert A. Slayton, *Empire Statesman: The Rise and Redemption of Al Smith* (New York: Free Press, 2001); and Bernard Sternsher, *Rexford Tugwell and the New Deal* (New Brunswick, N.J.: Rutgers University Press, 1964).

The Depression has also inspired an outpouring of oral history, beginning with Studs Terkel's *Hard Times: An Oral History of the Great Depression* (New York: Pantheon, 1970). Other oral histories include Benjamin Appel, *The People Talk: American Voices from the Great Depression* (New York: Simon & Schuster, 1982); Ann Banks, *First-Person America* (New York: Alfred A. Knopf, 1980); Andrew J. Dunar and Dennis McBride, *Building Hoover Dam: An Oral History of the Great Depression* (New York: Twayne, 1993); Katie Loucheim, *The Making of the New Deal: The Insiders Speak* (Cambridge, Mass.: Harvard University Press, 1983); and Tom E. Terrill and Jerold D. Hirsch, *Such As Us: Southern Voices of the Thirties* (Chapel Hill: University of North Carolina Press, 1978). Supplementing these are the unpublished interviews conducted for the presidential libraries and the Columbia Oral History Research Office, together with the relevant manuscript collections at the Herbert Hoover, Franklin D. Roosevelt, and Harry S. Truman presidential libraries and the Library of Congress.

INDEX

House of Representatives, U.S., 8, 10, 16, 21, 41, 82, 84, 107, 123, 163, 194, 207
  apportionment of, 13
  and FDR, 184, 189, 204
  and Hoover, 47, 49, 53–54, 58, 60–61, 167–168, 187
  pork-barrel politics, 46, 53, 65, 67, 145
  See also Garner, John Nance
Howe, Louis McHenry, 175, 180, 186
  and FDR's nomination, 38–39, 70, 74–75, 78–80, 87, 103, 109, 122
  and 1932 election, 120, 125, 138, 141, 155
Howell, Clark, 82
Hull, Cordell, 39, 81, 102
Humphrey, Hubert, 204
Hurley, Patrick, 119
Huston, Claudius, 42

inflation, 8, 9, 52, 115, 136, 209. *See also* deflation
interregnum, 5, 161–172
Irwin, Will, 33, 55
isolationism, 10, 13–14, 52, 192, 195

Jackson, Andrew, 18, 101
Jews, 14, 15, 158, 160, 182, 186
Johnson, Hiram, 22, 47, 96, 132
Johnson, Lyndon B., 60, 203
Josephson, Matthew, 149, 182–183
Joslin, Theodore (Ted), 58–59, 92, 124

Kennedy, John F., ix, 203
Kennedy, Joseph P., 106
Kent, Frank R., 56, 78
Kerry, John F., 208
Keynes, John Maynard, 136, 191
Kirby, Rollin, 110
Kleberg, Richard, 60
Knox, Frank, 181, 193
Krock, Arthur, 167, 176, 184
Ku Klux Klan, 15, 32

La Follette, Robert M., 15
La Follette, Robert M., Jr., 132
LaGuardia, Fiorello, 63
Landis, James M., 181
Landon, Alfred M. (Alf), 129, 160, 188–189, 193, 203
Lane, Franklin K., 22
League of Nations, 9, 10, 14, 22–23, 84, 133
Lee, Ivy, 89
Lemke, William, 189–190
Liberalism, 28, 30, 112, 115–116, 150, 168, 190, 198
  defined, 2
  Democratic, 28, 30, 61, 65, 76, 85, 91, 159, 204–207
  FDR's, 5, 71, 78, 86, 89, 110, 123, 132–133, 136, 138, 141–142, 186, 192, 198, 202, 209
  Hoover's, 20–21, 195
  Wilsonian, 4, 23, 67, 82, 106
  See also populism; progressivism
Liberty League, 186–187
Lincoln, Abraham, 10, 18, 95, 142, 158, 220
Lindbergh, Charles, 62, 154, 195
Lindley, Ernest K., 87
Lippmann, Walter, 22–23, 30, 51, 91–92, 106, 116, 148, 150, 199
Literary Digest, 97, 152–153, 188
Long, Huey, 101, 153, 167, 185, 189
Longworth, Alice Roosevelt, 26, 121
Longworth, Nicholas, 26, 60
Los Angeles Times, 14, 133
Lubell, Samuel, 1
Lucas, Robert, 43

MacArthur, Douglas, 119
MacLafferty, James, 122
Marsh, Bill and Bub, 121
Martin, Joseph, 98
Marx, Groucho, 50
Mayer, Louis B., 99, 106

Roosevelt, Franklin Delano (FDR)
(*continued*)
   radio use by, 86, 88, 94, 105,
      124–125, 130, 144–145, 147–148,
      176, 178, 211–218
   relations with vice presidents,
      107–109, 123, 129, 157, 160,
      166, 168, 194, 197–198
   speechwriting, 74, 85–86, 109–
      110, 129–130, 132, 137–138,
      140–142, 175
   vice-presidential campaign of, 23,
      40, 71, 73, 79–80, 180
   and World War I, 20, 70
   and World War II, 192–200
Roosevelt, James, 72, 88, 134, 139, 174
Roosevelt, Sara Delano, 68–70
Roosevelt, Theodore (TR), 8, 21, 45,
   68–70, 121, 130, 132
Roosevelt, Theodore, Jr., 121
Rosenman, Sam, 74, 85, 109, 110,
   138, 142
rural Americans, 3, 9–13, 15–16,
   53–54, 170
   and election of 1928, 27–30, 33, 41,
      47, 73, 75
   and election of 1932, 75, 110, 124,
      129–130, 135, 142–143, 157, 159
   and New Deal, 3, 170, 177–178, 189
Ruth, Babe, 54

sales tax. *See* taxation
Sanders, Everett, 99–100, 127, 128,
   153, 157
Scopes Trial, 12–13
Scripps-Howard, 91, 110, 148
Secret Service, 25, 46, 118, 139, 144,
   155, 166
Securities Act, Federal, 169, 177
Securities and Exchange
   Commission, 169, 178, 181. *See
   also* stock markets
Senate, U.S., 8, 16, 21, 58, 118, 159,
   163, 194, 207

Banking Committee investigation,
   168–169
FDR and, 69–70, 132, 145, 184,
   189, 192
Hoover and, 20, 25, 27, 41–43,
   48–49, 51, 53, 56, 61, 64, 67,
   99, 119, 139, 167–169, 172
pork-barrel politics, 46, 53, 67, 145
Shachtman, Max, 113
Shipstead, Henrik, 61
Shouse, Jouett, 41, 76, 80, 90–91,
   101, 186
Shuler, Robert Pierce (Holy Bob), 133
Smith, Alfred E. (Al), 198
   and election of 1924, 15
   and election of 1928, 1–2, 28–36,
      114, 136, 146, 148, 189, 201–
      202
   and election of 1932, 110, 120, 123,
      143–144, 153–155
   and nomination in 1932, 67, 78–
      82, 84–86, 88–92, 101–109
   relations with FDR, 38–39, 70,
      72–76, 82, 143–144, 171, 187
Smoot, Reed, 48, 159
Smoot-Hawley Tariff, 47–48, 56, 135,
   143, 147, 154. *See also* tariffs
Snell, Bertrand, 98–99
Socialist Labor Party, 112, 157
Socialist Party (U.S.), 3, 75, 111–113,
   116, 150–151, 153–154, 157, 190
Social Security, 185, 188, 189, 191,
   207. *See also* old-age pensions
southern states, 11, 13, 16, 65, 170
   in election of 1928, 1, 27–28,
      30–31, 36
   in election of 1932, 79, 81, 88, 101,
      105, 111, 115, 122, 124, 143, 154,
      158–159
   and New Deal, 186, 192, 205
   and Republicans, 10, 27, 30, 42–
      43, 158, 204–205
Soviet Union, 21, 112, 113, 149, 190–
   191, 196, 199–200